THE ACCOUNTABLE LEADER

Developing Effective Leadership Through Managerial Accountability

Brian Dive

KOGAN PAGE

London and Philadelphia

*In memory of my sister Susan
and my lifelong friend Phil Mears*

First published in Great Britain and the United States in 2008 by Kogan Page Limited

120 Pentonville Road
London N1 9JN
United Kingdom
www.koganpage.com

525 South 4th Street, #241
Philadelphia PA 19147
USA

© Brian Dive, 2008

The right of Brian Dive to be identified as the author of this work has been asserted by him in accordance with the Copyright, Designs and Patents Act 1988.

ISBN 978 0 7494 5160 8

British Library Cataloguing-in-Publication Data

A CIP record for this book is available from the British Library.

Library of Congress Cataloging-in-Publication Data

Dive, Brian.
   The accountable leader : developing effective leadership through managerial accountability / Brian Dive.
       p. cm.
   Includes bibliographical references and index.
   ISBN 978-9-7494-5160-8
   1. Leadership. 2. Organizational effectiveness. I. Title.
   HD57.7.D587 2008
   658.4'092--dc22

                                                             2008017598

Typeset by JS Typesetting Ltd, Porthcawl, Mid Glamorgan
Printed and bound in Great Britain by MPG Books Ltd, Bodmin, Cornwall

Contents

Foreword

What company does not want to describe its organization as 'high performance'? To achieve this goal, a variety of continuous improvement (eg lean six sigma) and annual 'enterprise wide' re-engineering initiatives are often put in place, to engage the entire organization from the bottom to the top. Yet, as Brian Dive demonstrates in *The Accountable Leader,* there is much more to achieving organizational effectiveness than simply optimizing business processes. In particular, the power of a leader depends on the power of the context: the structures in place that, depending on their design, can either support or constrain people as they try to perform.

The core elements of organization design include structure, decision rights, information flows and motivators. (At our own firm, we call these the 'building blocks' of an organization's DNA; together, they determine its culture and collective capabilities.) Brian's previous book *The Healthy Organization* correctly emphasizes the roles of decision rights – or as he calls it, Decision Making Accountability (DMA) – and their direct linkage to appropriate organization structure. It is not by accident then that one of the frequent areas of rapid cost reduction that we find with our clients (often representing up to 20 per cent in headcount reduction by function or business unit) is in delayering their organizations by clarifying DMA up and down the organization spine.

What is new about *The Accountable Leader?* It provides a critical piece of the organization design and strategic leadership puzzle, one that is often overlooked. It turns the focus on the application of organization accountability principles from efficiency to effectiveness, especially in the area of leadership development. Far too many companies cannot develop leaders effectively because of a dearth of leadership roles where the incumbent has clear accountability established through well-defined decision rights up and down the organization.

For example, the most important decisions are often made by a process of multiple layers and committees of review, followed by an ultimate decision made only at the top 1 or 2 layers. Brian makes a key point that 'managerial leadership', especially in up to Levels 3 or 4, cannot be developed in this environment. Organizations at their core are created and designed to execute against a set of stable processes that can be measured and improved upon over time. Managerial leaders are put in charge of functions or business units to get results from resources applied against these processes. As Brian defines accountability of a managerial leader, it includes this 'goal oriented behavior, a role that is neither shared nor conditional, that is meaningless without consequences, and that applies to individuals'. This description appears quite apt when applied up to Level 3 or 4.

But leadership changes when the role transitions from primarily 'operational' to 'strategic' – or to what Brian terms 'Strategic Accountability'. Here *The Accountable Leader* provides detailed descriptions, in the form of 'seven elements of a role' (Nature of Work, Resource Complexity, Problem Solving, Change, Internal Collaboration, External Collaboration, Time Frame) for each of the levels. In the management consulting vernacular we often call the operational tasks required of a business the 'running and fixing', while the strategic tasks are the 'changing' of the business. And we also say that 'Change Leadership is a **TEAM** Sport'.

When it comes to leading change, the best CEOs are not capable in all dimensions. But they know how to bring together a team that represents a full range of ability. Any individual leader typically is strong in just one or at most two 'leadership spikes' from four main change leadership attributes:

Thinking creatively and innovatively;
Empowering others through focus on execution;
Aligning through the ability to integrate across disparate insights and perspectives; and
Mobilizing through motivating and encouraging the organization.

The most successful CEOs are aware of those change leadership attributes where they are themselves not strong, and they compensate by teaming against strategic change initiatives with other executives who have complementary 'spikes'.

This is consistent with Brian's views that the nature of the collaborative elements increases dramatically as organization levels increase. It also explains in part why the vast majority of strategic change initiatives at corporations fail to achieve their original intended target – failing to understand the important distinctions between managerial and strategic leadership. If for only this key insight, Brian's latest book, *The Accountable Leader* will be a valuable book for senior executives, CEOs and Boards of Directors who are involved in top leadership development and CEO Succession.

Steve Wheeler
Senior Vice President
Booz Allen Hamilton

Acknowledgements

The evolution of ideas underpinning this book took many years of fieldwork in many countries to germinate and come to fruition. I am indebted therefore to a great number of people along the way who have enabled me to identify and refine the ideas that form the basis of this book. I referred to the lineage of thinkers and the key events that first sent me down this path in *The Healthy Organization* (2002) and others subsequently in the second edition (2004).

Since then I have worked with others who have helped me further test the assumptions that now form the basis of this book. Many of these leaders have moved to other organizations since, but they include Valerie Scoular (Aegis Media and Barclays), Mike Cutt and Stephen Lehane (Alliance Boots), Fiona Rodford (BAA and Alliance & Leicester), Rachael Mason (Air New Zealand), Pavita Walker, Sue Turner, Adam Pearce when at Barclays and latterly as an OD colleague, Malcolm Saffin and Peter Dugmore (Cable and Wireless), Shaunagh Dawes (Orange), Claire Davies (QBE), Iain McDonald (Royal Bank of Scotland), Catherine Glickman and Jane Storm (Tesco Stores), Joe Singleton (New York DEP), Chris Johnson and Paul Fretten (UK Cabinet Office), John Fingleton and Sarah Kaye (The Office of Fair Trading), Judy Vezmer (Reed Elsevier), Chris Dik and Luc de Baets (Ahold).

I have also enjoyed working with key players in Booz Allen Hamilton such as Dave Mader, Martina Sangin (USA), John Potter (UK), Marco Kesteloo, Robert Spieker and Ralph Maenen (The Netherlands), with support from Vinay Couto, Gary Neilson, Tim Hoying and Giri Rao in the USA.

The work in Chapter 10 in New Zealand and Australia was carried out with the support of Janne Pender, Collene Roche, Eileen Henderson, Chris Faisandier, Phil Mahoney and Pat Lynch.

Many others have helped with the improvement of the ideas and their expression in this book. Chief among them is Steve Wheeler of Booz Allen Hamilton, who strongly supported this book from the outset, given his interest in strategic leadership and organizational change. He read the first draft and made many suggestions. I am so pleased he agreed to write the Foreword.

My colleague, Adam Pearce, a leading authority in organization design and the implementation of Leadership Levels, also read the drafts in detail. He has been a tower of strength in challenging my logic and key concepts while suggesting areas for improvement and the inclusion of new material.

I was fortunate to be able to draw on the experience of Robert Kramer, Principle Researcher at the New York Conference Board, who has conducted distinctive research into global organization design for over 30 years and who has also written on the development of leaders in international companies. Robert and I have worked together on a number of projects over the years. He also kindly read my early manuscript and suggested a number of refinements.

A number of the ideas presented in Chapter 3 were first set out in a series of articles in *Croner Pay and Benefits Briefing*, where my key contact was Colin Keating.

Art Kleiner, the Editor of *Strategy and Business* (Booz Allen Hamilton) and author of a number of business books in his own right, was another great source of help. He also introduced me to Adrienne Crowther and Steve Coomber, who have helped steer the book towards completion.

Sam Gilpin read the early draft and made helpful suggestions for improvement. Helen Roberts and Lisa Cramp provided the insight for the categorization of personality and behavioural types and their alignment to DMA Competencies and levels of accountability, set out in Chapter 9. Ania Jaskiewicz toiled on the drafts, helping to produce and improve the layout and diagrams.

The initial draft was critiqued in great detail and improved by my son Bernard. Nothing escaped his penetrating eye and formidable logic. I am both extremely grateful for and proud of his contribution. The final outcome owes much to his erudition, attention to detail and creativity. His involvement also helped shorten and soften the frustrations felt by Anne and Lizzy, when so much of my spare time was otherwise spent locked away, preoccupied with the various versions that preceded the final outcome.

A key player in the final stages of getting the book ready for the publisher was Steve Coomber, who helped refine the argumentation and the style of the book. His professional input was much appreciated.

While I gladly acknowledge this book has been enhanced by input from these many sources, nevertheless given that accountability is its key theme, I have to accept that any errors of fact or omission remain solely the responsibility of the author.

Praise for *The Accountable Leader*

"Simple organizational structure and clear accountability are necessary conditions for the exercise of effective leadership. In this comprehensive book Brian Dive has made a most useful contribution in reminding us of these fundamentals."
John Adair, the world's first Professor of Leadership Studies

"In a fast-changing and increasingly complex world, accountability of leaders is acquiring a renewed focus. Brian Dive's book clearly articulates how management can inadvertently make the contours of accountability fuzzy. How do we recognize it? More importantly, how can we set it right? These and many other questions are covered in a simple way. An eminently readable and refreshing book. More importantly, it is a must-read for operating managers, not just HR professionals."
R Gopalakrishnan, Executive Director, Tata Sons Ltd, and author of
The Case of the Bonsai Manager

"An excellent read. The benefit of truly accountable leaders is that they are able to create effective structures where their staff know what is expected of them, and can improve the business for customers."
Jane Storm, Group Head of Talent, Organization Design and Performance at Tesco

Introduction

Millions of words have been written about leadership – transactional, transformational, charismatic, inspirational, authentic and many other kinds. As the countless books, magazine articles, academic papers, blogs, reports and other musings are fond of emphasizing, leadership is an exciting, if challenging, undertaking. (Managers, those dull administrators, are largely ignored.)

What these publications tend to do is to describe what good leadership looks like, to explain the mechanics, detail the characteristics, traits and attributes of good leaders. What most fail to do, however, is to focus on an essential element of the leadership equation, without which effective leadership is simply impossible – the organizational context within which leaders are able to flourish. After all, what use are potentially brilliant leaders (or managers), if an organization is structured in a way that prevents them from using their skills to the advantage of that organization?

Moreover, while HR departments complain about the shortage of talented people, and senior executives fret over the lack of suitable leaders, perhaps both should consider that there might, in fact, be too many leaders in their organization. Having too many leaders, at any level of hierarchy, is counter-productive, bad for both the organization and its employees. But then, without knowing what optimal organizational structure looks like, how can anyone know what constitutes too many leaders?

So I make no apologies for saying at the outset that this book is no racy account of the latest leadership theory. You will not find leadership the Shakespeare way, the Genghis Khan way or the Babe Ruth way among these pages. Or 10 terrific tales of leadership. It is not a discourse on leadership traits, or what great leaders look like.

What you will find in this book, however, is an explanation of how the structure of organizations has a profound impact on the ability of managerial leaders to perform their job effectively. And how organization design has a huge impact on the individual well-being and happiness of those people earmarked for future promotion, so much so that talented staff may well leave an organization rather than suffer the effects of operating inside a poorly designed organization.

My decision to focus on organizational structure and its relationship to leadership is no accident or whim. I have spent 40 years considering the following key question: why do so many organizations, despite an abundance of talented leaders, still fail to perform to their maximum potential? And what have I learnt about leadership in these last four decades, from working with a variety of organizations, from multinationals to small family businesses, in about 70 countries, across all continents and over 20 different industries, both in the private and the public sector?

For a start, that there are no easy answers to such a question, no panacea, no magic bullets. There are plenty of fads and fashions, but few fundamental truths. But perhaps the most important thing that I discovered is that 'clear accountability', a concept I describe in detail and at length in this book, is the bedrock of successful leadership.

If organizations are really concerned about creating the climate for their people to fulfil their true potential, to create an energy that drives success, that makes people want to join and work for that organization, they cannot afford to ignore the link between structure and effective leadership. It may be one of the most overlooked aspects of leadership, but it demands attention.

So, if you read this book as a senior executive you will learn how to test your organization's design, and diagnose if and where it is preventing your people from achieving maximum performance; how it is preventing your organization from being as successful as possible. Alternatively, if you read this book as a manager and leader, you may discover the reasons for those feelings of frustration you experience at being unable to make the impact on your organization that you know you are capable of. And how to go about changing that.

Because while this book may not be the latest in leadership fads or fashions, it is a practical how-to guide to understanding and constructing the most effective organizational design that will allow leadership to thrive. Or, to temporarily adopt the snappier style of the leadership genre, this book is not about leadership by chance – it is about leadership by design.

A note on the structure of the book: it is divided into three sections. The first four chapters in Section 1 outline the key concepts and provide the theoretical underpinning for the practical approach that follows.

Section 2 has a practical focus; it describes how the ideas introduced in Section 1 cover the work of well over 95 per cent of those employed in organizations of all shapes and sizes. It covers operational work, defined in detail and illustrated with examples, and then moves into the strategic challenges of leading in an international setting.

The third section makes the link between organization design and leadership more explicit. It describes why many leadership development schemes are not wholly effective and then looks at a case study showing how the assessment of levels of accountability lays the foundation for successful leadership development. Finally, it plots the career of a manager moving through all the levels of accountability during a lifetime career, which illustrates how the nature of accountable leadership changes at different levels in an organization.

Part 1

1 Accountable for success

'The basic building block of organizational action is not the job, the team, the project, the process, the share or even the dollar. It is the decision.'

Art Kleiner (2006), *Who Really Matters*

Held to account – what does it mean?

In 2003, a major international financial services company ran into trouble. Struggling to meet market expectations, and operating in a highly competitive sector, the company needed to identify the source of its problems and quickly. After some internal debate, management decided that one of the main reasons for the firm's malaise was a significant human resources problem: a shortage of leaders.

This conclusion should come as no surprise. It is a common assumption among organizations when corporate performance is sub-par that somehow the people in the company are to blame – it is a 'capability problem'. Of course, when results are going well, senior management is usually happy to claim responsibility.

In this case, to its credit, the financial services company decided to get a second opinion, and asked me if I could analyse the firm's capabilities and identify any deficiencies. The first thing that I did was to analyse the company's management structure, based on the methods outlined in this book. The results showed that the company had 12 layers of hierarchy as detailed in Figure 1.1. As this book will show, *no* organization can have 12 layers of hierarchy and remain effective.

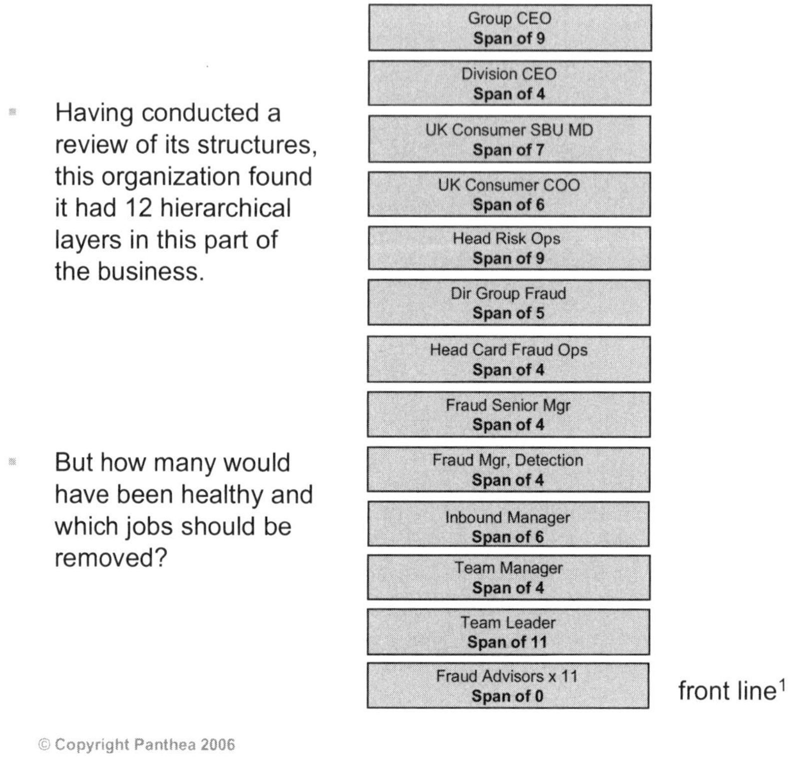

- Having conducted a review of its structures, this organization found it had 12 hierarchical layers in this part of the business.

- But how many would have been healthy and which jobs should be removed?

Group CEO **Span of 9**
Division CEO **Span of 4**
UK Consumer SBU MD **Span of 7**
UK Consumer COO **Span of 6**
Head Risk Ops **Span of 9**
Dir Group Fraud **Span of 5**
Head Card Fraud Ops **Span of 4**
Fraud Senior Mgr **Span of 4**
Fraud Mgr, Detection **Span of 4**
Inbound Manager **Span of 6**
Team Manager **Span of 4**
Team Leader **Span of 11**
Fraud Advisors x 11 **Span of 0**

front line[1]

Figure 1.1 Leadership accountability health check

It was clear from my investigation of the organizational structure that there were a number of factors having a directly negative impact on the company's performance:

Hierarchy heavy

As my analysis revealed, there were too many layers of hierarchy; more leadership roles than were required. Worse, even if the company had known this, it could not have fixed the problem as it had no idea how many layers it did need, nor did it know which layers in the reporting chain from the front line to the CEO at the top of the organization – the spine of accountability – were failing to add value.

Poor grading

Grading of jobs was an issue[2]. Nearly every layer of management right up to the senior management team was given a separate grade, which was unnecessary, but then, at the top of the organization, the most expensive and senior layers of management were all in the same grade.

Career dead ends

And that was not all; there were several other problems. The company could not identify its top 100 jobs; there were no reliable career paths for developing leaders; spans of control, the number of people an individual managed, were widest at the bottom (the front line of the organization) and at the top and smallest in middle management; plus the company was carrying millions of dollars of excess cost.

A problem of accountability

The senior management approached me because they suspected that the company had a capability problem. What I discovered instead were different and unsuspected problems, at least from the organization's perspective. The company had plenty of jobs without apparent purpose, which subtracted rather than added value. (And a job without purpose, understandably, impairs the person in that 'non-job' from being able to lead effectively.)

In essence, the company had an accountability problem – its leaders were not clearly held to account, as it was impossible to assess their true impact. Unfortunately, because of insufficient attention to the effects of an organization's architecture on leadership and performance, there was no way that the company could have known this. Without a method of assessing the levels of accountability of the managers, there was no way of telling where the non-jobs were located. Nor was there any way of telling which individuals were capable of top performance, and which were not, or even which had the potential to be senior managers.

It had apparently not occurred to the company that the root cause of its performance issue might be faulty organization design.[3] Its plans for rejuvenating the management team with a more aggressive hiring and firing regime would therefore have failed to resolve that basic issue.

The company in question deserves some praise, however. After my evaluation, using the processes described in this book, it became clear that 6 or 7 layers of hierarchy were more appropriate than the existing 12. Painful though it must have been, the financial services company took the results on board and subsequently reorganized, stripping out the excess layers. The quest to reinvigorate leadership and performance was enhanced in the process. The change in organizational architecture and hierarchies gave more meaning, purpose and satisfaction to the employees' work and performance.

The effects on the employees throughout the organization should not be underestimated. Recent research on employee engagement, and work by occupational and social psychologists, has demonstrated that 'people want meaning in their work and life, and they want to make a difference.'[4] Or as management guru Charles Handy suggested: 'The quest for purpose has to be an attempt to leave the world a little better than we found it.'[5]

Most importantly of all, as far as the senior team was concerned, business results improved. Whilst many other factors may be involved in the company's improvement, and it would be wrong to claim a one-to-one causal relationship, there is little doubt that the restructuring had a significant impact on the improved performance.

Unfortunately, far too many companies suffer from similar problems. Yet, as my experience with this organization demonstrates, it is possible to implement a solution and with dramatic results. It is just a question of diagnosing the problem, making the necessary adjustments and then benefiting from the results. The rest of this book aims to illustrate how any organization can do the same, if and when necessary.

Recurring questions

There are some questions that relate to organization design that management must ask. They are questions that apply to private corporations, public institutions, voluntary organizations and cooperatives. They apply to both small organizations such as internet start-ups and to huge global entities.

Do you know the answers to these questions, for your organization?

- How many layers of management are necessary and why?
- How should functions and processes be aligned as a result?
- How should spans vary and why?
- How should employees be rewarded?
- What are the logical steps of their personal development?

Accountability, organization design and effective leadership

The case described earlier in the chapter highlights a problem that is common among many organizations. It concerns three inextricably linked factors:

accountability, organizational design and leadership. Over the following chapters I will show how these three concepts are related and how accountability is at the heart of sound organizational architecture, which in turn is a pre-condition for truly effective leadership, leadership development, and a rewarding career path.

This book will address the problem of poor organization design and the resultant leadership issues, and demonstrate how to diagnose the organization and decide whether it is healthy (a healthy organization is one that meets its purpose, and where employees add value to each others' work while they simultaneously learn and develop, because they are held to account for their work). It will also illustrate how to identify and remove purposeless jobs, and show how leaders can be assessed, identified and developed across the organization.

Accountability: what does it mean?

Accountability is a key concept in leadership and the design of organizations.[6] It occurs when one individual is answerable to another for work (a goal-oriented behaviour), resources, results and/or services, which can be measured in quantity, quality, cost and time.[7]

Accountability stems from the tasks inherent in a role; it indicates what the person in that position has the authority to do within that role. Success in carrying out those tasks should lead to reward and recognition from the person or persons who set up the role in the first place. Conversely, failure to deliver what is specified in the role should lead to some sort of sanction.

This last point is important, as any disconnection from performance and its consequences is debilitating for the person in the role. Consider the example of bureaucrats (and those served by them) who work in an accountability vacuum, which customers, clients and patients will recognize as a total imperviousness to their needs and desires.

I have seen public sector organizations that are totally internally focused – concerned only with the well-being of their staff to the total exclusion of those they are allegedly serving. They do not calibrate or reward good performance or customer service. Indeed, I have seen such organizations decide first what they wish to pay and then play the system to find the grade and job title from the HR library to deliver the desired reward for the employee. Accountability to the customer or patient at the front line is totally ignored in this search for 'promotion' and more money. For the disconnected bureaucrat, lack of performance or service does not matter.

Beyond this definition of accountability, others have proposed some fundamental ideas of what accountability is, to stimulate and guide properly accountable conduct. So, for example:

- Accountability is a statement of personal promise, both to yourself and to the people around you, to deliver specific defined results.
- Accountability for results means activities are not enough.
- Accountability for results requires room for personal judgment and decision-making.
- Accountability is neither shared nor conditional.
- Accountability is meaningless without consequences (rewards, sanctions).[8]

Why is accountability important?

'Total liberty for wolves is death to the lambs.'

Isaiah Berlin, *The Crooked Timber of Humanity*

Accountability is vital to organizations for many reasons. Lack of true accountability causes excessive cost, both economic and psychological, de-motivation in those who work for the organization, dissatisfaction in those served by it, and sub-optimal performance in general.

Who decides what?

The basic premise of an accountable organization is the following: managerial leaders only take those decisions that the people that report to them are unable to take due to a lack of knowledge, skill and/or experience. The person to whom that managerial leader reports must also make decisions, which are both different from and add value to the latter's work. As the work becomes more complex, so the decisions being taken differ in nature.

A compressive regime

For an effective organizational structure, there must be a clear boundary of accountability between the individuals above the manager and those below. Otherwise, compression occurs. This is when two or more layers of people are working in the same decision-making zone or level of accountability.

What results from this situation is micro-management, or supervision that is too close and oppressive. The person in the apparently more complex role ends up occupying all or most of someone else's actual and psychological workspace. That senior job is then surplus to requirements; it duplicates the work of another and does not add value. In its hollowness, it does not enable the person in the position to learn or to develop; likewise, the person whose job is being encroached upon is deprived of opportunities for learning and development. The most talented individuals quickly become disenchanted with this type of job situation.

Compression is the opposite of empowerment. It results in the suppression of the spirit and enthusiasm of those subject to it and limits the freedom of the individual to do the legitimate work of their choice. It results in not being able to take any real decisions. Empowerment, by contrast, calls for the addition of something of value to the work of others by the person at the higher level, enabling them to achieve more than they would otherwise.

Accountability: positive or negative, direct or indirect

Accountability is related to the concept of liberty or freedom. You may well wonder what that has to do with the work of people within an organization. However, in an age when the talk is of customer service excellence and empowerment of employees, think of accountability as defining the boundaries of the decision-making freedom an individual enjoys within an organization.

Thus accountability can afford greater freedom for leadership, or deny and constrain the individual's ability to perform effectively. In this sense accountability can be positive or negative; both are important.

Negative accountability

Negative accountability occurs when there is interference with or blocking of the free exercise of positive action. For example, I once worked with a talented young marketer who was posted to the Philippines early in his career. Probably the most creative marketer I have seen, his time in the East was marked by a number of brilliant, innovative launches that took market share from other multinational companies.

Not surprisingly, promotion followed (he was given a higher job grade) – in this case to Germany. But a new pan-European organization had emasculated the German job. The marketer grew bitterly disappointed and frustrated. He tried to innovate and make the sort of changes he had previously managed in Asia, but, he said, his hands were tied. He took this up with the top of this mega-organization but the response took ages.

The result? 'My head was telling me I had a great job but my heart said if you can't even decide the colour of a product wrapper, what is the point of staying? So, I left.'

I have heard many more anecdotes such as this, from very talented people, where the outcome has been similarly frustrating for them and the organization that employed them. Individuals want to be, and are entitled to be, free from unnecessary interference in their work.

Negative accountability is one of the most widespread malaises in 21st century organizations. It is typically manifest in a cluttered, non-value-adding hierarchy, with excessive layers of management and small spans of management – that is, those averaging less than eight reports per manager.

Positive accountability

It is not much use being free from interference if you are not then able to use that freedom to do something worthwhile, like fulfilling your potential. Accountability implies a freedom to do something; it moves beyond the mere absence of interference or coercion and implies a definite sphere within which an individual can act to get things done. In this sense such a person is free to make a positive contribution to their organization. In the context of working for an organization, this might be some particular, definite achievements. Also, if an individual is to be answerable for something, that individual must be in a situation in which it is fair for them to be answerable in that way.

Positive accountability should operate at all levels in organizations, whatever their size and mission. This is distributed accountability, or, indeed, distributed leadership. In this context, there is no difference between the concepts of management and leadership, more of which later. The levels of positive accountability stem from the mission, purpose, scale and complexity of an organization.

> Positive accountability occurs when one is answerable to another for the provision of work, husbanding of resources and the delivery of a service, product or set of results that can be measured in terms of quantity, quality, cost and time.

Direct accountability

Direct accountability is synonymous with management accountability, ie direct accountability for others. It typically involves authority to manage a team, deciding who comes into the team, what work they will do, how they will be rewarded for that work, how they will be trained and developed and on what basis, and when they will leave the team.

There are 10 core direct accountabilities that enable a manager to add value on the spine of accountability, and these are listed later in this chapter. If this authority is effectively discharged, the team members will enjoy the benefits of positive accountability and true empowerment, and the organization's performance will benefit as result. If these accountabilities are not clearly present for a particular job, then that job is superfluous and is actually a source of interference in the work of others. Accountability is then negative.

Indirect accountability

There are a number of job types that derive their legitimacy from indirect authority.[9] These are known as support jobs, and although not required on the spine of accountability, they do add value to it.[10] Support jobs are not, however, to be confused with span-breakers; jobs that exist solely for the comfort of the accountable manager immediately above – typically to reduce the span of management – but that do not add value to the work of others.

The key thing to remember about jobs with indirect authority and accountability is that those who do these jobs are not the bosses of the managers' team members. The critical differences between line (direct) and support (indirect) accountability will be developed at greater length in Chapter 5.

The link to authority

Authority and accountability are closely related concepts. The exercise of relevant authority is a critical element of accountability. An accountable person is expected to exercise the relevant and appropriate authority for their role. In this context, authority is of two broad types: line authority and supporting authority.

Authority can relate to a position or a person. The ideal is the seamless integration of both. That is, the person in the role should have the personal qualities, know-how and expertise to ensure that the affairs they have authority over are carried out effectively. This is particularly important for support roles in, for example, research laboratories, regional headquarters (RHQs) and corporate headquarters (CHQs), where the *raison d'etre* should be the provision of value-adding knowledge to the field operations.

This book assumes that the people in the particular roles described have the requisite abilities to discharge their responsibilities in reality, ensuring that fit is a major HR challenge.

Teams and shared accountability

Popular wisdom has it that teamwork involves shared accountability. But this is a common mistake. Teamwork is shared endeavour, not shared accountability. A team is led by an individual who is personally accountable for the team results. Current management fashion may encourage CEOs to talk of 'we', 'the team', and 'consensus decision-making', and favour democratic leadership over autocracy, but whatever the language, noone usually doubts who is the boss.

This is clearest during a crisis. It is also a reason for the short CEO tenures we have today – according to research by Booz Allen Hamilton, annual CEO turnover grew by 59 per cent between 1995 and 2006 – as CEOs are ejected following poor corporate performance. This has been the case even at blue chip companies such as IBM, General Motors, Home Depot, BP and Marks & Spencer, to mention but a few. It is equally clear that in cases of malpractice it is key individuals who are cited, depending on the nature of the case: as at Enron, World Com (in the USA) and Ahold (in the Netherlands), where the legal process (and in some cases even prison) have removed CEOs and/or CFOs from the C-Suite.

Accountability assumes a proactive and conscious commitment to the purpose of an organization by an individual. It also presupposes clarity, transparency and participation, which enable contribution to that purpose. Single-point reporting (reporting to one person, not many) enables the ultimate enhancement of the individual's performance. This is why the once popular matrix structures of the past have been abandoned by the likes of Hoechst, Shell and Philips.

What is management accountability?

Management accountability can be viewed from above and from below – in relation to the commitments the manager has made to those in the level above him or her, and in relation to the obligations of the manager to his or her subordinates – obligations connected not only to the accomplishment of the work for which they are being employed, but to their learning and development. The accountabilities of employees, for example, in relation to their work commitments, have been described in terms of 'commitment' and 'adherence'.[11]

Commitment: employees must fulfil their output commitments exactly, in terms of quantity, quality, and time parameters, as defined in the assignments, projects, services and other deliverables – unless the manager agrees to alter them. The employee should not surprise the manager at the due date with unexpected changes that have not been agreed in advance.

Adherence: Employees must simultaneously observe and work within defined resource constraints – that is, the rules and limits set by policies, procedures, contracts, law and managerial guidelines. At the same time, 'managers have to be clear with their subordinates about what (quantity and quality of output) they are expected to deliver, and when. They are also accountable for providing the relevant resources.'[12] This means employees must bring about the results expected of them and do so in the correct manner, that they may reasonably expect that their goals should be made clear to them, and that they should be provided with what they need in order to achieve them.

Accountability is concerned with expectations, obligations, commitments and adding value. It encompasses rights and responsibilities. A competent manager fulfils commitments both to those above and to those below him or her.

The 10 key management accountabilities

As we have already seen in the case of the financial services company, levels of accountability can be assigned to organizations depending on a variety of factors, not least the types of decisions taken by people in various positions within the organization's hierarchy. And these levels of accountability only rarely correspond with the existing management layers.

Managerial accountability typically commences at the second level of accountability (the first layer of management), when there is a front-line team of subordinates at Level 1. (Although the front line may be higher than Level 1, as will be explained later.)

In order to meet the criterion of value added decision-making, a *bona fide* line manager must be accountable for the following:

1. Deciding (or at least having a veto on) who comes into the team, negotiating and managing a budget for that team, and being held to account for its expenditure.
2. Deciding who will work where, in which jobs and when (eg on which shift), as relevant.

3. Securing employee commitment to attain the relevant goals and providing them with the means – the authority or the resources, especially financial – they need to deliver their goals.
4. Giving constructive feedback and deciding upon individuals' performance and appraisal ratings, agreeing their training and development needs, and ensuring these are acted upon. Deciding appropriate rewards on the basis of performance and contribution in relation to the agreed commitments.
5. Ensuring the members of the team meet all their obligations, and, if necessary, changing the goals, obligations or team members, as appropriate.
6. Providing solutions when confronted with problems. The underlying thinking required for effective problem-solving starts in the concrete domain in operational jobs and moves into the increasingly abstract domain for strategic accountabilities.[13] This process is sometimes referred to as the different degrees of abstraction. At strategic levels the problem is known but the solution is not, in the initial stages. Accountability entails finding a new solution.
7. Making change happen. Change management is an integral part of any management job in the 21st century. In the first couple of management layers (Levels 2 and 3), leaders are expected to deliver change that is essentially a modification of an existing product, process or service. For Levels 4 and above these changes move into areas of breakthrough, 'first in the industry' type changes, which usually call for new knowledge when faced with new problems or new (eg market) opportunities. These are the basis of sustainable competitive advantage.
8. Achieving results from peers and colleagues over whom they do not have direct control. It is often necessary to win cooperation of others across the organization in order to complete one's own tasks and objectives. This can extend from the local and proximate to the global and increasingly remote. At strategic levels this can involve working across the entire organization.
9. Achieving results with and through external agencies, such as consumers, customers, suppliers and shareholders. This can also extend from the local to the global. The key difference is the nature of the accountability, which moves from the merely reactive response to the proactive, where the leader is called upon to influence and change the external environment on behalf of the organization.

> 10. Setting timelines and establishing goals, broken down from the leader's own targets, which then need to be achieved in terms of quality, quantity and service.
>
> These are the 10 key accountabilities that enable a leader to add value on a spine of accountability.

It is possible that not all the 10 accountabilities are present or mastered in a given role. Nevertheless they strongly correlate, so you would expect the majority to be present. If not, then accountability is diluted, which may be an indication that the role overlaps with that of the job to which it reports. In which case, it is not adding value to the work of others.

It is hard to visualize an effective role that just calls for strategic problem-solving and operational change management within very limited time frames. In fact, if after investigation a spectrum of operational and strategic accountabilities emerges from the examination of a certain job, experience suggests there is a high probability that the job in question is compressed by one or more jobs above it. Another possibility, if not all of these accountabilities are in evidence, is that the job in question might be a support role (this will be explored in depth in Section 2, Chapter 6).

The accountabilities in these definitions vary depending on the person's position in the hierarchy. This is broadly as follows:

- financial resources – from dealing with expenses to capital and investment expenditure;
- problem solving – from concrete to abstract domains of thought;
- change – from the modification of what already exists to invention and discovery;
- internal and external networks – from the proximate to the remote;
- time – from short to long term.

Finally, if it cannot be placed in the hierarchy of jobs that add value, or cannot be shown to be a support job, then the job is hollow and we have 'a straw boss'.[14] The job is surplus: an unnecessary cost of no value to the organization or the incumbent.

I cannot stress enough the importance of the first of the 10 accountabilities listed above. If managers cannot decide who comes into and who leaves their team, they cannot be held accountable for the team's performance. The absence of this fundamental tenet of management accountability is a key flaw in the so-called accountability of many organizations, both private and public sector.

Personal fulfilment on the front line

I once interviewed a district nurse working for a major public sector health supplier. Her role seemed to belong to the first layer of management – but she had no budget and no control or say over who joined the team, nor how the team was to be deployed on an ongoing basis in the community. She had no budget accountability, other than when told, 'The budget is now spent so you need to cut back on expenses.'

Apparently in order to ensure objectivity in the promotion process, nurses seeking promotion attended a selection panel that asked standard questions. They were able to apply as often as possible for promotion to the next grade until the questions (which often came to be known in advance by those applying several times) were correctly answered. There was apparently no assessment of performance in the process! Furthermore, on any given day she could find the nurses that reported to her removed to work elsewhere. The organization design (or lack of it!) was hindering the effective discharge of the role in question.

And it gets worse. Although this person had joined this particular health service with the highest motives of service and concern for others, after 16 years she was close to despair. She felt trapped in an organization that loaded her with more work than she could carry out as she had no real or meaningful accountability to get things done. Her job satisfaction had been totally eroded by a heavy burden of frustration, exacerbated by multiple layers of management above her that were a non-felt presence. They were not adding anything to help her or her team.

Needless to say, those supposedly being served by this organization – the patients – also suffered from its organization design faults. Sadly, the more conscientious the personnel working in an unhealthy organization are, the greater their frustration.

The Accountable Leader Chapter 1: Key points

1. Do you know the answers to these questions for your organization?

    - How many layers of management are necessary and why?
    - How should functions and processes be aligned as a result?
    - How should spans vary and why?

- How should employees be rewarded?
- What are the logical steps of their personal development?

2. A definition: Accountability occurs when one individual is answerable to another for work (a goal-oriented behaviour), resources, results and/or services, which can be measured in quantity, quality, cost and time.

3. The basic premise of an accountable organization – a managerial leader takes only those decisions that cannot be taken by those reporting to him or her. Not because they are not permitted to take those decisions, but because they do not have the knowledge, skill and/or experience to do so. The person to whom that managerial leader reports must also make decisions, which are both different from and add value to the latter's work. As the work becomes more complex, so the decisions being taken differ in nature.

4. For an effective organizational structure, there must be accountable space between the individuals above the manager and those below. Otherwise, compression occurs. This is when two or more layers of people are working in the same decision-making zone or level of accountability.

5. There are 10 key management accountabilities that enable a leader to add value.

Ten indicators of unsound accountability – a checklist for CEOs

There are several signs of faulty organization design:

- unclear purpose and priorities;
- a lack of timely and appropriate decisions;
- duplication of work;
- too many ineffective meetings;
- a culture of long and excessive hours at work;
- managers working in their team members' decision space;
- multiple, small authorization steps leading to 'organizational treacle' that slows down decisions;
- quantitative grading systems that generate unnecessary jobs (and therefore structure) to provide administrative 'promotions';[15]
- undue loss of good people;
- top management thinks there is a capability problem.

Do you recognize any of these signs in your organization?

Notes

1. The front line is not included in the count as it is not a leadership layer.
2. I use the term 'grading' synonymously with terms such as job evaluation and job classification.
3. Clearly it had occurred to the executive who initiated the project!
4. Bains, G *et al* (2007) *Meaning Inc.: The blueprint for business success in the 21st century,* Profile Books, London
5. Handy, C (1997), *The Hungry Spirit,* Hutchinson, London
6. Here, and elsewhere in the book, organization design refers to the challenge of designing an optimal structure – the healthy corporate skeleton needed for a healthy corporation, the foundation of good leadership distributed at all levels of the organization.
7. The concepts of accountability and responsibility are synonymous and interchangeable. The two words tend to cause confusion in English because people like to think the words represent different concepts. For the purposes of this book, 'accountability' may be taken as synonymous with 'responsibility', and *vice versa.*
8. Klatt, B, Murphy, S and Irvine, D (1999) *Accountability: Practical tools for focusing on clarity, commitment and results,* Kogan Page, London
9. These main types of authority are described in Chapter 4.
10. The four reasons that justify the need for support jobs are also outlined in Chapter 4.
11. Kraines, G A (2001) *Accountability Leadership,* Career Press, Franklin Lakes, New Jersey
12. Kraines, G A (2001) *Accountability Leadership,* Career Press, Franklin Lakes, New Jersey
13. Concrete thinking is characterized by immediate experience rather than by abstraction.
14. Brown, W (1971) *Organization,* Heinemann, London
15. An administrative promotion is a change in grade, but not a real change in accountability or the quality of decisions taken.

2 Organizing for accountability

*'The quality of management throughout the company
– not just the quality of the most senior executive leaders
– matters.'*

Glen Hubbard (2006) The Productivity Riddle,
Strategy + Business, (45) winter

Hierarchy: the response to increasing complexity

Hierarchy is an inevitable aspect of organizational life, yet the term 'hierarchy' is often misunderstood; seen as synonymous with top-down command and control. It is also incorrectly linked with the word 'authoritarian', a management style out of vogue today. However, hierarchy in the context of organization design, as described in this book, has nothing to do with an authoritarian style, nor is it the equivalent of top-down command and control.

Hierarchy is a common concept in mathematics, biology and information theory, where it refers to qualitative increases in complexity. It is the association with complexity that is important, relating, as it does, to the increase in complexity of work and concomitant increase in the quality of decisions needed in an accountable organization that requires layers of value-adding management. Organizational hierarchy is associated with accountability for more complex decisions. In many organizations it is the misalignment of accountability and complexity that leads to empty jobs, cluttered bureaucracies and frustration.

The theory is clear. The problem for managers is how to put it into practice. How many vertebrae should there be in this spine of accountability? One too many layers, or one too few, are equally debilitating. Both result in slow decision-making and frustration for subordinates. Too many layers and decision-making slows down, but too few and it also slows down, as the key manager gets overloaded.

The challenge remains. Which are the key jobs? How are they to be identified? What is the impact of removing a job from this spine? What impact will this have on the development and motivation of the incumbents? Surprisingly, at the beginning of the 21st century this is still an area of guesswork in many organizations. In 2007 I ran a webcast with the Conference Board in New York on the subject of organization design and leadership. In answer to a poll question, 72 per cent of participating companies (about 40, mostly North American) indicated they felt they had too many layers of management and did not know what the right number should be.

The challenge in the 21st century is to build accountable organizations: those in which the accountabilities of the individuals who work in them are clearly defined, differentiated and understood in a way that is motivating and meaningful.

The importance of a sound organizational platform

Since Alfred Chandler, Professor of Business History at Harvard Business School, presented theories on the multi-divisional form of organization, and organizational strategy, it has been generally recognized that organization design should be aligned to organizational purpose and strategy. But there is not the same widespread awareness of how a sound structure can assist efforts to identify, test and develop successful leaders.

A well-designed organization enables individuals to give a good account of themselves. It enables people to demonstrate and develop their potential. An accurate plotting of key accountabilities is a crucial part of designing an effective organization. 'To be truly effective, an organization requires healthy informal connections that ensure agility, as well as clear vertical accountabilities that foster a culture of execution', argued Emmanuel Gobillot, Director of Leadership Services at the Hay Group consultancy.

The fact that the world in which modern organizations must act is an increasingly fast-moving one simply makes the task more urgent. In the telecommunications industry, for example, the ceaseless reinvention of technologies intensifies the need for cost-effective organizations of motivated, talented people. The industry has – so far – struggled to cope with these pressures.

Top down or bottom up?

The 'structure follows strategy' school leads to top-down design (from the CEO) of organizational architecture. That is logical, but it is not enough. Good organization design should also work upwards from the front line at the same time. This latter aspect is invariably overlooked, but it is the most reliable way to identify which roles in a spine of accountability add value to the customer and are fit-for-purpose. The relevance and importance of the 'bottom-up' perspective will be emphasized throughout this book.

Effective organization design is not unlike the building of the Sydney Harbour Bridge. Construction started from each bank of the harbour and met successfully in the middle. Effective organization design has to be tackled simultaneously from two directions: top-down and bottom-up. The top perspective provides the link to purpose and strategy; the bottom one the equally important link to the customer. The two approaches need to be complementary to ensure they link up appropriately in the middle. When this does not happen there is invariably a bulge in middle management, as was the case with the financial services company in the first chapter, with its narrowest spans of control in the middle.

The scope for improvement and success afforded by sound and accountable organizational structures is unlikely to be appreciated if the very concept of accountability is misunderstood and misapplied. This, unfortunately, is often the case at the present time – particularly in the public sector. Bottom-up empowerment is regularly confused with top-down control in an effort to meet largely political targets. Professional people near the front line are being made to perform tasks that they should not have to undertake – tasks beneath the level of accountability for which they have been trained.

The frustrations involved in such a situation are obvious, and they proceed from confusion about what accountability means, and give rise to an improper distribution of work. It is a waste of talent, allegedly in short supply.[1] If this trend is not redressed, accountability will become – like bureaucracy before it – associated with all that is obstructive, oppressive and unwieldy in organizations.

What makes for an accountable organization in which leaders are held to account?

An accountable organization is one in which the responsibilities of the individuals who work in it are clearly defined and understood and are not overlapping. It is one in which those individuals know what they must answer for and are properly equipped for the work for which they are answerable, in which what they must answer for is aligned to the purpose of the organization, and in which their various contributions to the fulfilment of that purpose are properly coordinated.

An accountable organization is one in which the people belonging to it know what they should be doing, how what they are doing relates to and furthers the efforts of those they are working with, and are competent and empowered to do it. Their performance is measured against objective yardsticks, for which they receive rewards or sanctions, based on clear feedback.

In an accountable organization people know what they will be rewarded for, and how those rewards are set and calibrated. They know they will be given the means to carry out the objectives they have agreed to. They also know what the consequences will be for not completing the tasks and assignments they have agreed to complete. Things happen in an accountable organization; performance counts. A bureaucracy, by way of contrast, is an organization that is disconnected from performance. It does not deliver its mission and noone in the organization cares, or suffers as a result. Things don't happen as they should.

An organization can be said to have vertical and horizontal aspects to its architecture. The vertical aspects relate to its height – the number of management layers. The horizontal aspects relate to its reach or span of management (or span of leadership, often referred to as the span of control). It covers how work is grouped or chunked together, and how groups of teams interact, which calls for integration and coordination.

In a properly accountable organization these two dimensions are in a state of dynamic equilibrium. But the majority of large organizations have too many layers and their average spans of management are too narrow. Organizations like this – with their horizontal and vertical aspects out of kilter – can be hell to work in.

The importance of organizations being 'in flow'

Mihaly Csikszentmihalyi is a distinguished Professor of Psychology at Claremont Graduate University in the US. His research has focused on the importance of people being 'in flow' in their work – in a state in which their capability matches the challenge of the work they are doing. When people find they are working outside their comfort zone they become anxious and are unable to cope. And the converse applies. When people do work that is beneath them, they become bored, frustrated and so on. The key question is: 'Are you big enough for your job? Is your job big enough for you?'[2]

Organizations can also be in flow. An organization is in flow, or in a state of equilibrium, when the required number of management layers matches the effective reach over the relevant resources that the organization needs in order to deliver its purpose. When organizations are not balanced – not in flow, not in a condition in which their structures are adapted to their purposes – those who work in them cannot get in flow either. This is because their personal accountabilities will be blurred and unclear.

Sustained competitive advantage

An organization in flow is a basic requirement for sustained competitive advantage. Once purpose and strategy are agreed upon, the key to finding an optimal structure is to focus first on the requirements of the vertical axis. The driving question is: 'How many layers of management are required to add value to the customer front line?' If an organization has too many layers of management, a narrow management span of control is inevitable. The opposite approach, though – focusing first on the horizontal axis – is not as rigorous a means of identifying precisely where the obstacle exists.

For example, my colleague, Adam Pearce, and I undertook a review of a public utility in New York in 2007. It had three more layers of management than it needed. The deputy CEO role had a span of 13, while a middle management field role in the same chain of command had a span of 2. Using the span measurement only as the path to effectiveness, the tendency was to delete the role with the smaller span. But analysis of the spine of accountability revealed the latter role was adding value (albeit in a poorly designed structure), while the former role was a non-job with no distinct or discrete accountability of its own. In other words, the role with the wider span needed to be deleted. This is counterintuitive for most CEOs.

Good organization design calls for equal attention to both these dimensions of the overall architecture.

Overloading the levels: a US example

A good illustration of why organizations need to have the vertical hierarchy of work levels and the horizontal spans of control balanced – or in flow – occurred when Unilever purchased Breyers ice cream business in the United States. Unilever was the largest ice cream business globally, and Breyers was the biggest ice cream operator in North America. At the time, one of Unilever's North American operations, T. J. Lipton, had an ice cream division called Good Humor. So the original plan was to absorb Breyers into Lipton. These two companies each had a turnover in excess of US $1 billion. Lipton was essentially an ambient foods company, which happened to have an ice cream division, at Level 4.

When the plan to merge the two companies was announced, the president of Lipton proposed an additional layer of management, an Executive Senior Vice President or COO, as his deputy (two dubious titles that often signal a non-job). But on examination it was clear that both companies operated at the same level of accountability. They were both at Level 5 (often a key general management role, as in this case) and adding two Level 5 roles together did not change the quality of the president's decision-making and creating a Level 6 role (though the traditional, quantitative approach of job evaluation schemes would not highlight this organization design shortcoming). There was therefore no justification for another layer of management, which would have made the structure sub-optimal.

This was a case where the horizontal reach was out of kilter. The span of management was too wide and could not be managed by the president. He quickly recognized this – hence his request for another layer of management. However, this response, though common, could not solve the problem. In fact, it signalled that the organization design was sub-optimal.

A closer examination of the original idea revealed that there were very few overall synergies between these two businesses. The customers were often different, purchasing the respective products at different outlets; the two supply chains were different, one relying on a network of cold-stores, the other on ambient warehouses; and finally the marketing approaches were different, given the different consumers. One was essentially targeting the impulse market with seasonal products, the other the more traditional grocery retail market.

The correct organization design decision was to separate the two companies – shift the Good Humor division from Lipton to Breyers, and thereby create two stand-alone Level 5 companies (Lipton excluding Good Humor and Breyers including it) in which the vertical and horizontal axes could be in flow. This is in fact what happened. Both companies have prospered since.

A level of confusion: a European example

Two retail companies in Europe took different approaches to organizing the horizontal reach of their geographical stores networks. One retailer, Tesco, recognized it had stores of differing sizes and complexity appealing to different markets. It realized it had stores at differing levels of accountability, which needed to report to field management at different work levels. Thus a Level 2 store manager would report to a Level 3 regional manager, while a Level 3 hypermarket manager needed to report to a Level 4 stores director.

At around this time the company also reorganized its stores into different formats, which made the overall stores structure doubly focused and effective. This sound structure also enabled a clear approach to career steps and leadership development. As is well known, Tesco has prospered and continued to grow throughout this period.

This is in stark contrast to the action taken by another retailer at the same time. The company's results and stock market position were both deteriorating at the time I conducted fieldwork in the stores side of the business. This second company was under a good deal of public pressure and had taken a number of cost reduction measures to improve results, as the top line was not growing. But this second retailer had no reference frame to guide the decisions on organization design.

There were two tiers of supervision in the stores. One, assistant supervisors, was between the front line sales staff and the store supervisors. The assistant supervisory roles were removed. Then cluster managers were appointed in place of the store supervisors. These would each run three stores, not just one as in the past. This saved the salaries of the redundant store managers but broke the principle of single-point accountability.

Single-point accountability refers to the fact that one person is accountable for the unit, in this case the store. The cluster concept meant there was noone physically present in the stores who was accountable for the resources in them. This led to delays, confusion and missed sales opportunities. Supervisors were very stressed and results declined.

When this did not work, the company was about to put back all the store managers, a correct decision, and the assistant supervisors – a wrong decision. Furthermore, the existing supervisors were demoralized by the recent changes, which had made their jobs more difficult and unclear. The company had a major morale problem now and store sales continued to plummet.

The great majority of the stores were at Level 2. Some of the largest stores, which were critical to the company's growth plans, were at Level 3. But all stores reported to area managers at Level 3, who in turn reported to Level 4 regional managers. The key retail managers who were needed to drive new growth were not empowered. The regional managers, to whom they reported, were not adding value.

The company was badly organized and was not releasing the talent of its key leaders. There was a clear case for organizing into different formats, as indeed Tesco had done at about the same time. But this second company was taking ill-advised organization design and leadership decisions driven by a desire to cut costs. The counterbalancing need to consider the effect on performance and accountability was ignored. This clearly resulted from the lack of sound organization design principles. The overall company performance did not improve and not long after this the CEO and the stores director left the business.

Lessons to be learnt

The message from these two examples is the same. In order to gain sustainable competitive advantage from organization design, companies must take into account both the vertical and the horizontal elements of their structures. Both are inextricably woven together. They must be in flow. Historically, most consultants and managers have tended to focus only on the horizontal dimension. This has been accentuated by both an inability to assess the height and effectiveness of the structure and an undue concern with process and the need to work effectively across an organization. The latter is very important but is only half of the picture. The key to deciding how business units, regions and functions should be grouped together comes from having an accurate grip on accountability in the vertical structure.

Why are organizations so often lacking clear accountabilities?

There can be a number of reasons, the most notable of which are:

- unclear direction or purpose;
- faulty strategy;
- key roles not linked to strategy;
- lack of understanding about accountability;
- poor organization design, which is not in flow because of the lack of a framework of principles;
- negative company culture and history;
- genuine capability problems;
- an obsession with continuous cost reduction;
- lack of feedback from the external environment;
- lack of performance measures;
- lack of consequences for action;
- the adoption of management fads and fashions, which lack sound theoretical underpinnings.

In the private sector an obsession with continuous cost reduction is the most recurring of these problems. It is in part driven by the pressure of stock market scrutiny, but since the late 1980s, ill-advised re-engineering and endless process mapping initiatives have not helped.

Well-intentioned CEOs set out to empower their people, but in this more competitive age they are soon driven by a need or desire to cut costs to improve profitability. This pressure is most intense in those businesses where the top line is not growing, and profitability is therefore not growing or is even declining. And as long as an ill-informed surgeon has a scalpel, he can continue cutting until the body fails.

It is not difficult to find and remove costs in a large organization. That is not the challenge. The real challenge is in knowing when to stop and why. The crucial question for a CEO is: 'Am I cutting fat or muscle?' In other words, will the desire to cut costs result in negative performance?

If that question cannot be answered with certainty, it is unlikely that a truly cost-effective organization will be the result. The desire to cut costs is apt to go to extremes, which then adversely affects performance. This is why some organizations can actually fall into the trap of being too flat.

In the public sector, insulated from these economic pressures, the problem stems often from the lack of a performance culture, grading systems that serve the interests of staff but not the patient or customer, a stream of politically correct measures undermining merit and a lack of urgency or any real desire to rectify rich structures that stem from an institutionalized lack of clearly defined accountabilities. France Telecom is an interesting example. Like many telecom companies, FT had a heritage of fixed line technology and a public sector monopoly prior to privatization. Although it bought the more nimble and entrepreneurial Orange, prospering in the mobile sector, it seems old habits die hard. Fairly soon after the acquisition the culture of the old French operation sustained around 65 per cent of the people, but less than half of the profits.

The Accountable Leader Chapter 2: Key points

1. An accountable organization is one in which the responsibilities of the individuals who work in it are clearly defined, understood, and not over-lapping. Those individuals are answerable, and what they must answer for is aligned to the purpose of the organization.
2. In an accountable organization people know what they will be rewarded for, and how those rewards are set and calibrated. They know they will be given the means to carry out the objectives they have agreed to. They also know what the consequences will be for not completing the tasks and assignments they have agreed to complete.
3. An organization has vertical and horizontal aspects to its architecture. The vertical relate to its height – the number of management layers. The horizontal relate to its reach or span of control.
4. An organization is in flow, or in a state of equilibrium, when the required number of management layers matches the effective reach over the relevant resources that the organization needs in order to deliver its purpose.
5. An organization in flow is a basic requirement for sustained competitive advantage.

Notes

1. See Baroness O'Neill's Reith lectures in 2002, 'A question of trust', for an insightful presentation of the consequences of this approach.
2. As McMorland (2005) put it very succinctly: Are you big enough for your job? Is your job big enough for you? *University of Auckland Business Review,* **7** (2)
3. In this context, 'customer' covers all external stakeholders.
4. 'Work levels' is the term that Tesco and a number of other companies have used to describe their levels of accountability. Tesco implemented levels in 2001.

3 Leaders and leadership development

'The roles of both the manager and the leader are critical. Successful organizations are run by men and women who are in combination both managers and leaders.'

Robert P Neuschel,
The Servant Leader

The corporal with a squad of 10 men, the night shift supervisor of a team of 30, the production manager with a department of 80, the call centre manager with a staff of 900, the business unit manager in charge of 3,000, the country manager with an organization of 12,000, the General in charge of a Corps of 30,000, or the CEO of an international company of 200,000; these are all leaders. They all have to lead. They are all held to account; albeit in fundamentally different ways.

The Napoleon syndrome

One of the major weaknesses of most treatments of leadership is the tendency to zero in on the person at the top who leads everyone else: the '1 in 100,000' leader. Thus people study the deeds of Napoleon Bonaparte, but tend to overlook the officers and leaders who fought and led throughout Napoleon's

Grand Armée. Napoleon is not the only person who made decisions in his army. And, it might be argued, he wasn't necessarily the best decision-maker either. Should we really be taking how-to lessons from a leader who twice lost 95 per cent of his men – from an army of 500,000 in 1812 – and twice abandoned them in the field? Is this the kind of leader that you want in the echelons of your organization, let alone at its head?

The focus in this book will not be on the CEO, but on leaders all the way from the front line up through the organization – the '10,000 leading the 90,000'. It will be on distributed leadership, the leadership required at each level. Such leadership is the heart and soul of any successful organization, whatever its size and complexity. Also, I will concentrate on the practical substance of leadership and on the conditions for facilitating leadership, and not on style or charisma, which are singular and individual.

Leadership versus management: a barren dichotomy

There is a widespread tendency for leadership to be separated from management. In the management literature, for example, leadership guru Warren Bennis, distinguished Professor of Business Administration and founding Chairman of The Leadership Institute at the University of Southern California, describes the manager as someone who 'administers, maintains, focuses on systems and control, has a short-term view, who asks how and when and focuses on the bottom line', and the leader as someone who 'innovates, develops, focuses on people, inspires trust, asks why, has a long-term view and an eye for the horizon.'

In the conduct of business, however, the debate seems largely academic, as whether it is management or leadership, it is exercised in different ways by the same individuals.

Interestingly, according to the likes of Frederick Taylor and Henri Fayol, early 20th century pioneers of business research, management is not about administration; it is about 'getting things done through a community of people'. Exactly what is required in the modern world of networked organizations and distributed leadership.

In this book, the terms leader and manager will be applied to the same individuals and used interchangeably.

A key distinction

A key distinction in leadership is between the leader of an organization and a leader in an organization.

Leaders of

Leaders of organizations are those at the top of the organizational tree; the US President, the CEO of General Electric, or the Secretary-General of the United Nations. They are the charismatic, transformational leaders so popular in the leadership literature.

Notably, leadership theories tend to concentrate on aspects of leadership such as the leader's own personal traits, the followers, and the situation. There is, in some theories, a strong focus on behaviour appropriate in a given situation in terms of leadership style.

What these theories lack is a focus on substance, an acknowledgement that the behaviour and performance of a supervisory leader at the front line of an organization would be quite different in substance, not just style, to that of a middle or senior manager. There is nothing in these theories that differentiates between the quality of work, and therefore leadership required, at different layers of management in an organization. This is a core weakness. The preoccupation is always about looking for the 'right way' to lead.

Leaders in

Invariably, leadership studies tend to focus on leaders *of* a community or organization. They do not concentrate on leaders *in* the community or organization. The search is for outstanding examples of leadership; leaders at the top of an organization who have stood out in their time above peers and competitors.

The focus of this book, however, is on the 99.9 per cent of distributed leaders in and throughout the community, on the situation or accountable context in which that leadership takes place, and on the behaviours required at varying levels of accountability in an organization. Because the most widespread leadership need is for those who can take the helm at various levels in society and organizations, and add value as leaders and managers. Ensuring that organizations have such leaders is a complex challenge, as it means designing organizations with the right number of value-adding layers of leadership and ensuring that the leaders at each level are capable of making the appropriate decisions required of them.

What is meant by leadership?

Leadership does not exist by itself. It can only be really understood in relation to the role in which it is discharged. Furthermore, it does not help to manufacture a distinction between leadership and management as if they are completely different. They are not. Hence I will often refer to 'managerial leadership' or 'managers' throughout the book.

Leaders are required throughout an organization, but we need a theory that explains what leaders do at different levels within an organization. Effective leadership is not simply situational, but contextual – linked to a level of accountability, and dependent on the competence of the occupant to handle the demands of a specific role. The importance of context is to provide meaning and satisfaction to individuals. 'The drive for contextualization and coherence is an essential cognitive tool for dealing with a complex and bewildering environment,' says Gurnek Baines.[1]

A key tenet of this book will be to show how an effective, accountable organizational structure provides the context for effective leadership, as it is the foundation of both leadership and leadership development. Effective managerial leadership depends on the ability of the occupant of a role to lead other people (management accountability below). In some roles, leadership will devolve from various types of authority rather than the mobilizing of people.

Leadership is a process whereby an individual sets out a meaningful direction or line of action in such a way that others will willingly move in that direction to the best of their ability.

Effective leadership depends upon three critical variables:

- an accountable role;
- a healthy, effective organizational infrastructure of roles;
- a well-balanced, competent individual.

Most organizations tend to concentrate only on the third of these factors when assessing leadership capability. The first two, especially the second, are often ignored. This explains why so many leaders are not truly held to account and why so many leadership development schemes fail.

Strategic leadership

Strategic leadership is not simply about the people at the top of an organization occupying strategic roles. It has a wider canvas than that. Strategic leadership is the capacity, among the person or people at the highest levels of the hierarchy, to both maintain high performance and to sense change and guide the organization through a shift in direction. There are four interrelated components to this capability.

At the core is the ability to set a course that inspires the organization to win. Strategic leaders must establish and articulate a compelling story that aligns the top team, informs the prioritization of campaigns, and motivates the organization.

The second component is an aligned top team, one level below the CEO or top executive leader. Critical roles for this team include developing a balanced action team that builds on each member's individual leadership strengths, and developing a CEO and top team succession pipeline (linked to campaigns).

The third component is a small set of prioritized and focused campaigns that are supported by the top team. Campaigns must be designed for success, each with its own balanced leadership team, clear goals, metrics and incentives.

The last component is an empowered organization, one that is culturally fit and with a structure that allows individuals to participate and be accountable for their results.

These four components must be dynamically balanced and in equilibrium. Each component must be strong in itself; but in a world that is ever changing, the ability to build new capabilities that sustain competitive advantage comes from simultaneously leveraging all four variables.

One common problem today is that many leadership teams focus on only one component. In particular, they focus exclusively on strategy (through their campaigns); but they do not link strategy to the organization's capability, they try to do too many things at one time, and they lose a sense of overall direction and how to win. The job gets only partially done and the top team cannot understand why their strategy is not achieving results as planned.

The strategic leadership model that I find most instructive, developed by Booz, is summarized in Figure 3.1.

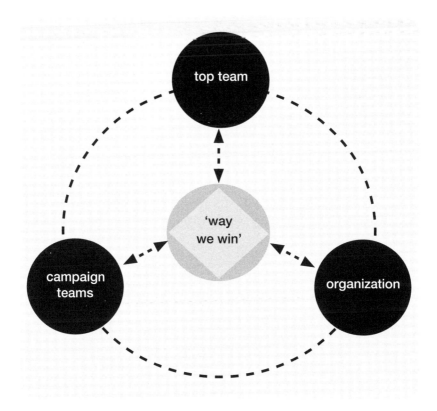

Figure 3.1 The strategic leadership agenda

It is important to bring together expertise from strategy, assessment, psychology, and organization design and development in order to align and manage the leadership agenda. These four variables mutually influence one another and need to be synchronized to ensure an effective outcome. You cannot lead or produce leaders in an organization that does not know where it is going, does not have a healthy structure and does not have capable people held to account.

The issue of talent

Although the financial services company in the opening example was not a truly accountable organization and was over-managed, such organizations tend to be noteworthy for two things; everyone is working hard, and they are putting in long hours. Unfortunately, if corporate performance is below par, top management tends to believe that there is a capability problem. This is seen as a shortage of true talent; a shortage of leaders.

In 2005, Infosys (the IT outsourcing providers based in India) set out to recruit 10,000 IT engineers. It received 1 million applications for those vacancies. The logistics of fairly and accurately assessing 1 million applicants is not a problem that most HR managers today would know how to handle. And yet some still maintain that there is a war for talent.

Even more importantly, many companies have an abundance of talent right on their doorstep, within the organization itself. The challenge is identifying that talent. The contribution and performance of individuals cannot be accurately assessed in an organization with a cluttered hierarchy of unclear and ill-defined accountabilities. Likewise, it is difficult to make a strong contribution in a situation in which it is not clear who should do what.

This situation is often found in organizations that believe they are short of leaders and genuine talent. Indeed, there is much talk of a talent shortage today, when arguably there has never been a greater abundance of educated and talented people available to take on challenging work. Far too many organizations – both in the private and public sectors – do not know how to build sound structures designed to deliver their core purpose and to enable people to learn and grow by undertaking demanding and fulfilling work; to build, in short, accountable organizations.

Organizations will need to rectify this situation. Talent will follow a challenge. Talent today is more internationally mobile than ever before. The best people do not have to stay in a stultifying environment, stifling their initiative with no or few opportunities for learning, job satisfaction and growth. They can move on. Just ask the new technology companies in developed countries competing for talent with China, India and Korea.

So, the real problem does not seem to be a shortage of talent, but rather a shortage of organizations that know how to organize, harness and develop their talent.

Leadership pipeline – what pipeline?

At the end of 2004, in New York, I addressed a number of managers responsible for developing leaders in their respective global companies. I was surprised to see how many were following the precepts of a book by management guru Ram Charan, called *The Leadership Pipeline: How to build the leadership powered company*.

Charan's model talked of 'self-management, management, managing managers, functional managers, group managers and enterprise managers'. Once the CEO was included, it assumed seven levels of accountability, apparently following Canadian-born psychoanalyst Elliott Jaques' seven-strata model of the Requisite Organization.[2] But Jaques had suggested that there were 'up to seven or eight strata of accountability available', not that most companies had seven levels.

Even in the US, not that many companies can justify seven levels of accountability. Yet it was clear from the presentations I witnessed that many of these companies assumed that Jaques' seven strata, and consequently Charan's model, fitted their business. They had not thought about the possible scenarios where the front line might not be at Level 1, in terms of accountability. They had no way of assessing the top level of accountability in their corporations.

So, for example, Charan's pipeline answer would have self-management at the first level of accountability. In my experience this covers most companies, but, in this age of technological innovation and offshoring, not all.

Next the pipeline model talks of management, without describing what that entails. Then we have managers of managers, which, as the front line can be at Level 2 or even Level 3, would make 'managers of managers' Level 4 or 5 respectively. The next level in the pipeline solution is jobs classified as 'functional managers'. This is an extremely ambiguous title, which depends on the size and complexity of the organizational infrastructure under review. Functional managers could be anything from Level 2 to 5, but in this solution they seem to be universally positioned at Level 4.

The next two levels in the pipeline are 'group' and 'enterprise' management positions. These are titles that I have found used in widely different ways around the world to indicate jobs at very different levels of accountability. To simply assume they might indicate jobs at the fifth and sixth levels of accountability is naïve and dangerous.

Charan's pipeline model is not the only flawed talent management model. What was telling though was how organizations presented their experiences as examples of best practice in global leadership development. It had not occurred to them that they might well be working on a false organization design premise. Their stories seemed to suggest that they were treating the pipeline model as a fixed, 'one size fits all' solution. It was a good example of why leadership development programmes fail.

> The first step towards ensuring effective leadership exists throughout an organization is to design a sound platform of challenging roles. This means the organization's structure must be designed with the right number of meaningful jobs, and these jobs must be aligned to the purpose of the organization. They must add value to the work of others while at the same time allowing individuals the opportunity to learn and grow.

Leadership development in the organization

It takes time to develop leadership abilities in an organization. But it takes more than time. It involves taking the right steps, making the right moves, at the right time; and it involves a clear understanding of what these steps are.

As part of a case study into leadership development at Unilever (related in more detail in my previous book, *The Healthy Organization*, 2004) I looked at 10 variables to assess which had the most impact on leadership development. A period of time spent at Level 3, and again at Level 5, was a critical factor in determining who operated successfully at Levels 6 to 8.

When it comes to the personal growth of leaders throughout an organization, especially those who get to the top echelons, there is no substitute for experience and clear accountability. Accelerated development sounds exciting but it is full of pitfalls, especially if the organizational architecture is flawed. There is also compelling evidence to suggest that skipping a level of accountability in a career is a recipe for failure.

Later chapters address the issue of the boundary moves that underpin successful leadership development. Suffice it to say here that a boundary move is one that takes leaders or potential leaders outside their comfort zone without progressing beyond their learning zone. This process is really only a muddled lottery unless the people planning the leadership development programme accurately pinpoint different levels of accountability within an organization.

Finding the appropriate number and quality of leaders to ensure the organization succeeds, or at least does not fail, is about orchestrating the training and development of leaders in the community – not something that is addressed much in the current literature on leadership.

Job evaluation: status, grades and ranks[3]

If accountability is so important in leadership development, why then do so many companies and public agencies fail in this regard?

One answer is the historical use of a system of grades and ranks. While these started out being used primarily for job evaluation, almost unconsciously grades have come to drive organization design – something for which grading systems were never designed. Moreover, these structures often acquire a link with matters of status, and this contributes to ineffective structures, unwieldy bureaucracies and promotions that do not reflect substantial changes in responsibility. The upshot is cost drift, hollow jobs and dissatisfied staff.

Status

Status is the position of an individual in relation to others, and it assumes considerable importance in many cultures. Unfortunately, a desire for status can work against recognition given for work done well, and prove the enemy of merit.

Issues relating to status often encourage the existence of non-jobs, which are detrimental to the development of effective leaders. There is a tendency to create positions of honour to recognize the perceived importance of certain individuals. The forms of expression may differ markedly from culture to culture, but the essential process is there just the same.

Status is universal

It would seem there is not a country or organization in which status is not an issue. Although some countries, for example Germany and India, might be more noticeably prone to a hierarchical culture with clear boundaries, less overt forms of deference exist elsewhere.

Take the United States, a country that prides itself on its robust individualism, and with good reason. Even there status is a fixture in the organizational climate. The issue of titles is simply one indicator of how embedded status can become. Large, complex US companies almost universally talk of non-exempt (normally unionized) and exempt categories of staff. The latter are referred to generally as managers, although more senior individuals are executives. The different tiers are typically demarcated in the junior layers as: managers, who invariably report to directors, to vice presidents, to senior and/or executive vice presidents, to a COO, to a CEO.

There seems to be only one valid reason for the role of COO; when the person in the role of COO is the Dauphin – the heir apparent – being prepared to succeed the CEO within months.[4] Otherwise, this US practice is in essence a status-driven approach reinforced by different benefits, bonus plans and long-term incentives. The problem, which I have observed again and again in the United States, is that often the layers in which these titles reside belong to jobs that are not needed because they do not add value.

Status becomes a problem when it undermines efforts to build a genuine meritocracy. Status can become focused on who you are, not on how you perform or what you are accountable for. In this sense status is not seen as appropriate in an egalitarian setting where performance should drive rewards. Most modern organizations have rightly done away with the trappings of status, such as executive car parks, special carpet and curtains for senior managers, private dining rooms and other associated perks. These trappings were also usually aligned to grades, which further heightened resistance to their removal.

Curing the grade obsession

Grading systems are widely used in both the private and the public sector. They are usually underpinned by a system of job evaluation. These systems aim to lay the foundations for a rational, fair and equitable system of pay or reward. The focus is on the job, not the jobholder. This is in contrast to status, which is more concerned with the person and the need to embellish his or her standing in an organization.

But the fundamental problem with job evaluation is it simply measures the job as it exists. It does not ask whether it *should* exist and, if so, whether it adds anything to other jobs around it.

Systems of job evaluation enable the comparison of grades in different organizations. This becomes the basis for pay comparisons in a given market. Organizations can then correlate their respective systems to make the capture of market pay data more easy and reliable. A correlation of this kind could establish that grade 3 in one system is equivalent to 24 in another, and 56 in yet another. On this basis, the reward packages can be assessed.

Many international companies have correlated their job grading systems for market survey purposes, and reward consultants have similar approaches with their bespoke grading systems. But this approach has simply spread problems that arise when there are (as in most cases) too many grades. Where there are too many grades, so there are too many layers of management, and leadership development programmes are undermined.

Figure 3.2 illustrates the relationship between grades and levels in a real company that has subsequently been analysed according to the principles of accountability. Each pie represents a different level and, as is apparent, the distribution of grades does not correspond to differences in level.

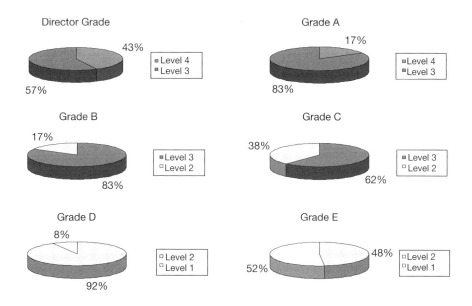

Figure 3.2   Misalignment of grades and levels

Figure 3.2 is one of many examples I have encountered where grades are scattered across different levels of accountability. In this example, all of the grades are split between more than one level of accountability. This completely undermines leadership development because the company is not able to identify a real promotion. For example, a person could be steadily promoted from grade E, to D, to C, to B, without leaving the second level of accountability. Similarly, an individual could move from grade C, to B, to A, to Director and not leave Level 3. Thus a series of supposed promotion steps could occur and yet all still be within the same level of accountability. These would be merely administrative or paper promotions.

In a worst case scenario, a person could be promoted from grade B to grade A and jump from Level 2 to Level 4. As will be demonstrated later in the book, this is a recipe for disaster for the individual concerned. There is robust evidence to suggest that you cannot successfully skip a level of accountability.[5]

The problem for companies like this is that they do not know where their true decision-making levels reside. This company was not aware of the problem it had. A reliance on grades for determining promotions is not a reliable basis for the development of leaders, and yet most organizations make this mistake. But when individuals associate grades with promotions, a grading obsession soon develops, with managers chasing grades by constantly switching jobs across the organization. This is unhealthy for the individual and for the company. This company, incidentally, was carrying millions of dollars of unnecessary cost in its management structure.

Having a small number of grades does not necessarily help either. An international media company that we worked with operated with only five grades, but some of those grades tended to straddle more than one level of accountability. Job evaluation grades are not a guaranteed basis for real promotion, but levels of accountability are and therefore provide a better platform for the development of leaders.

Although the public sector does not tend to correlate its job evaluation systems with global companies, it is still guilty of faulty internal comparisons. For example, it seems that some civil service grades were originally aligned to military ranks. But while the army, for example, had 19 ranks, it only had 7 battle echelons as a rule. Most public sector organizations, including the UN, seem to have little or no idea as to where their 'battle echelons' or levels of accountability reside. For example, most of my work in this area suggests, rather worryingly, that the civil service in the UK is broken at Level 3; precisely the level that is the backbone of successful organizations.

The great danger, which has subsequently plagued public sector organizations, is the assumption that grades can be aligned to layers of hierarchy. This inflationary alignment of grades and hierarchical layers has spawned public service organizations of diluted accountability that are a byword for lack of service and lack of job satisfaction. They are noted now more for job titles (driven by status concerns, perhaps) such as Deputy-This and Assistant-That. But what value are these jobs adding to the mission of the organization when they are not deputizing or assisting?

In one massively over-managed organization in India that I recently examined, 42 per cent of the titles of management included either 'Assistant to' or 'Deputy'. And they had worries about the leadership capability of their management!

Ranks

So, is a system of ranks the answer then? Well, not necessarily. First, let's look at the system of ranks in a police force.

The 52 police forces throughout the UK seem, like the civil service, to have aligned their ranks to a military model. In which case it is intriguing to note in the current police careers booklet that: 'The current rank structure has not varied a great deal (*apart from adding sub-divisions to the higher ranks*) – my italics – since the introduction of Peel's New Police'. The sub-divisions added seem to be ranks of deputy chief constables and assistant chief constables. With only 150,000 constables in total these are not large organizations, so why the extra ranks and layers of bureaucracy? It would seem the police – notwithstanding the plethora of ranks – are not too clear on where their true levels of accountability reside.

Not so long ago I worked with a major metropolitan police force in the United Kingdom and we concluded that there were a number of cornerstone problems:

- no unity of purpose;
- organization too self-sustaining because of rank obsession;
- ill-defined roles/boundaries;
- organization strangled by Head Office.

Among the root causes identified were:

- order/disorder struggles;
- an illusion of order;
- confusion because of system upon system;
- a rule-bound dependency structure.

Some of the recommendations were:

- reduce senior posts;
- merge intermediate levels;
- revise top roles;
- give guidelines not instructions;
- rationalize Head Office functions;
- devolve as much as possible.

This is not to imply any criticism of police endeavours in the United Kingdom, but this example dramatically underlines the shortcomings of a rank system not based upon clear levels of accountability.

In 2006, an excellent initiative to amalgamate police forces in the United Kingdom seemed to meet the needs for more effective organization design, leadership development, improved accountability and lower cost. Politicians turned it down.

Do the armed forces have the answer? It would seem not. In 1995, the Bett Independent Review, also in the United Kingdom, suggested, in the polite language of such reviews, that the military had too many ranks and that not all of them were adding value to the mission of the three forces. It was suggested that this situation should be reviewed. Apparently it was. The outcome was the removal of the rank of Field Marshall (a five-star rank not then occupied by any serving officer). The rank infrastructure of the forces was not affected. Or, putting it another way, the professionals outwitted the politicians.

But the real problem with the Bett Review, as with so many organizational reviews, was the fact that those who carried it out did not have a set of accountability principles to guide their conclusions, even though common sense was taking them in the right direction.

Self-actualization

An individual can reach personal fulfilment (self-actualization) at any level of accountability, provided that this level reflects and is aligned to their personal capability. They are then in flow as a person. But this is easier to describe than to achieve.

Abraham Maslow, the US psychologist, put forward a theory about self-actualization as part of his hierarchy of needs concept. Self-actualization involves the full realization of a person's desires and potential, an objective placed within a hierarchy of lesser needs, also calling for fulfilment. In short, personal fulfilment comes from stretching yourself to be what you can be.

In practice, this is the major challenge and ultimate justification of the HR profession. It needs to be able to ensure that employees are both personally in flow, and in productive roles aligned to the organization's mission or purpose. When this is achieved the individual is balanced, not stressed. The accountability and challenge of the role is matched by the ability of the incumbent.

Organizations owe it to themselves and their staff to deal with what is a critical question for the senior management team: 'Is the talent properly organized in real jobs that add value?' Only then can talented people fulfil their true potential.

The Accountable Leader Chapter 3: Key points

1. An effective, accountable organizational structure provides the context for effective leadership, as it is the foundation for both leadership and leadership development.

2. Strategic leadership is about setting a clear course for how to win and then ensuring that the links between an aligned top team, focused campaign teams, and an empowered organization are dynamically balanced and in equilibrium. In today's fast-changing environment, the ability to build new capabilities that drive sustainable competitive advantage comes from simultaneously leveraging all three variables.

3. The first step towards ensuring effective leadership exists throughout an organization is to design a sound platform of challenging roles. The organization's structure must be designed with the right number of meaningful jobs, and these jobs must be aligned to the purpose of the organization. They must add value to the work of others while at the same time allowing individuals the opportunity to learn and grow.

4. There may be a shortage of talent, but there is definitely a shortage of organizations that know how to organize, harness and develop their talent.

5. Grading systems were never designed to drive organization design. Where there are too many grades, there are too many layers of management, and leadership development programmes are undermined.

6. Job evaluation grades are not a guaranteed basis for real promotion. Levels of accountability are, and therefore provide a better platform for the development of leaders.

7. An individual can reach personal fulfilment at any level of accountability, provided that this level reflects and is aligned to their personal capabilities. They are then in-flow as a person. (This is easier to describe than to achieve.)

Notes

1. Gurnek Bains in his book, *Meaning Inc.: The blueprint for business success in the 21st century*.

2. Jaques, E (1989) *Requisite Organization*, Cason Hall & Co, Arlington, Virginia

3. I first set out a number of the ideas in this section in a series of articles for *Croner Pay and Benefits Briefing* during November and December 2005.

4. Kramer, R J (2006) *The Role of COOs*, The Conference Board, New York

5. See also Chapter 8 of *The Healthy Organization*.

4 Holding leaders to account: leadership by design

'Lack of accountability is a fatal flaw of leadership.'

Zenger and Folkman,
The Handbook for Leaders

We have established that leaders must be accountable for their work. The problem is that most organizations do not know how to make sure that this happens. They are not sure how to hold leaders to account, or indeed what leadership means for different jobs throughout an organization.

This uncertainty is invariably because organizations lack a logical framework or set of principles that can guide their organizational design and the empowerment of their people. The Decision Making Accountability (DMA) Solution Set provides the principles needed to address this problem.[1]

The DMA Solution Set

The DMA Solution Set is the product of extensive fieldwork, not merely speculative guesswork or theorizing. The ideas have been tested and refined in many industries and numerous countries.[2] They emerged from efforts to find solutions to real problems in leading companies, such as:

- How tall or flat should this organization be?
- How do leadership requirements change at different levels?
- How can potential leaders be identified?
- How can they be developed?
- How should they be rewarded?

The Solution Set is a way of arriving at solutions, not a 'one size fits all' approach. The solutions are flexible and can be variously applied to any number of different organizations.

First the needs of a specific organization have to be identified and understood. Then the appropriate solution can be provided. While the principles are universal, the applications are specific and particular. They help identify the specific and optimal architecture for many different types of organization.

Whatever an organization's age, size, complexity or mission, the DMA Solution Set is a powerful X-ray tool with which to discover what the most effective form of an organization should be. It is a key approach to organization design.

What is Decision Making Accountability?

A decision is a considered act in response to a demand or need. It can involve moving a process forward, changing a state of affairs, solving a problem or delivering a service. Decision Making Accountability is positive accountability.

DMA is the process of taking decisions in seven key decision-making zones called Elements (defined in detail later in this chapter) that align with the purpose and strategy of the organization and add value to the work of others, while at the same time enabling the individual taking the decisions to learn and grow.

We are dealing with a set of principles, which underpin a process aimed at identifying the required levels of decision-making in a given organization, together with the corresponding layers of management it needs. This process identifies whether or not people are being held to account in an organization. It determines the vertical dimensions of an organization's architecture, the spine of accountability, which is a key step in identifying any organization's ideal design.

The Accountability Probe

This process, known as an Accountability Probe, will be described in more detail later. It is one thing to know that an organization depends on sound levels of accountability, but quite another to detect whether it is in perfect working order. In most organizations this is still very much a matter of guesswork. The Accountability Probe plots what decisions people make and whether those decisions add value to the work of others. It reveals how many decision-making layers of management are required.

In the case of Unilever, for example, operating in 100 countries around the world, a total infrastructure with more levels of decision-making is required than, say, Amersham (prior to its takeover by GE), which has less international reach and less complexity. National operations, such as the Alliance and Leicester bank or a New York public utility, would, as a rule, require less again. It depends upon the complexity and size of an organization, which in turn drives the infrastructure needed to support the front line.

The number of jobs and levels of accountability needed determine an organization's infrastructure: the network of total jobs across all levels of accountability. One could, however, imagine a huge national organization such as the Indian railways or the Chinese Post, each with over 1 million employees, that might need the same number of management layers as a large multinational company.

The number of management layers is not fixed. Any of these organizations could change in the future, through acquisition or a major sale of assets, for example, which may alter the total number of management layers. The solutions suggested here are flexible and adaptable to the context and the needs of the particular organization being reviewed at a given point in time.

> The Accountability Probe plots what decisions people make and whether those decisions add value to the work of others. It reveals how many decision-making layers of management are required.

The importance of conceptual integration

The DMA logic integrates everything involved in the management of people. It is based on one simple idea: 'Are you making decisions that add value to the work of others in the same organization?' The Solution Set is therefore unique in its conceptual integration. Most other HR approaches to the management of people are only administratively integrated. This is a key difference.

The DMA Solution Set is holistic, not fragmented. Most traditional approaches such as job evaluation are quantitatively based, with points awarded for size of budget, turnover and number of subordinates. The DMA principles have a qualitative focus.

This model concentrates on the added value of decisions taken and how they differ from those of subordinates and superiors. It reveals which jobs must exist if an organization is to fulfil its purpose. No more, no less. This is an obvious first step to underpin who should be paid what and how they should be individually developed. But not a first step that traditional HR approaches and consultancies adopt.

The DMA Solution Set helps to identify the optimal organization structure. The approach starts at the bottom of the organization, at its front line. It is not a top-down process. Starting at the bottom is the only way to ensure an organization has the correct number of roles in total. This in turn provides a platform of real jobs for personal growth and leadership development, which facilitates meaningful coaching.

Although very few companies have adopted this approach to date, those that have tend to be successful organizations, and include companies like Tesco (with its international Leadership Framework) and Unilever (which introduced work levels in about 100 countries in 1998 as part of a global change in its reward strategy and practice), as well as B&Q and Orange. These firms have also variously aligned (linked) rewards to work levels in different parts of their organizations.

Malcolm Saffin, a leading authority on executive compensation and pensions, has underpinned some of his reward work at Amersham and Cable and Wireless on the logic of levels.

The link to business strategy

Determining the levels of accountability in an organization by exploring decision-making in a number of areas is essential. And as a number of companies have discovered, the framework of work levels revealed during this process can then be used to create reward systems and leadership development programmes.

Before determining levels of accountability or indeed devising leadership development programmes, however, the organization must understand itself and its core purpose. Effective people-development programmes reinforce the organization's purpose and strategy. Only once the organization's mission

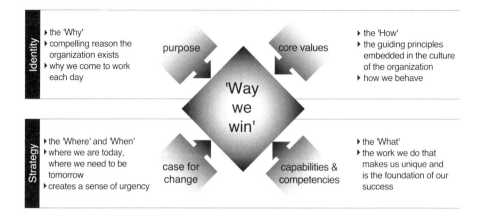

Figure 4.1 Booz's The core of strategic leadership

or purpose has been established can the boundaries of accountability be determined and measurable campaigns be orchestrated to deliver the organization's strategy.

Drawing again from Booz's strategic leadership framework, this critical area is addressed by establishing a compelling 'way to win' by addressing key themes across identity and strategy, as Figure 4.1 shows.

Each of the four variables (purpose, core values, case for change and capabilities & competencies) must reinforce the others in an ongoing, iterative and dynamic way, as each box assumes priority for a period. All the elements in the chart are relevant, even though the focus here is on the organizational dimension and its link with the top team, because issues of organization must always be considered in relation to the particular context in which the organization functions.

There are a number of key considerations relating to organization design and effectiveness. It is important to help an organization:

- define and communicate a compelling sense of direction – a 'way to win';
- ensure that identity and strategy are well aligned and that the strategy is robust;
- render strategy actionable by breaking it down into a small set of campaigns with measurable targets;
- review organization, ensuring it is culturally fit and that its structures of accountability are clear and efficient;
- assess the leadership talent available and match it to its strategy and campaigns;

- develop leadership talent through not only customized coaching, but also campaign team leadership;
- ensure that board and senior teams have balanced teams that are fit for the tasks in hand and are well aligned to the overall direction.

How might this play out in practice? In 1997, Tesco was the number two grocery business in the United Kingdom. A decade later, it had created about five times more value than two of its local retail rivals, Sainsbury's and Marks & Spencer, put together. Today, Tesco is the world's number three retailer.

How did Tesco make such significant progress? Partly by setting a strategic leadership agenda, one that included many of the factors mentioned above. The company focused on issues such as purpose, direction, talent and values. Significantly, Tesco has also implemented work levels and has aligned its leadership development framework to those levels.

Tesco's approach and the Booz strategic leadership model provide an insight into the complex interlinkages involved in the successful development and delivery of strategy through people. The two vital intertwined components that are most often overlooked or taken for granted are the aspects of organization design and the consequential leadership required. The mastery of this critical interlinkage is the subject of the rest of this book.

The DMA Solution Set explained

DMA is called a Solution Set because the appropriate action required in a given context depends upon knowing the needs of the particular individual and organization. It is a blueprint for holding leaders to account. The key premise is: jobholders must take decisions that cannot be taken at a lower level and that need not be taken at a higher level.

The Solution Set consists of a set of principles, which can govern:

- how work is organized;
- how the organization is designed;
- how performance is rewarded;
- how individuals can be fulfilled in their work;
- how performance and potential can be assessed;
- how the growth and development of individuals can be orchestrated;
- how challenging future assignments can be planned.

The hierarchical levels in an organization emerge from increasing complexity in work, and from the concomitant need to manage the infrastructure of jobs required to ensure successful delivery at the front line or customer/consumer interface.

The three key principles of DMA

This approach is based on three fundamental principles, in an organization fit for purpose:

1. All organized work falls into a hierarchy of discrete levels or strata of increasing complexity. At each successive level the objectives to be achieved, the complexity of work to be mastered, the changes to be managed and the decisions that therefore have to be taken become broader in nature. The range of environmental circumstances to be taken into account becomes more complicated and more extensive, and it changes in quality. The discretion and authority required correspondingly increases, as does the geographical reach. Finally, more time is required to assess the impact of these decisions.

2. The second key principle is that for any assigned job, the balance of major tasks falls into a single leadership level. The balance of tasks comprises more than 50 per cent of the burden of accountability. A good indication of this balance or burden is to identify which tasks take the most time.

    In some cases, however, work will be spread over more than one level. For example, an executive who is accountable for strategic decisions may also need to spend some time on less challenging administrative matters, ensuring that subordinates are carrying out key responsibilities. But if the major portion of the superior's time is spent on lower-level tasks, then this will lead to organization development and culture problems, as the manager supposedly in the higher level is working in the wrong (ie lower) level. If this is happening regularly then the junior person's role is being compressed.

    Compression is the opposite of empowerment and usually occurs when there is more than one layer of management in a single level of accountability.

3. The third principle is that each accountability level above the front line requires one and only one layer of management. This is the Golden Rule of DMA. (Hence the formula: the total number of levels − 1 = an optimal depth of structure).

Management layers and work levels

The distinction between layers and levels is critical. A layer is not a level.

A level refers to the decision-making zone or area in which a person is working. It is identified by focusing on the type of work a person does by analysing their unique decisions (or lack of decisions) in relation to the seven differentiating Elements outlined later in this chapter.

A layer of managerial leadership is a job on the spine of accountability in a hierarchy of increasing complexity. A layer of management is required only where the leader really is accountable for making decisions that cannot be taken by the direct reports – not because they are not permitted to, but because they lack the know-how, expertise and/or relevant experience.

Principle 3 emerged from fieldwork when it was found that if there were two or more layers of management within a single level of accountability, the junior incumbents were inevitably very frustrated. In fact, the most talented were the most frustrated, as their work was being duplicated and re-worked. There was no value being added by the layer above, as all of the key players were operating in the same decision-making space.

In the treacle

I recall a case in India when a particularly highly thought of manager resigned from a senior financial post. The CEO was very disappointed as he had high hopes for this individual. I was able to point out that the manager in question had been interviewed earlier in the project as part of the Finance Accountability Probe and was in a compressed job. He was unable to make any real decisions, despite the fancy trappings of his job and office.

People in compressed jobs like this talk of being mired in 'organizational treacle' or 'bogged down'. The culture becomes one of 'doing less with more'. Some might call it hamster management, as everyone feels like the hamster in the wheel; no matter how hard or for how long the hamster runs, it still goes nowhere.

No wonder the highly talented manager was frustrated. Fortunately, the story had a happy outcome. The manager in question was moved to another job with real accountability. As a result he stayed with the organization and prospered.

In this sort of organization there are often far too many meetings involving multiple layers of management. They tend to be undisciplined in terms of time-keeping and decision-taking. One problem is that the multiple layers of management present each tend to have many small authorization steps for budgets and expenditure.

In one European insurance company I worked with during 2006, the authorization levels for underwriters reduced in percentage terms as you moved upwards through the management layers. The second authorization limit was 100 per cent above the first, the third 70 per cent above the second and the fourth 50 per cent above the third. Authorization limits in over-managed organizations, increasingly obsessed with control and compliance as a result of the Sarbanes-Oxley legislation, are usually arithmetic in progression when they should be geometric.

The fundamental reason why reporting relationships in the same level do not work is that a genuine leader must have the authority to make decisions that take into account and integrate a genuinely broader and more complex area of work than those their team members must take. Otherwise there is duplication of effort and decision-making. If a boss and subordinate are accountable for identical planning cycles, such as an annual plan, this is usually a sure indication that they are operating in the same work level. The inevitable consequences are organizational blockages, individual frustration and personal unhappiness.

As already demonstrated, the main cause of confusion about work within an accountability level stems from unclear authority and quantitative grading systems. If individuals are to have full accountability for their work, they must have the commensurate authority to ensure that the right people can achieve the work in the right order, in the right way and in the right time frame.

The key ideas of the DMA Solution Set relating to organization design, the varying nature of accountability, and the identification and rewarding of talent are summarized in Figure 4.2, which happens to be an example of an organization with six decision-making levels.

The special feature of the DMA Solution Set is its conceptually integrated logic, about decisions adding value to the work of others, which underpins everything that needs to be mastered in the management of people.

The components of other models are at best only administratively integrated. For example, a job might be calibrated in job evaluation points, to which a salary is aligned. The points might be used as a basis for promotion to a job with more points. But the fundamental problem with these job evaluation systems is that they do not ask: 'Should the job exist? Does it add value to other

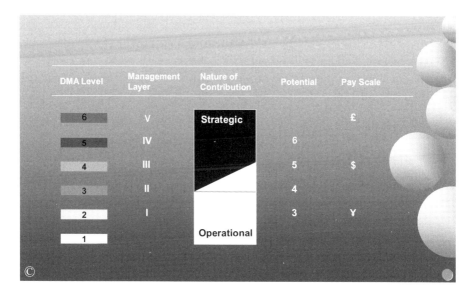

Figure 4.2 The DMA Solution Set[3]

work?' They take the job as a given and then measure it in accordance with their preferred factors, such as number of subordinates or size of budget.

Every organization in which I have worked that had a job evaluation scheme was over-layered. There was no rigorous testing of whether the role in question added value to the work of others or the stated purpose of the organization. It is self-evident that if these job evaluation systems are not able to demonstrate whether a job is required, they are not appropriate vehicles for organization design or personal development, since hollow jobs lead to hollow development and unnecessary cost. By way of contrast, the focus on accountability and quality of decisions does establish why the job should exist; thereby ensuring that it adds value to the organization's purpose and is a sound platform for personal development.

Furthermore, given the one layer per level principle, a person reporting to someone in a Level 3 role cannot be more than Level 2, as this would lead to compression. This means there is no 'level drift upwards' and consequently no loss of cost control in the leadership levels approach. This is quite different to traditional job evaluation approaches, which are invariably bedevilled with cost inflation and a breakdown in equity within an organization as a result of unchecked grade drift. Cost drift is also the main reason why so many broadbanding initiatives have failed. This is inevitable if broad categories of accountability have not been identified first.

As the model in Figure 4.2 illustrates, the same guiding principles identify the type and level of work to be carried out and the number of organizational layers required, and provide insight into the development and growth of individuals (which in due course can impact on their career development and on career planning for the organization as a whole). Finally, it can help establish how people should be paid by linking the level of work or responsibility to a national or industry market.

Nature of contribution

One way of determining the nature and level of a particular job is to work out the nature of the contribution it makes to the organization (see Figure 4.2). Virtually all jobs seem to have elements of work related to operational tasks and strategic tasks. The key point though is to determine the balance of accountability (principle 2 of the three key principles of the DMA). It has been found that, up to Work Level 3, accountability for work is essentially operational.

Operational work involves accountability for existing resources – whether they are physical assets, systems, ideas in the form of patents, money, people or services to be delivered – and, in particular, it involves ensuring that, increasingly, they perform better.

By Level 3, the emphasis is on achieving continuous improvement or productivity from existing assets. There are very clear plans to meet, which are often specified in terms of volume, quality and time. Operational managers are not held accountable for the change of location, type of technology or reconfiguration of these existing resources.

From Work Levels 4 and above, the balance of accountable work is strategic. At the strategic levels, the constraints of operational work are removed. Now the jobholder must make authoritative (because of expert competence) recommendations for change, based on analyses of gaps in the availability and performance of key resources, product portfolios, systems and technology, knowledge (eg science), services and people. The key accountability here is identifying opportunities and constraints and initiating the introduction of new resources as well as the withdrawal of old ones.

An important point to bear in mind though is that strategic accountability does not necessarily mean that all the best strategic ideas come only from the jobholders at Level 4 and above. This is the mistaken identification of accountability with control. Often, subordinates will suggest new ideas for promotions, products and new developments.

The key accountability of the leader is to set the framework of priorities, and to recognize which new initiatives should have support and extra resources to ensure that the unit or company objectives are met. In strategic leadership terms this means managing the dynamic interplay of the variables covering direction, people and organization. Thus the strategic manager frequently has to assess and choose between ideas for new directions or developments, since inevitably the resources available are not unlimited.

Potential

In the column 'Potential' in Figure 4.2, there is a series of numbers one higher than the DMA level. This shows how levels of accountability can drive individual development. Thus a person in a Level 2 role with potential for one in Level 3 can be seen as 'potential 3'.

In order to use this approach effectively it is important to identify what behaviours individuals need to exhibit before moving up to the next level of accountability. (This will be covered in considerable detail in Section 3 of the book, where a differentiating competency model will be outlined and applied.[4])

It is evident though that even in large organizations with perhaps only six levels to traverse in a career, the time spent at each level is considerable – about six to seven years on average, even for those proceeding to the higher strategic levels. This is why it is important that individuals have many different work experiences in the same level to ensure that they continue to learn and grow throughout their working life.

Research has shown that dwell-time in two levels, 3 and 5, is critical to preparing people for success at Level 6 and above. Conversely, there is evidence that being accelerated through Level 3 has a very detrimental effect on the growth and development of the individual concerned.[5]

A promising manager at Level 2, for example, is promoted to run a hypermarket at Level 3. This store has been doing very well for some time, and has a highly motivated workforce and a stable community of middle-class customers. After the first year this manager meets all the KPIs (key performance Indicators). The manager has performed well, but in a relatively easy situation, and if this manager is promoted to Level 4 on the basis of it, the evidence suggests the likelihood of failure at the higher levels, such as 4 and 5, is very high.

However, if after 18 months this manager is moved to another hypermarket in a deprived area, also at Level 3, then the new challenge is very different. Now we have a turnaround situation, where sales have been drifting down, shrinkage (loss of product) is drifting upwards, staff morale is low and labour turnover is high. If, after one-and-a-half to two-and-a-half years the stores ratios are improving, the learning curve for this manager would have been significant. Now the manager is ready for a start-up situation, still at Level 3, involving choosing a team from scratch, training them and turning them into effective performers.

Each of these three roles was at Level 3, and each offered significant learning opportunities. Given five to seven years' experience of this sort at the same level, when promotion occurs this person will have direct experience of the major store types likely to be in the region. Success in the new job at the next level of accountability is more likely as a result.

Link to the compensation market

Once the levels of accountability have been established, the organization can then the appropriate market pay (or price) per level. This can apply around the world – which is not to say pay per level would be identical. Pay for a Work Level 3 role in Australia would differ from that for a similar role in Zambia. However, a consistent measure of responsibility makes it easier to construct fair and relevant expatriate packages. This is of obvious value for an international organization wanting to build a multicultural workforce with cadres of genuinely international management.

In the DMA Solution Set, organization design drives job evaluation and pay, not the other way round. This overcomes the weakness of traditional systems, which have led to grade and cost drift. Since there can be only one layer per level there is no scope for upward grade and cost drift. As more companies adopt levels, it will become easier to make market comparisons and to match responsibilities across companies.

The Seven Elements of DMA

About twenty years ago I was wrestling with the following conundrum: 'How many layers of management are justifiable in a global organization and how can they be identified?'

At the time I was a member of the New York Conference Board's Council on International Management. It consisted of about 24 multinational companies and included most of the leading organization design and development managers in the world. One manager, Don Kane, reported to Jack Welch, then CEO of GE. GE had just removed the layer of sector management (one below the top executive team). These were very senior, powerful individuals working at the top of one of the world's largest companies.

So I asked Don: 'How did you know sector management was the layer to remove?'

I listened carefully to Don's reply: 'Well, Jack and I know the business well.'

'What if it is the wrong layer?' I asked.

His answer shocked me somewhat: 'Well, we would put it back.'

I was shocked because this seemed to be a formula guaranteed to traumatize employees, which of course is exactly what re-engineering initiatives were doing at the time. After a few more conversations of this kind, it became clear that I would have to find my own answer to the question: 'How tall should an organization be?'

As I was working on organization reviews around the world at this time, I set out to find the answer by asking top managers that I worked with the following:

- What decisions do you take that cannot be taken by your team members?
- What decisions do you take that are not taken by the manager to whom you report?

This work took many years to complete and involved about 1,000 man-hours of interviews across about 40 countries in around half a dozen different industries, which were subsequently written up. As I analysed the material, a general picture began to emerge of what differentiated the decisions that managers were making. It eventually became clear that managers were making decisions in seven areas, or decision-making zones, which formed the basis of their added-value contributions.

I labelled these seven areas the Seven Elements and have used this framework ever since. Indeed a large part of the potential intellectual challenge and excitement of every subsequent interview has been the prospect of finding perhaps an eighth element. But that has not happened, despite thousands of additional interviews in subsequent years in which the interviewees have been asked: 'Is there anything else in this role that has not been covered so far in the interview?'

The model has worked in a great variety of settings, and each experience of using and applying it around the world, in about 20 different industries now, has confirmed its value. These Seven Elements are a touchstone for determining whether a job adds value, and they are a compass for determining the location of a job in the landscape of the organization.

The Seven Elements are not just a theoretical model; leaders in major corporations are held to account against them every day. They were initially introduced at Unilever, for example, in 1997/98, and then by Tesco in 2001.

An example of the Seven Elements, using Tesco's terminology, is summarized in Figure 4.3.

Other companies, such as Amersham (now part of GE), Barclays, Orange and Unilever have used different headings for the same ideas. The nomenclature is not critical; it is the ideas that matter. As already indicated, the skill in a given situation is to establish terms that resonate and mean something to the individuals in that particular organization, while retaining the integrity of the essential ideas. As is the case with job titles, the trick is to find the terminology that works in a given situation.

1. Nature of work

This first Element covers the work expected of a role – not an individual. It focuses on the core reason for the existence of a particular job and where it differs in essence from those below and above. Given the purpose of the role, the focus is upon the three to five key decision areas or objectives that need to be delivered to know the job has been successfully carried out.[6] The nature of work necessarily becomes more complex at each successive work level.

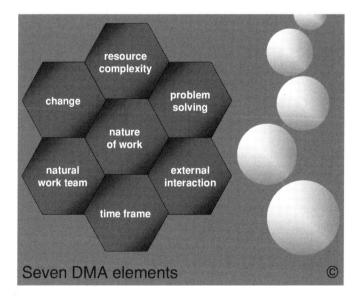

Figure 4.3 The DMA Solution Set (Tesco's terminology)

One of the key issues in this whole process is: how do we distinguish between the person and the job? Clearly, people are more or less capable, and matching an individual's skills and competencies to a job remains a fundamental challenge for managers. The task here is to identify the work entailed by or associated with a particular role in the organization. This Element refers to what the organization expects and determines the individual should do – their role. It defines the nature of their accountability for a distinct area of work. It establishes the degree of complexity that characterizes that area of work.

When undertaking the Accountability Probe interview, it is a good idea to interview a good, solid performer, who can give an accurate picture of the role in question.

2. Resource complexity

This Element defines accountability for resources: people, technology, budgets and know-how or knowledge. Accountability for these resources starts at Level 2, assuming a front line, the lowest level of accountability, at Level 1. In the new 'knowledge age', know-how is rapidly becoming the critical resource, something that is apparent from a global recognition of the importance of skills and competencies in delivering sustainable competitive advantage.

Roles in ascending levels are accountable for an increasingly extensive and complex array of resources. At Work Levels 1, 2 and 3, the balance of physical resources is specified. For example, the manager of a shoe factory cannot decide to make ice cream. At Work Levels 4, 5 and 6, gaps in resources, such as factory capacity, for example, or opportunities in a given market, have to be identified. This entails planning and negotiating for the relevant and necessary resources, since these are rarely available in either sufficient or unlimited quantities. Jobholders are expected to make authoritative recommendations to add or delete resources within their specific area of accountability.

Thus someone at Work Level 4, a supply chain director, for example, would be expected to draw up a plan to add to existing manufacturing capacity, output and efficiency, or to re-balance production between a number of different factories. At Level 5, the resource configuration within a France Telecom or a Barclays could be a company or a national business unit; someone at this level would be accountable for a complete value chain of activities with full accountability for the bottom line. Otherwise they might not justify Level 5.[7]

At Level 6, on the other hand, the resource infrastructure is a network of such self-sustaining Level 5 entities, frequently spanning more than one country in the context of an international or global business. At this level, the boundaries of previously self-sustaining business units may themselves be reconfigured as part of the more comprehensive Level 6 network.

3. Problem-solving

The type and nature of the problems that need to be solved change at each successive level of accountability.[8] This Element is concerned with the type of thinking that is required to solve a particular problem or set of problems. The mental path taken to solve the types of challenges confronted at the different levels of accountability can be observed and mapped. This is where intellectual capability is taken into account; an important factor in the assessment of individuals' ability to cope with the demands of increasing levels of accountability.

At Levels 1, 2 and 3, problems are concrete and operational in nature. Individuals are working with given concrete resources or assets. The problem-solving Element is influenced by the type of thinking that different tasks require.

Wilfred Brown aligned different levels of abstraction in thinking to the respective work levels. With the first level of abstraction, Perceptual Concrete, the object of the task must be physically present. At the second level of abstraction, Imaginal Concrete, physical or visual contact isn't necessary, so long as sufficient contact has occurred in the past. At the third level of abstraction, Conceptual Concrete, the job-holder must be able to deal with the future using mental models based on past experience of concrete tasks.

For Abstract Modelling, the fourth level of abstraction, the job-holder must have the capacity to discard past experience and think afresh. This is the first level at which breakthrough thinking or 'thinking outside the box' is required. Accountability for solving problems of a strategic nature, at Level 4, requires abstract and conceptual analysis to identify problems and assess potential solutions, including new formulae, products, technology, systems or policies. Tomorrow's solutions may not yet physically exist and therefore have to be conceptualized. This mental modelling process entails identifying the causes of patterns and linkages in consumer or customer behaviour and the performance and capacity of plant, people and systems. At these higher levels this is the thinking process that underpins the discovery of new knowledge stemming from applied or pure research.

Levels of accountability: a thoroughly tested idea

When I first presented the idea of introducing work levels and replacing the 17 job class structures for 20,000 managers around the world to Unilever's top management, I was asked: 'Who has done this globally?' When I replied 'Noone that I am aware of', there was a very long silence. The Board of Unilever was being asked to implement a system and approach which at that stage was only an idea. Wisely, it asked for another year's fieldwork and testing to see whether the idea was viable and could be implemented in 100 countries. It was.

4. Change

The essence of strategic leadership is sensing and then ultimately managing change that leads to building a new competitive advantage. Change management is at the heart of modern management accountability. Perhaps it represents management's greatest ongoing challenge. This demanding Element is concerned with accountability for driving innovation in its various forms. The key consideration here is: 'What can the jobholder change without referring to the next level?'

Whilst new ideas can come from anywhere in an organization, not all levels are accountable for ensuring that innovation takes place, or that these new ideas are implemented. Levels 1 to 3 work with existing technology, systems and products. The work at Levels 1 to 3 is essentially developing, modifying or improving something that already exists. At Level 3 the leader is trying to maximize the performance of the resources and assets for which they are accountable. It is not part of Level 3 responsibility to decide whether the unit should be closed, or whether the work could be done elsewhere.

However, from Work Levels 4 to 6 there is a need to discover or invent new solutions. At Level 4, for example, the jobholder is accountable for thinking about resource allocation. 'Are my factories making the right products? Are my hypermarkets in the right cities? Should my call centres be offshored?' At Level 4 and above, increasingly the challenge is about studying, understanding, accommodating and shaping the future.

Accountability for true research emerges at the fourth level of accountability. In research laboratories a scientist at Level 4+ would be trying to establish new linkages among existing bodies of knowledge or ideas. This can lead to totally new products or services, rather than simply adaptations of existing ones. The jobholder spots gaps in received wisdom and know-how, and discovers ways and means of closing those gaps.

It is then the person with Level 5 accountability who has to manage the integration of the relevant resources and ensure that the solutions identified are successfully implemented. A typical example of change at Level 5 is organizational change, where the chief executive of, say, a national business unit would be accountable for boundary reconfiguration of the company.

A scientist at Level 5, on the other hand, would be driving blue sky or pure research. This is the work that entails scientific discovery, new knowledge and invention leading to groundbreaking changes, which can redefine the confines of an industry. For example, if a scientist invented a way to clean clothes with a laser, the result would be leadership of the global homecare market and the decimation of the white goods market. Consumers would no longer need washing machines. The consumer behaviour for cleaning clothes, at least in the developed world, would be fundamentally changed. The commercial and personal impact would be enormous. Companies spend billions on research, hoping to find new scientific and technological breakthroughs worthy of a Nobel Prize that would redefine markets to the advantage of the innovators.

The extension to Level 6 would entail boundary reconfigurations that would involve a number of business units/companies and/or countries. A typical Level 6 decision would be deciding whether to enter or leave a country.

5. Internal collaboration

This Element refers to the lateral interaction or collaboration with peers within the organization to complete common tasks. It is this network that allows an individual to get their job done successfully.

At the lower levels, teams are accountable for outputs that tend to be localized; at the higher levels teams have outputs that are more distant geo-graphically. Thus at Work Level 1 a team may be limited to a production line in a factory, a work bench in a laboratory, or a work station in an office. These teams can be increasingly international or even global in very large organizations at Level 6 or above.

Again, it is important to stress that the key is accountability. Being a member of an international team contributing, for example, to the development of a new product does not of itself raise the level of accountability. It depends on what the individual is accountable for. For example, the accountability for leading an international project team is more demanding than simply being a member of that team.

Nevertheless, plotting the natural peers of common roles within the organization is a very powerful indicator of the nature of the work required, in other words the accountability level. These Elements tend to reinforce one another, so that it would be unlikely for a role to be established or to be assessed as being at Level 3 in expected work and resources, and yet only at Level 2 in terms of lateral teamwork.

In my experience, over-managed organizations have great difficulty establishing effective networks across their operations. There is a tendency for too many layers of management to become engaged in meetings, for example, where the junior person cannot provide the information needed to progress a decision. The net result is that the decision is held up while the lower level person endeavours to find the answer and bring it to a subsequent meeting. This is why so much teamwork breaks down or is ineffective.

In one case, a US$15 billion US multinational was asked by an international retailer to tender for a major piece of business. It took a month to respond, by which time the retailer had already purchased from a competitor. A key reason for the missed sale was the fact that this company had two unnecessary layers of middle management. This meant it was too slow to respond to a major opportunity and fell further behind the market leader as a result.

There is a tendency in some organizations to believe that the presence of teams can offset the need for hierarchy and clear accountability. Not so. 'Contrary to some popular opinion, teams do not imply the destruction of hierarchy. Indeed quite the reverse', writes J R Katzenbach in the *Harvard Business Review* article 'The myth of the top management team'.[9] 'Teams and hierarchy make each other perform better because structure and hierarchy generate performance within well-defined boundaries that teams, in turn, productively bridge in order to deliver yet more and higher performance.'

6. External interaction

The previous Element, internal collaboration, covers lateral interaction within a global company. This Element covers the need for collaboration outside the organization. For example, the consumers, customers and suppliers, who are all part of the lifeblood of a company, are covered by this Element.

The increase in global competition since the 1990s has intensified the external challenge of doing business. Many public sector agencies or organizations have been privatized and transformed by the need to respond to and cope with competition. Total quality initiatives, supplier partnerships, more powerful trade groupings and increasing numbers of strategic alliances, not to mention the increasingly active non-governmental organizations (NGOs), have added to the external pressures on organizations over and above the traditional institutions such as governments, the media, financial institutions and trade unions. The latest pressure is the increasing influence of private equity deals.

Many jobs in a large multinational are accountable for achieving results in the external domain. In a business such as Procter & Gamble, the prime focus is on the individual consumer, but the interface with trade customers and suppliers is also a critical area of commercial accountability. A company like Wal-Mart will focus on individual customers and commercial suppliers. A financial services organization such as Citibank will target both personal and commercial customers.

At the operational Levels 1 to 3, for example, roles work with clearly defined customers and suppliers. At Level 3, external contacts could be at the national headquarters level, where tailor-made solutions or responses might be required to maximize the performance of a network of customers or suppliers. External interaction in these operational levels is largely reactive. It is a matter of responding to the external body, eg a demand for more pay or another threat of a strike by a trade union.

By contrast, at Levels 4 and above more proactive action is required to be effective. The jobholder has to positively influence the environment, be it national, regional (EEC, NAFTA) or global (IMF, World Bank). It is not enough to simply react to someone else's decision.

At Level 4 the environment is likely to involve national government and other similar institutions. Supply networks are likely to be international and similar customer developments are quickly emerging around the world. A number of major retailers such as Wal-Mart, Carrefour, Promodores, Ahold and Tesco are expanding on the international stage. International hotel chains and airlines are now international customers of multinational suppliers.

By Level 5 the manager has to both reconfigure elements of the internal organization to reflect significant external developments while at the same time manage the environment, which at times may work against the aims and interests of the organization. At Level 5, in self-sustaining, fully equipped operating units, this is apt to be in a national context, whereas at Level 6 the external reach would be international and would affect business results in a number of countries.[10] A clear example of this is the emergence of international customer bases that wish to negotiate across more than one country. The response would probably require orchestration at Work Level 6.

Ongoing new developments, such as the removal of a myriad of customs barriers, tariffs and regulations in Europe, have in turn led to the establishment of pan-European organizations and structures. This means that the external network is widening and deepening and there is a greater need for strategic and proactive collaboration with more and more external organizations.

7. Task horizon

Timescales drive large organizations. Most activities are framed by deadlines, which are usually subservient to the planning process. Thus starting at Level 1, a jobholder might be responsible for a customer check-out or check-in desk where tasks can be assessed in seconds or minutes. Increasingly higher levels may then be responsible for a night shift, monthly production, quarterly results, the annual budget, the mid term plan, the long term plan, or a seven year FDA (US Food and Drug Administration) project at Level 6.

The accountability being assessed here is: 'How long does it take to know whether the work covered in the first six Elements of the DMA Solution Set have been successfully completed?' If someone spills orange juice at a customer check-out desk in a hypermarket, it is known within seconds whether that upset has been satisfactorily redressed. But if the CEO of a company decides to take it into another country in another continent, it will be some years before that decision can be effectively assessed as a brilliant step or a disastrous failure. In other words, the time taken to assess the effectiveness of decisions varies according to the level of accountability. The task horizon is the longest time on average it takes to complete the balance of tasks for which a person is held accountable.

Based on work in 20 different industries around the world, these time frames can vary by industry, particularly in the operational levels of accountability. Retailers, for example, seem to take pride in the statement 'retail is detail', and as a result the industry tends to be very short term and reactionary at Levels 1 to 3. Nevertheless, the best also do the strategic things well, such as site selection for new hypermarkets, where Tesco, for example, has left its UK competitors behind.

Factories' activities are divided into shifts, and production plans into days, weeks and months. Sales results are monitored on a daily, weekly and monthly basis. Management accounts mirror these same reporting periods. Statutory accounts are available quarterly and consolidated on a yearly basis. These are usually referred to as budgets or short-term plans. Longer-term or strategic plans are often up to three years on a country basis. Regional plans are more typically up to five years and global planning tends to take a somewhat longer perspective. Levels of accountability tend to lock into these time zones.

Although new technologies, like the fax, e-mail, the internet and computer simulations are compressing the time available for decision-making, accountable tasks clearly fit into time frames and business planning cycles. Thus roles at Work Level 2 often operate within the boundaries of an annual plan. Managers at Level 3 are, in addition, accountable for contributions to the policy and substance of the following one-year plan. By Level 4, an authoritative contribution to the next strategic plan (ie up to three years) is expected. At Level 5, one would be expected to deliver the current strategic plan and play a key role in establishing the next strategic or long-term plan while ensuring all interim plans and results are achieved. This typically requires a task horizon of up to five years. At Level 6 this time frame stretches a little further, as an authoritative contribution to the long-term global plan as a whole is also required.

Identifying true timescales

Time frames are prone to inflationary claims since individuals know that they can influence their work levels and therefore, in many cases, their compensation. It is important, therefore, to establish the true balance of task accountability.

This is particularly important where individuals are working in teams and/or on research assignments. Identifying budgeted milestones usually helps provide realistic answers to these conundrums. I remember discussing accountabilities of scientists with the head of research at a biosciences company. Much of the work in the laboratory had to cover a seven-year time span owing to legislative requirements. His explanation of how he managed this process was as follows.

'Look, I would not give someone the whole seven-year task. I would not sit back and wait seven years. I would set the first major assignment with a 12 month deadline. After a month I would be checking progress. "Have you finished phase one yet?" And so on.'

Another problem that can inflate time frames is the issue of queuing, or dead time. I recall a tax manager in Belgium explaining that his task horizon was seven years. What he meant in reality was that it had taken seven years for the last tax case the company had taken to get through the courts. The length of time for the resolution of the case was a factor of the inefficiency of the legal system, not the amount of time it took to assemble and defend the case. Most of the seven years referred to was dead time, waiting to get into court.

Perhaps the most amusing case I encountered was the following. A worker planting palm trees on a plantation in Malaysia informed me he had a task horizon of up to 25 years – a longer time frame than that allocated to the CEO of that company! His logic for telling me this was that he planted palm trees that have a 25 year life cycle. On closer examination, though, it became clear that his actual task horizon was just a few days. The job in question involved the task of successfully planting a sapling and watering it to ensure it did not die. The success rate of these plantings could be assessed by a supervisor within a couple of days, by which time the plant was either thriving or had wilted.

A task horizon, then, extends from minutes in some front-line jobs to many years at the higher work levels. Accountable completion times for tasks are normally set by the boss and sometimes approved by even higher authorities.

The Accountable Leader Chapter 4: Key points

1. The DMA Solution Set helps provide answers to problems, such as: how tall or flat should this organization be? How do leadership requirements change at different levels? How can potential leaders be identified? How can they be developed? And how should they be rewarded?
2. Decision Making Accountability is the process of making decisions in seven areas, or decision-making zones, which form the basis of their added value contributions. These areas are the Seven Elements.
3. The Accountability Probe plots what decisions people make and whether those decisions add value to the work of others. It reveals how many decision-making layers of management are required.
4. DMA logic is based on one simple idea: are you making decisions that add value to the work of others in the same organization?
5. Before determining levels of accountability or devising leadership develop-ment programmes, the organization must understand itself and its core purpose. Only once the organization's mission or purpose has been estab-lished can the boundaries of accountability be determined and measurable campaigns be orchestrated to deliver the organization's strategy.
6. Jobholders must take decisions that cannot be taken at a lower level and that need not be taken at a higher level.
7. The three fundamental principles of DMA in an organization fit for purpose are: all organized work falls into a hierarchy of discrete levels or strata of increasing complexity; for any assigned job, the balance of major tasks falls into a single leadership level; and each accountability level above the front line requires one and only one layer of management.

8. A layer is not a level. A level refers to the decision-making zone or area in which a person is working. A layer of managerial leadership is a job on the spine of accountability in a hierarchy of increasing complexity.

9. Up to Work Level 3, accountability for work is essentially operational. For Work Levels 4 and above, the balance of accountable work is strategic.

10. In the DMA Solution Set, organization design drives job evaluation and pay, not the other way round.

Notes

1. I first used the term DMA Solution Set in my book *The Healthy Organization*, 2004. In this book it will be used synonymously with accountability levels and leadership levels. The concepts behind these different terms are constant and consistent. Decision Making Accountability is the substance of levels. It represents a set of principles that can be applied in different situations to arrive at the appropriate answer or 'solution'. Similarly, some companies refer to levels as accountability levels, leadership levels, work levels and so forth. The key is to use language that works in a particular situation, provided the integrity of the ideas is not devalued.

2. Following extensive fieldwork I led from 1987 to 1995, Unilever implemented work levels in about 100 countries 10 years ago.

3. This diagram is based upon a six-level organization. Organizations in fact vary between two and eight levels of accountability (I have not yet encountered a nine-level organization). Given a six-level organization, one can then plot the consequences as per this diagram. This Solution Set provides the logic that underpins leadership or accountability levels.

4. Differentiating DMA competencies was outlined in *The Healthy Organization* – see Chapter 7 – and an example of their application will be illustrated in Chapter 9.

5. See chapter 8 of *The Healthy Organization*.

6. Note that these are three to five decision areas within the Element of 'nature of work', not to be confused with the fact that nature of work is itself only one of the Seven Elements.

7. This paragraph is not arguing that *all* national business units in France Telecom or Barclays are Level 5.

8. Note that the problem-solving referred to is not the same as that in some job evaluation schemes, such as the HAY system. The focus here is on what psychologists refer to as the degrees of mental abstraction, which underpin the way we think, moving from the concrete domain to the increasingly abstract.

9. Katzenbach, J R (1997) The myth of the top management team, *Harvard Business Review*, November–December
10. The mere fact that a company is international (operating in more than one country) does not guarantee that the top job is Level 6. I have worked with international companies where the top job was only Level 5. Because the infrastructure of jobs only went up to Level 4, some key functions, such as manufacturing, were missing and/or were covered by a Level 6 operation somewhere else in the international organization.

Part 2

5 Held to account at the front line

'I am held to account for managing myself and my time to provide a good quality service to customers, suppliers and/or colleagues.'

Tesco Work Level Workbook

On the level

The next four chapters outline what decisions are expected of a role at a particular work level in an organization. This is done with reference to the seven decision-making zones described in Chapter 4 – the Seven Elements of DMA.

What is important, however, is not the terminology, but the concepts described. With the Seven Elements, for example, while I use the term 'external interaction' when discussing decisions relating to links outside the organization, another term would be just as acceptable. Whatever the term used, it must still retain the integrity of the ideas and reflect the decision boundaries outlined in the book. Calling the 'external interaction' element something entirely unrelated, for example, would not be sensible.

At the sharp end

Every day we encounter people working on the front line. They are invariably at the sharp end of customer service, whether it is the public or corporate customers that they are dealing with: the customer service reps at the airline check-in desk; the shop staff at the supermarket checkout desk; the telephone operators in the call centre; the sales reps on the road; the medical centre receptionists; or the person manning the help desk.

It is essential to identify what roles are on the front line, and where the front line lies in different parts of the organization, as it provides the base work level in a bottom-up process. Start by delineating the decision zones for the Level 1, front-line employee, and we begin to ensure that there are no other overlapping jobs hampering the ability of the Level 1 worker to get their job done – in the case of a customer-facing Level 1 role, to provide great customer service.

So, what does a front-line worker do? What decision-making accountability do they have? We can find out by looking at the Seven Elements.

The Seven Elements at the front line

1. Nature of work

Founded in 1909, Kirin is part of the Mitsubishi Group and one of the two leading companies in the Japanese beer market. Kirin lager, for example, is the oldest beer brand in Japan. A while ago I visited the Kirin brewery plant at Hokkaido, one of the company's most modern breweries. The visit followed an earlier visit to one of the firm's original breweries in Tokyo.

When I arrived, one thing was immediately noticeable – the relative lack of people at the plant. Within the plant, the process control room was one of the most staff-intensive sections; a company operative monitored a bank of computers that controlled the brewing and bottling processes.

While training was required for this work, which called for considerable judgement and expertise, the desired outcomes and the ways of achieving those outcomes were already determined in advance. The control room operative was not required to think up new ways of tackling the problems they might be confronted with. There were clear guidelines and procedures laid down for what to do in the event of particular data or flashing lights appearing on the screens. The computer programs had been designed by systems staff in the IT department, and these were based on the process control elements designed by the engineers and brewers.

For the control room operative at the Kirin plant, like the majority of employees at Work Level 1, the decisions to be taken are prescribed in advance. This is why work at this level can be, and increasingly is, automated, like airline check-in processing, for example.

The output or outcome is specified in advance, and it cannot be changed without the agreement of someone at a higher level. Tasks are, for the most part, predictable and can be explained in a manual or imparted during a period of training, usually on the job or as part of an apprenticeship. The tasks may still be complex, though, such as removing and replacing an engine on the wing of a commercial aircraft.

The person may have access to a relevant database of information via an intranet or process control facilities, as, for example, in a modern robotic factory. The important point is that although the person doing the job might need to be skilled, and might be expected to use some judgement, the process and outcome are laid down in advance – even though that too might be quite complex.

Work at Level 1 is often mapped out in guidelines or defined processes, which ensure maximum consistency and effectiveness. The work may vary from unskilled to semi-skilled to skilled. The level of skill required by engineers at an airport preparing an aeroplane for its next flight will be a lot different from that required of a skilled operative working the night shift at a chocolate factory. Equally, their appropriate levels of pay will be different – but it is important to note that while their pay may be different, their work level is the same.

Time at Level 1 often forms a key part of a training programme. In a number of situations and professions, trainees will enter at the top of Level 1 and are expected to rapidly progress, within one to three years, on to Level 2. This trainee experience provides an important initial understanding of the business.

2. Resource complexity

At Level 1, resources for jobs are restricted to the resources required to achieve the prescribed output. The person doing the job does not have the authority to change or make key decisions about those outputs, and is not accountable for decisions about those outputs.

Job-holders at Level 1 do not have accountability for budgets or people. They do, however, have accountability for a very important resource, the efficient use of their time, as well as for any equipment or systems they need to use to do their jobs. This accountability for the use of their time – self-management – is the essence of Work Level 1 resource accountability.

The education required at this work level varies. A person working in a research laboratory, for example, may require more qualifications than someone working on the shop floor in a factory or hypermarket, or working in a call centre or on a customer service desk, or at a work station in an office.

However, the fact that different levels of education may be required does not mean that the jobs are at different work levels. For example, in research laboratories the work undertaken at this level is predominantly directed towards a predetermined output and follows agreed procedures and bench routines. It might involve assisting with laboratory experiments, including undertaking relatively straightforward analysis, and specific educational qualifications might be required in order to ensure that the correct protocols are understood and followed.

3. Problem-solving

The problems faced at Level 1 are concrete, real world problems that are familiar and recurrent. They are often referred to as demands – 'do this', 'provide that', and so on. Usually there are guidelines, either hard copy or accessed via an electronic database, to help employees at Level 1 to resolve these problems. If there is an unfamiliar problem not covered by the standard guidelines, it would usually be referred upwards to someone at Level 2+, who would then be required to resolve the issue – to modify a system, or if necessary take the issue further up.

Managers are often on call, in multi-shift operations for example, for precisely this purpose. They help manage the exceptions. The manager is authorized to devise an entirely new approach to a problem or to change the proposed outcome. While it is often the case that the exceptions that lead to this type of intervention may also have been predicted and guidelines for appropriate action specified, in some situations, such as night shift work, a duty manager on call would be expected to resolve a totally unexpected or unpredictable event, such as a major technical breakdown in equipment or technology.

Managers' guidelines are different from those at Level 1; they can deal with less frequently encountered problems and have more discretion in how to solve those problems.

4. Change

Although job-holders at this level are not accountable for making changes outside guidelines, or for making changes to specified processes, operating procedures or IT programmes, they are expected to respond to changes, and if the relevant schedule is not working, to seek improvements. Many of the better workers will suggest improved ways of working and can often point out the need for refinements or improvements that their boss was not aware of. If road works on a particular route threatened to disrupt the timings of a regular delivery schedule, for example, the driver would be expected to point this out and suggest alternative timings if there was no other route that met the original schedule.

5. Internal collaboration

Internal collaboration refers to a worker's network of contacts within the organization. Front-line team members normally work closely with colleagues at the same level, in the same department and at a single location, whether it is around a workstation, a lab bench, a production line or a customer help desk. Contacts are likely to be frequent and face to face, although the increase in offshoring of business processes means that customer contacts are frequently managed over the phone.

Roles at this level require the employees to act, primarily, as channels of information. Decisions are taken at a higher level and the relevant information conveyed to customers, suppliers and employees via individuals at the Level 1 front line.

6. External interaction

External links and interfaces at this level are likely to be with specified customers or suppliers, within a framework for regular contact and liaison.

The majority of key decisions on things like pricing, discounts and exceptions will have been anticipated, often as a result of previous experience. Consequently, many of the typical manoeuvres involved in the selling or buying processes will be outlined in advance. For example, in telesales there will usually be a script or a number of listed steps that the telesales staff should follow when making sales calls. The boundaries within which the telesales operator has freedom to act or manoeuvre are therefore set out in advance.

More extensive use of IT and the internet may increase the frequency and remoteness of these relationships, but not the underlying purpose, which is to promote sales and increase orders and information in line with overall frameworks, agreements and targets.

The fact that a company has a wide geographical spread – for example, call centre operators working across many countries – doesn't mean that the level of accountability changes. This only occurs if the complexity of decisions changes. Where international interaction occurs it is usually part of a regular prearranged pattern that has to be maintained by the job-holder. Product lists, pricing arrangements, terms of trade, delivery schedules and the like – all these are set by those in higher levels of accountability.

7. Task horizon

The results of unskilled and semi-skilled work are often evident within seconds or minutes. As the work becomes more complex, however, the timescale for successful completion becomes longer, stretching to hours, days and weeks. For activities such as the training of other colleagues at Level 1, it might be one or two months. Thus the task horizon for Level 1 is up to three months. The contributions expected from skilled workers such as supervisors might take a little longer to complete.

Challenges at the front line

Pyramid or Chinese hat?

Most people in most organizations are at Work Level 1. Traditionally, organizational hierarchy is depicted as a pyramid. In reality, though, the pyramid is more like the shape of a traditional Chinese peasant hat. It has a relatively sharp point – where the very few people with strategic accountabilities reside – while many more people are at the brim of the hat, at Work Level 1. Such is the popularity of the idea of the pyramid that the reality of the situation still seems to surprise many managers. It shouldn't come as a surprise though, as the Chinese hat shape is widespread, whether the organization is in the military, the public, the private or the voluntary domain.

Normally the percentage of employees at Level 1 would be above 80 per cent. In highly labour-intensive operations, such as tea estates, call centres and retail outlets, the number of people at the front line is likely to be well in excess of 90 per cent of the total number of employees. This is one reason why comparing the percentages of managers employed in different organizations is not a good way of determining best practice. Ideal proportions vary in relation to the nature of the business. It is also why some international companies totally misinterpret the performance of their operations in the developing world. On the other hand, capital intensive or knowledge-rich operations – such as research laboratories – would be expected to have substantially less than 50 per cent of their staff at Level 1.

Skill categorization at the front line

Many organizations, and trade unions, have hopelessly overcomplicated the division of work at Level 1. The complexity of their organization designs tends to outweigh the complexity of the actual work in question. As a result most job evaluation systems at this level have far too many grades or categorizations of work. This type of excessive granularity is not helpful. In the 21st century, work at Level 1 should, at most, be divided into three categories: unskilled, semi-skilled and skilled; with possibly a fourth category – the supervisor.

The crucial issue here is to define what these terms mean in a given organization. It is no secret that a semi-skilled worker in telecommunications will have more expertise and training than a semi-skilled worker in a retail shop or bank branch. This is because the nature of the technology driving these different industries is fundamentally different. Salary levels will be different as well, especially if one of the skills – for example in telecommunications – is in short supply. Companies such as France Telecom have found that mobile device technologists are currently in short supply, for example, because companies from the Middle East, India, China and Korea are competing for their talent.

But the major point here is that each industry can define what is meant by unskilled, semi-skilled and skilled. Indeed, some might argue that they do not have unskilled or semi-skilled work, only skilled work. This is really immaterial, since these terms are relative, not absolute, and therefore can actually be applied in any situation where skilled work is required. But the reason why it remains at Work Level 1 is that, as already outlined, its decision-making differs in nature from that in the level above.

The supervisory role in the first level of accountability

One of the main problems with handling large numbers of people is that you need help. That support is often to be found in an important role at the top of Level 1, often referred to as a supervisor.

The supervisor is usually a support role and so is not accountable for budgets or for staff recruitment, development or discipline – they don't have a budget and they don't have the authority to decide who comes into a team or what that team member does when they are in the team. Instead, the supervisor exists to assist a manager in the first layer of the hierarchy – at Level 2 – to manage the department, particularly when the number of subordinates, or the sequence of work shifts, makes that task too burdensome for one individual. The key function of a supervisor is usually training subordinates and monitoring and auditing their performance on behalf of their manager, ensuring that their work meets prescribed standards within a specified time.

The supervisor's role has been a fraught one for some time. Often described as the 'meat in the sandwich' between the front line and management, it has long been recognized by trade union negotiators as a role having little or no power. Supervisor is also a role that tends to be surrounded with uncertainty and a lack of clarity, which then leads to unduly complex and confused organization design. Many organizations have yet to get to grips with the role and tend to have more layers of supervisors than they need. Despite the challenges involved, however, supervisory leadership roles are vital components of good organizational structures.

Line and support jobs

There is a key distinction, which impacts on Level 1, concerning the type of leadership roles within an organization, and that is the distinction between line and support roles. There are roles at Level 1 where leadership is required but where the leader is not a full manager with the 10 management accountabilities. Managerial leaders, which are line management roles, start at Level 2 (see the next chapter) and reside on the spine of accountability, but support roles do not, and are not a layer of management.

Support roles are usually Level 1 positions and support a layer of management, often as supervisory leaders. The supervisory leader is on the cusp of that continuum, starting to contribute to the 10 managerial accountabilities.

Assessment of the Seven Elements will establish the appropriate accountability level for a given job (see Figure 5.1).

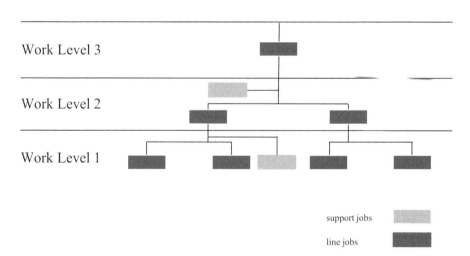

Figure 5.1 Line and support jobs

There is only one line or core job per accountability level in a given chain of command. The line job-holder is the boss or managerial leader who is individually accountable for the performance of those working in lower work levels. They have the authority to select staff and assign tasks, to set objectives and task horizons, to appraise performance and change plans and responsibilities, and, if necessary, to change staff. A managerial leader may ask others to contribute to the appraisal of subordinates, for example, which is typically a task for supervisors, but in the end it is the managerial leader who is accountable for the total department or unit. It is the line job, or that of the managerial leader, that is justified as a value-adding layer on the spine of accountability, and that is responsible for the 10 managerial accountabilities.

Support jobs are required when, for example:

- there are exceptionally large numbers of subordinates to be supervised;
- there are subordinates to be supervised who are widely dispersed geographically;
- there are multi-shift operations requiring continuous supervision;
- there is an absence of essential, specialist know-how within the team – this is particularly important in head office scenarios.

There are line and support jobs in all aspects of an organization's activities, both direct (in production for example) and indirect (in human resources for example), and at all levels of accountability except that of the CEO.

There are some apparently confusing situations where certain jobs have both support and line accountabilities; an auditor in a support function, for example, who is also accountable for a team of more junior auditors. The key in this situation is to look closely at resources. If the job under review is accountable for subordinates, then it can still be a support role to a boss on the main spine of accountability while also functioning as the managerial leader of a small off-line department. An example would be an HR manager supporting the manager of a large factory, who is not therefore the boss of the production managers and the factory engineer, but who is the managerial leader of the factory HR department.

Support roles and their link to authority

Support roles are not second-class roles. Their legitimacy stems from the authority they exercise, which is different to that of line roles.

Value-adding authority for support roles

There are five main types of value-adding authority that underpin support roles.

1. Auditing

This is the authority (sometimes called 'prescribing', eg the work of doctors in hospitals) that ensures activities are carried out in the correct way to meet legal, technical and/or policy requirements. Auditing is a vital governance function demanded by various legislators and regulatory bodies, including, in the case of listed companies, financial bodies like the Securities Exchange Commission and the London Stock Exchange.

Unfortunately, however, in the wake of recent corporate scandals such as Enron, there is an over-reliance on legislation and regulation, and an increasing obsession with control and compliance. This in turn has been a major factor in the growth of red tape, bureaucracy and the over-layering of management in many financial services, banks and insurance organizations.

In 2006, for example, I worked with an insurance company that had unnecessarily overcomplicated its underwriting operation. The company had created four levels of internal audit, three of which were at Level 1. On top of these four layers there were a further three additional layers of external audit, driven by recent legislation.

The bureaucratic overlay was not improving customer service or standards of performance in the industry. All that was being achieved was additional administrative cost, which in due course would be passed on in increased insurance premiums.

2. Coordinating

The coordinating authority ensures that work is completed consistently, cohesively and effectively across a number of separate operations. An example would be a brand manager managing the critical path for a product launch. The brand manager is at the hub of a network of different departments, the activities of which need to be orchestrated within a tight time frame to ensure all components of the marketing mix for the brand are delivered in time for the launch date.

3. Specialist

Often linked to coordinating authority, specialist authority consists of the provision of expertise that does not reside elsewhere in the team. These are roles where the authority is based on particular know-how: 'The work must be done in this way'. This is often the critical added value required in a national, regional or corporate head office.

The classic support function based on specialist knowledge is finance. A number of financial activities call for specialist expertise, such as taxation, statutory accounting, treasury management, and indeed auditing. Given the need to produce accurate figures for annual accounts, and presentations to the stock market, finance functions are prone to excessive control and emphasis on compliance, which in organization design terms manifests itself in narrow spans of control and excessive layers of management.

4. Quality

Quality is the authority of legitimate inspection that ensures technical standards are complied with and key specifications are met. Sometimes described as a monitoring activity, authority derived from quality allows someone to stop an operation until a quality issue or shortcoming has been successfully resolved. This form of quality assurance is akin to auditing, which often calls for specialist technical knowledge, but where auditing tends to be associated with finance, this authority is associated with quality assuring non-financial activities.

5. Supervisory

This is the most widespread and important of the various forms of indirect authority. These jobs are critical support roles in the management of large teams (such as call centres) or of sales staff who might be spread across a number of different locations. They typically manage activities such as induction, training, auditing of performance and handling of grievances and discipline, together with other departmental procedures such as absences and holidays. They are key roles in the management of shift patterns, often known as duty managers, night-shift managers or superintendents.

These different types of authority, together with the correct number of layers, ensure that an organization is in flow. They influence how work – processes and activities – and people are chunked together to ensure a state of equilibrium and balance between the number of management layers and the spread of activities across an organization.

The legitimacy of support roles, especially in corporate offices, is usually infused with one of these types of authority. They help ensure the horizontal reach or span of management is feasible, and thereby help ensure that the line-accountable people are able to manage their work effectively. Sometimes line managers need to widen their spans of management with support roles in order to carry out their own responsibilities more effectively.

An example of a common support role would be the HR manager in a factory, a call centre or a hypermarket. The HR manager is not the boss of his or her colleagues in the unit, but works across the unit on behalf of the accountable manager. Although not a line role, this support role is adding value to the work of others on the basis of particular professional knowledge (specialist authority).

Line roles add value on the spine of accountability. Support roles add value to that spine. Both are essential for an effective, truly accountable organization.

Differences between line and support jobs result from different relationships to a common area of work and concern. The support jobs contribute to the achievement of the work for which a particular person in the line is held accountable. Support roles are essential. They are not second-class roles.

The supervisory challenge at the front line: a 'spanner in the works'?

The leadership role of supervisor is often the spanner in the works of organization design. This is because supervisory roles are often not well understood or clearly defined, usually due to confusion about line and support accountabilities.

If the true role of the supervisor is misunderstood, its purpose and accountability are not likely to be clearly defined, which in turn inevitably contributes to over-layering. This is especially the case in organizations with large numbers of staff at the front line involved in a $24 \times 7 \times 52$ day operation. In fact, multiple layers of unnecessary, non-value-adding supervisors seems to be an endemic problem in the 21st century, leading to poor morale at the front line as things don't get done as they should.

Four critical questions need to be answered:

- What is the role of the supervisor?
- Why and when is it required?
- What are the key duties?
- What is effective supervision?

What is the role of the supervisor?

The essence of the supervisor's job is to oversee (to 'look over') the work of others. A supervisory job is a support role, which does not discharge the 10 management accountabilities outlined in Chapter 1. If it does, then although labelled 'supervisor', the role is actually at Level 2, as the first layer of management – a good example of why comparing jobs according to their titles is misleading.

In reality, there is great confusion over the role of the supervisor, its authorities and accountabilities. In my experience it is the job that tends to have the highest dissatisfaction rating in company morale surveys. Those working in such roles frequently complain of a 'lack of authority and power' or of being 'pulled in different directions'.

The confusion is not helped by the plethora of titles given to this type of role. These can vary from team leader to superintendent, night-shift manager, duty manager, section manager and so on. The situation can be further confused when some companies insist that their supervisors are not in the union 'because they are part of management' (undefined), while in other industries they are unionized.

Sometimes national practices muddy the waters further: in France, for example, supervisors are invariably given the grand-sounding appellation '*cadres supérieur*'; while in Sweden they are part of a national bargaining agreement that reaches into the second and third levels of accountability. The national contracts in Sweden have a legally binding status, which has to be taken into account when implementing work levels. In short, there is no consensus on whether supervisors are really part of management. It is not surprising, therefore, to find that in practice some jobs with the title 'supervisor' are in the second level of accountability, while many jobs with the title 'manager' are actually in the first level of accountability (not discharging the 10 management accountabilities).

Why and when is the supervisory role required?

The true role of the supervisor in the first level of accountability is to support a fully accountable management in Work Level 2 – the managerial leader – while also adding to the work of the front line. Training the front line is a typical supervisory accountability. Thus a supervisory role has two dimensions: one is to assist the level above – aiding those at that level to manage their accountabilities; and the other is to add value to and contribute to the efforts and training of those working in the lower level.

The main reasons for having supervisors at Level 1 are:

- There are large numbers of people to oversee doing unskilled or relatively unskilled work, as on a tea estate, for example.
- The front line is spread across a number of locations, as with a national sales force.
- They are needed to help manage a 24×7 shift process, as with a call centre.

What are the key duties?

The supervisor role is an advisory role that has authority to make key recommendations in areas relating to:

- Appointing of new team members. The manager will make the recruitment decision, or at least has a veto, but the supervisor will often be involved in the recruitment process. In some cases, for example, the supervisor might ask a template of set questions in the selection or screening interview. (But the key point is to determine who designed the template.)
- Assigning specific tasks. The manager decides the type of tasks.
- Carrying out appraisals. The manager will decide the final ratings of all the supervisor's assessments (often in discussion with them) and will probably interview outliers (such as those with the best or worst reports) to ensure that the overall quality of appraisals is consistent and reliable.
- Initiating transfers. The manager then decides who gets transferred and when.
- Working out salary increases. The supervisor may be part of – but not accountable for – trade union negotiations and recommendations for salary increases, if a merit system is operating.

The role of supervisor might be legitimated by the need for certain types of authority, as described earlier in this chapter. Although these types of authority often apply to higher levels of accountability, supervisors at Level 1 would be working within clearly mandated guidelines and standards, and checking that those guidelines and standards have been adhered to.

Such a position would involve authority to:

- audit the work of others at the front line as part of compliance;
- quality-assure the work of front-line employees;
- train those at the front line;
- coordinate work to ensure consistency at the front line.

In the classic supervisory role, the supervisor is usually more experienced than the manager but does not have full accountability for the workers being managed by that manager, except in certain circumstances, such as the manager's absence. The supervisor will be the manager's key advisor, and in certain areas will know more than the manager; and therefore the manager would be wise to act on their advice. But the manager does have the prerogative to take a different course of action if more appropriate, and will be responsible for the consequences of all the decisions taken – whether they are in accordance with the advice of the supervisor or not.

What is effective supervision?

The role of supervisor is not a layer of accountable management. The role is a tier or rank within the first level of accountability. The spine of accountability should consist only of the layers of line jobs.[1] Most organizations tend to have too many supervisors and, more confusingly, too many tiers of supervisors. These jobs are invariably stacked on top of one another in Level 1. Some financial services companies have been known to have as many as three tiers of supervisors, where only one is justified.

This tendency to stack supervisors on supervisors seems to be a widespread shortcoming, found equally in the public sector, the private sector and the voluntary sector. In many cases it seems that the organizations have confused ranks, grades and layers of management, with disastrous results for both their employees and their hapless customers.

For good examples of severe over-layering at the customer front line, you need look no further than many of the call centres in operation today.

Multiple tiers of supervision: some examples

Once the importance of support roles is truly understood, it becomes clear that only one tier of supervision is required in Work Level 1. There could be many supervisors, depending upon the effective spans of control, but there should not be a stacking up of supervisors reporting to other supervisors, all at Level 1. This stacking of tiers of supervisors is still a common occurrence around the world and cuts across many industries: airlines, banking, biosciences, chemicals, conglomerates, construction, consumer goods, education, insurance services, retail, telecommunications and the public sector.

It seems to make little difference whether the employees are in a bank branch, retail store, factory, warehouse, customer service centre or finance department. In almost all cases they tend to have non-value-adding layers of supervision, something that generally undermines customer service.

Example 1

An example of this multiple supervision problem is outlined in Figure 5.2.

When I first came across this customer service centre I soon realized that there were two tiers of supervisor at the first level of accountability, but only

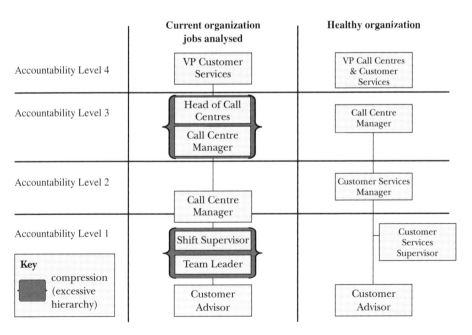

Figure 5.2 Supervisory compression in Level 1[2]

one was required. The shift supervisor had no more authority than the team leader to decide and resolve either staff matters or customer escalations.

This shortcoming was further aggravated by the fact that the call centre manager was not fully empowered to occupy the second level of accountability. For example, the call centre manager had no accountability for budgets or for the recruitment of people into the team, or any power to resolve performance issues.

The shift supervisor was also the union delegate, which served only to complicate the communication and management processes in the department. He also negotiated the annual agreement, with managers above the call centre manager, which invariably took months. Staff knew that with any grievance, the shift supervisor bypassed the call centre manager; and that there was no clear way of establishing which grievances were sound and just, and which were not. As a result staff came up with grievances all the time, most of which were not well founded, but there was no process for differentiating the well-founded grievances from the spurious ones. This is why the call centre manager role is depicted as straddling Work Level 1 and Work Level 2.

There was a lot of frustration and confusion about who could decide what in this organization. There were too many meetings, many of them with an industrial relations agenda that could not be resolved by the people sitting around the table.

The typical response from many shift supervisors was: 'My job is to motivate people' or 'to manage people'. But they had great difficulty identifying what they actually did and could decide on their own without needing to refer their decisions to someone else in the organization. They were not accountable for the management (not selection, recruitment or budget) of the customer advisors at the front line, and nor were the jobs in the two next two layers accountable for their management as the job design stood at that time.

The recommendation was to take out the two existing supervisory roles and replace them with one newly defined supervisor. As there were several teams in the department this recommendation meant removing a number of other jobs across the call centre.

As Figure 5.2 shows, there were also problems at Levels 2 to 4, but the confusion at these levels was a consequence of the mess at the first level of accountability.

If a supervisor does not decide who comes into the team, what the main tasks of the team will be, whether the members of the team work on day or night shifts, or what their merit pay will be (if they are not in a union), and if they do not have accountability for a budget, then that role should be placed in Level 1. There are still important people issues such as induction, training, auditing of performance and discipline for which the supervisor is accountable. However, these are not complex accountabilities requiring another layer of input from another supervisor who, regardless of grand-sounding titles (such as superintendent, coordinator, duty manager or night-shift manager) cannot decide any more than the junior supervisor.

Example 2

In another call centre situation that I came across at a financial services company, there were three tiers of supervisor. In this case the stacking was due to confusion caused by some incorrect assumptions about spans of control, an obsession with compliance, and the need to manage an onerous and very bureaucratic performance management system.

As a result of criticism over the lack of performance management and appraisal at the front line, a new system had been introduced. Unfortunately the new process was very bureaucratic, involving a lot of unnecessarily complex paperwork, adapted from the management performance management system. The supervisors had to appraise each of their team members every month. As part of that process the individuals were assessed against the company's values. Each month five people were approached in order to assess how the team members were living the organizational values.

As well as the values assessment, detailed comment was required on monthly performance and on whether the individual being assessed had the potential for further promotion. All this in an area of the business that had excellent performance data retained electronically (such as percentages of calls answered, how long calls took on average, etc), suffered from high labour turnover, and where hardly any of the front-line staff were ever promoted from the ranks into management.

The net result was that the supervisors could only oversee six to eight team members each, because a disproportionate amount of their time each month went into preparing, writing up and delivering the individual reviews. Performance management is important but this company had created a bureaucratic monster that actually interfered with effective supervision and limited the way the department could be structured.

Example 3

In 2007, along with my colleague Adam Pearce, I spent some time in the United States analysing the organizational effectiveness of a public sector office operating in a major city. The structure is illustrated in Figure 5.3.

Our main findings were that the office lacked a performance culture, accountabilities were not clear, and managers were not empowered. It was a

Selected roles analysed by accountability level

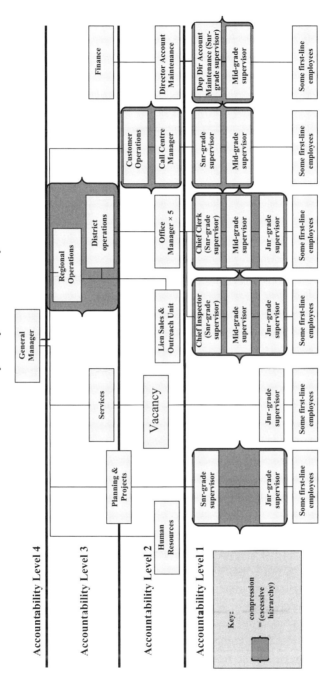

Figure 5.3 Organizational structure of a public sector office in the United States

graphic example of the unnecessary over-tiering of supervisory roles (and the knock-on effect at higher levels), and helped to explain why morale was low, the workforce unenthusiastic, and people on the front line felt that their work lacked any real meaning.

What does a typical supervisor's job – a support role at Level 1 – look like?

For someone in a support role at the top of Level 1 in a large retail outlet (for retail outlet you can substitute call centre, factory, etc) the key accountabilities might be as follows:

- Ensuring the product is effectively displayed in accordance with existing guidelines.
- Monitoring customer preferences and recommending (to someone at Level 2 as a rule) changes to display and presentation plans to help maximize sales.
- Training front-line staff in the relevant display and customer service guidelines and policies.
- Tracking ratios and contributing to statistical reports on sales, waste, cost-versus-expenditure estimates and plans on a daily or weekly basis.
- Acting as a role model for front-line staff and training them in ways of working to help ensure that best practice prevails.
- Possessing expert knowledge of the skills required for the various front line roles.
- Carrying out or organizing induction, training and coaching of front line staff.
- Auditing and checking the performance of front-line staff based on manuals and guidelines.
- Disciplining staff, usually as the first step in the grievance procedure.
- Recommending performance improvements and helping supervise their implementation.
- Ensuring that front-line staff are in the right place (eg on tills during peak periods) at the right time.
- Covering front-line skills for absences to maintain customer service.

- Monitoring front-line performance, attendance and management of holiday patterns within policy guidelines.
- Contributing to the recruitment process.
- Involved in conducting appraisals of front-line employees.
- Serving as a deputy for the manager in Level 2, if absent.

When assessing accountabilities it is important to note the verbs being used to describe them. Terms such as 'involved in' and 'contributes to' do not typically indicate managerial accountability. For example, supervisors might say that they do recruitment. But if that recruiting activity involves asking questions from a predetermined question template designed by a manager, with preferred answers already indicated, then that would not constitute managerial accountability for recruitment.

Similarly you will often find that supervisors conduct performance appraisals on behalf of their manager, especially if there are large numbers involved, and front-line roles are the same or very similar. But probe a little further and you will often discover that the approach, timing and ratings of the appraisals are agreed by the manager, not the supervisor.

Effective managers tend to conduct a sample of interviews themselves – a small selection of the best, worst and solid performers – to ensure that the correct benchmarks are available to assess the supervisor's ratings. Accountability in these cases still rests with the managerial leader, not the supervisory leader. It is important to remember that the manager does not have to do everything for which he or she is accountable.

Spans of control

It is unwise to give rigid figures for optimal spans of control – how many people should be managed by any one individual – for these supervisory roles. But generally ratios of 1:10 or less are too conservative. It may be surprising, but, as will be shown in the next chapter, a ratio of 1:30 is quite feasible, depending on the nature of the work, the clarity of the tasks, the quality of the training and the degree and effectiveness of the technology (eg the tills on a checkout desk, or the ticketing machines at an airport check-in desk, and so on).

The effectiveness of such spans also depends on the quality of the operating processes at the front line. A good example would be the Tesco front line 'routines' – processes designed to ensure consistency and reliability of behaviour and performance. These are the essential preconditions for empowerment at the front line. The quality of these guidelines, and the training given, seems to make the difference between being top or bottom class in an industry.

The well-organized customer service front line

Not all customer service centres are problematic when it comes to organizational design. Some companies are extremely adept at structuring their customer service provisions. One of the best examples of an organization at Level 1 that I have come across was at a Barclays payments centre in the United Kingdom, where work at the customer interface was divided into semi-skilled, skilled and supervisory. The semi-skilled work was in turn divided into two grades, 1 and 2; the skilled work was at grade 3; and the supervisory roles could be grade 3 or grade 4.

Employees in grades 1 and 2 were organized into teams of between 15 and 26, and reported to supervisors in grade 3. Each team, however, also had an expert or skilled customer advisor at grade 3 who was assigned to work with them as and when required, for training or technical advice, for example. These grade 3 advisory staff who helped the teams of semi-skilled advisors were more experienced, knew how most of the processes worked, and had a good in-depth knowledge of policy and how to handle exceptions.

So there were two kinds of employees at grade 3: those who were experts reporting to grade 4 supervisors; and those who were supervisors of staff at grades 1 and 2. The grade 4 supervisors led teams of about six; this number was about right, given the different nature of the problem resolution required and the fact that not many grade 3 experts were required.

The key point here is that the grade 3 supervisors did not report into grade 4 supervisors. Both grade 3 and grade 4 supervisors reported into the same manager. So although there were two types of supervisory jobs, they were not stacked on top of one another but reported in parallel to the same manager.

This parallel structure led to more effective ways of working. But this arrangement was not replicated throughout the organization, unfortunately. Other call centres in the same company had grades 1 and 2 reporting to grade 3 supervisors, who then in turn reported to grade 4. To compound matters, there were also additional grade 4 supervisors.

Whenever there is reporting within a grade, it is usually a sign of faulty organization design, something that frequently results in compression (that is, excessive and unnecessary hierarchy, where two or more layers of management exist at the same level of accountability). Compression is the opposite of empowerment.

Warning signs: typical issues resulting from multiple tiers of front-line supervision

When the platform of accountabilities is not clear across an airport, a call centre, a factory, a laboratory, an office, a retail outlet or a warehouse, a number of associated problems usually emerge, such as:

- insufficient and unclear definition of accountabilities at Level 1;
- lack of customer focus and timely problem resolution;
- insufficient knowledge of standards of performance and an inconsistent and irregular application of those standards;
- insufficient and/or inaccurate feedback to staff relating to the questions: 'How am I doing and where might I go?';
- insufficient communication and briefing, especially for part-timers and those coming on or off shifts;
- an absence of a robust competency framework to assess the potential of the individual;
- no training for the various team leaders, shift managers, coordinators, supervisors, duty managers, etc, on how to contribute to and manage standards of performance, feedback from and to individuals, and so on;
- the emergence of a blame culture;
- the lack of a performance-driven culture;
- little or no performance metrics to establish or to reinforce a performance culture;
- little focus on development and career planning even when the current demographics and levels of performance indicate likely succession problems are looming;
- concern that current recruitment practices are failing to get to grips with issues of development and career planning;
- lack of performance management in areas of sickness, absence and absenteeism;
- little or no real teamwork;
- an imbalance of stakeholder accountability between unions, staff and management;
- a need to build a stronger accountability bond between staff and line management.

If any of the above problems exist in your organization you might want to consider taking the following steps.

Possible next steps

A number of steps can help alleviate the problems outlined in the previous section:

- Design a healthy target organization of appropriate tiers of supervisory leaders, which over time removes the situation of unnecessary levels of hierarchy and blurred accountabilities.
- Define the new roles clearly at each level of accountability.
- Make clear which are line jobs and which are support jobs.
- Consider the value of introducing new titles as part of the change management programme this would entail.
- Assess the capabilities of the people working in the existing positions to clarify who should fill the roles in the redesigned organizational structure.
- Establish reward levels for the new roles.
- Plan the communication of the findings of the current review together with the agreed actions. Decide who should be involved and when and what contribution they can make.
- Decide how and when to involve the trade union(s), if relevant.
- Conduct information sessions on the reasons for the change and the new approach to clarifying accountability, improving teamwork and feedback, and to building a service-driven ethos and a collective sense of identity and purpose.
- Assess candidates and fill the new roles.
- Provide training for line managers and the new support supervisors – bearing in mind the needs listed above – to ensure that they understand how they can and should exercise their leadership responsibilities.
- Draw up a road map and project plan spelling out the key steps and deadlines for the implementation of this change management programme.

This is not a linear process. A good project plan will have these steps happening in parallel, where sensible and feasible. But the aspect that is most commonly neglected, or short-changed, is the communication needed to convince those affected by the changes, so that new actions and behaviours follow and become properly entrenched.

The Accountable Leader Chapter 5: Key points

This chapter defines what it means to be held to account at the front line of an organization. The most persistent organization design failing at Level 1 is the tendency to have too many tiers of supervision, needlessly stacked on top of one another, without any additional decision rights being involved. This chapter illustrates the sorts of consequences that can emerge and makes some suggestions for providing a solution.

The following key points are important:

1. Every day we encounter people working on the front line at Level 1. They are often, though not always, at the sharp end of customer service.
2. Most people in most organizations are at Work Level 1. Normally the percentage of employees at Level 1 would be above 80 per cent, and it is often well above this, depending on the nature of the work.
3. In the 21st century, work at Level 1 should, at most, be divided into three categories: unskilled, semi-skilled and skilled; with possibly a fourth category – the supervisor.
4. One of the main problems with handling large numbers of people is that you need help. That support is often to be found in an important role at the top of Level 1, usually referred to as a supervisor. The supervisory leader is starting to contribute to the 10 managerial accountabilities.
5. Support roles can be at any level up to that of the chief executive, and typically report to and support the layer of management at the level above their own. Managerial leaders, which are line management roles, start at Level 2 and reside on the spine of accountability, but support roles (such as supervisory leaders at Level 1) do not, and are not a layer of management.
6. There are five main types of value-adding authority, which underpin support roles: auditing (or prescribing), coordinating, specialist, quality and supervisory.
7. The supervisor role is an advisory role that has authority to make key recommendations in areas relating to: appointing of new team members; assigning specific tasks; carrying out appraisals; initiating transfers; and working out salary increases.

Notes

1. The confusion and over-layering in many organizations stems from unclear definitions about a value-adding layer of hierarchy. A layer of management like this is justified only if it is held to account for a clear majority of the 10 management accountabilities. Supervisory leaders do *not* meet this stringent requirement. These roles are in *Level* 1 but are not a *layer* of management. But as with management roles, only one supervisory leader is needed at Level 1. I will refer to supervisory roles as tiers of hierarchy within the first level of accountability needed to lead the front line.

2. Compression refers to an excessive number of jobs reporting to one another in a single level on the spine of accountability. It is the opposite of empowerment.

6 Managing the front line

'I am held to account to decide who is in my team, what they should do, how well they do it, ensure they have the resources to deliver good quality service to customers, suppliers and/or colleagues, matching appropriate solutions to their needs.'

Tesco Work Level Workbook

A few years ago two telecommunications companies were involved in a merger, following which, as is the case with most mergers, the combined entity undertook an organizational restructuring. I had already done some work for the larger of the two companies, and as a result was well aware how many layers of management would be required in the new company.

However, internal politics meant that the new structure was designed from the top down. This is often the case in merger and acquisition situations as senior managers seek to protect their protégés and other favoured staff.

In the case of the telecoms merger, the top-down restructuring led, predictably, to overstaffing and severe compression – that is, the unnecessary overlapping of accountabilities at Levels 2 and 3 in the company. This flawed approach to organizational restructuring undermined the cost synergies that the merger promised and the stock market expected. With many managers left in superfluous jobs, lacking the power to make an impact on organizational performance, the new company quickly haemorrhaged much of its best talent.

A rule of thumb: organize for value from the front line

The experiences of the two telecoms companies above demonstrates the value of adopting a bottom-up approach when establishing the first layer of management – a critical step in any organization design process. Unfortunately, the first layer of management (usually at Level 2) is often incorrectly positioned, as most CEOs tend to design organizations from the top down.

The reason for most organizations favouring a top-down approach to organizational restructuring throughout is that the usual place to start organization design is with the top team. This task involves consideration of the interplay of a number of core variables, such as technology, function, process, geography and product, market or business line, all aimed at delivering the agreed strategy. Starting with the top team is understandable; however, the temptation then is to continue organizing top-down. It is a common design mistake.

It is not that designing an organization from the top down is not possible. It is. The problem lies in the temptation to build in span breakers. These are layers of management that exist for the comfort of the boss, but which do not add value to the work of their peers or those in other levels.

The added value of work in an organization where leaders are appropriately held to account can only occur in a reliable manner once the front line service or task is agreed. Then decide what needs to be added to ensure the front-line level of accountability is fully and appropriately supported in those areas where it is not self-sufficient, and so on, until you get to the top of the organization. Once this infrastructure is in place, even if only at the planning phase, then and only then is it certain how many layers of management are required.

When you think about it, a bottom-up process is more logical. People at different levels in the organization see different aspects of the ongoing work of the organization. Surely it is best to design an organization by beginning with the perceptions of those at the bottom rather than the top, by considering the work that they undertake and the point at which an additional layer of management can make a genuine contribution to that work. By looking from bottom to top, rather than the other way around, it is possible to see precisely where and how the decisions of managers contribute to the work of others in the organization, relating those decisions to the specific areas of work with which they are concerned.

I have not yet seen this process work effectively in reverse, even though the practice is widespread. It is next to impossible to plot the value adding decision-making process from the top of the organization.

Why is this? The reason is that the top-down approach is based on guesswork, an assumption of where the senior management feels layers of management should reside. Whereas the bottom-up approach is not. It relies on an analytic and well-tested framework, using the Seven Elements to help clarify the differences in the levels of accountability. This in turn, given the golden rule of one layer of managerial leadership above the first level of accountability, establishes the right number of layers needed in a particular organization.

The Seven Elements at the second level of accountability

1. Nature of work

This is the level at which managers have full accountability for managing people at Work Level 1. They are managerial leaders. The work is no longer prescribed or following specified guidelines or routines. A job at this level always contains an element of judgement. This judgement is more than just common sense; it is derived from experience, and often from formal professional training.

The jobholder is required to make assessments in new situations or individual cases using analysis, diagnosis and judgement, before deciding on what action to take. As a rule, these cases or situations are handled on a one-by-one basis. They do not usually impact on one another, being discrete and particular. The leader in this type of role normally knows from experience or professional training that a number of solutions are feasible to resolve a given challenge. But, in the particular cases that the Level 2 manager deals with, it will not usually be obvious which solution is appropriate. Selecting and matching the right solution to the individual problem at hand calls for diagnosis and judgement.

Level 2 may be the front line. This is especially the case with certain types of specialist work – many professions, for example. It is often apparent that a front line position is at Level 2, because the person doing the job requires accreditation or certification by the relevant profession. These specialists use their technical knowledge to evaluate, assess and identify solutions to specific problems (there is more on this later in the chapter).

It is not always easy to spot the role of specialists in some organizations, since the degree of specialization is often relative. Many organizations would describe the IT function as a specialist area of the business. But for a company like Microsoft, IT is a core business and its definitions of specialist IT work would be more demanding and specific. The established professions, such as chartered accountants, certified engineers and so on, represent the most common specialist areas of work here.

2. Resource complexity

Where they have a team of Work Level 1 staff reporting to them, job-holders at Level 2 will be accountable for setting objectives, for the recruitment and release of people, for delegating main duties and work, for training and development, and for managing performance.

If they have subordinates, then employees at this level should be accountable for delivering against an operational expenses budget, including staff cost. They would be expected to negotiate this budget, with their own rewards influenced by their performance managing this resource. Accountability for a budget is a key difference between a supervisor at Level 1 and a managerial leader at Level 2.

A key resource for specialists at this level is their distinct knowledge, usually evident from a professional qualification, combined with several years of practical experience, leading to a professional accreditation. Sometimes these specialists will 'own' or will have designed a system or framework used by the employees working at the front line. An IT manager might, for example, have designed a stock control programme used by stock controllers, which helps guide their short-term ordering of seasonal products.

3. Problem-solving

If a person has a headache, goes to a pharmacist or drugstore and requests a packet of aspirin, this would be a Level 1 demand. As part of the service, the customer expects to be given aspirin and not paracetamol, to get the right change and, with any luck, a smile.

If the same person goes to a doctor complaining of persistent headaches, the doctor's training will suggest that there could be several reasons for the headaches: faulty eyesight; stress; even a brain tumour. The doctor will therefore set about identifying the most likely cause of the headaches so that they can be treated.

At Level 2, analysis and judgement are required. Even though in many cases problems will be discrete and non-routine, and the leader (from either experience or professional training at this level) will know that a number of solutions are possible – some fact gathering and diagnosis will still be required to enable the appropriate solution to be found. The challenge here is to discover which solution is best applied in a particular case.

Problem-solving at Level 2 is about investigating and evaluating the situation and then applying the appropriate form of treatment. So in the case of the patient with the persistent headaches, the patient might be referred to a surgeon if the doctor suspects a brain tumour.

The inventiveness of the solution required, which might need to be applied via known surgical techniques, would involve a higher level of accountability, requiring greater know-how, professional accreditation and experience, akin to Level 3. Whereas a surgeon-researcher interested in discovering new ways of dealing with brain tumours, for instance, would be at an even higher level.

It is expected that job-holders at this level will prioritize work and resources within an agreed plan (see the section on Task horizon) to ensure that the specific requirements of each situation are met. In the example above, once the situation is clear, the doctor will have a range of possibilities to consider. If the patient with the headache is suffering from stress, the doctor might want to suggest therapy, or anti-stress medication, or pain-killers for the headaches, or even a holiday, and that decision will be influenced not just by the nature of the particular case – the nature, degree, and apparent causes of the stress – but also by the availability and cost of the various forms of treatment.

4. Change

Unlike those at Level 1, managerial leaders at Level 2 are expected to make changes to operating guidelines and procedures as appropriate, so that Level 1 staff can improve their performance – they begin to be held to account for change at Level 2.

It is not enough for someone held to account at this level simply to carry on doing things the way they were done before. A performance improvement is expected from the team, territory or department. Job-holders are expected to find ways to use their specialist knowledge and experience to solve problems, to unclog systems, and to implement process and procedural improvements for those areas for which they are accountable.

5. Internal collaboration

At Level 2, managers work with colleagues at the same level, often, but not necessarily, within the same function or process at the same site; they could also cooperate with colleagues at different locations. This could be the case for a financial controller working on certain budgets and short-term planning activities. Or a brand manager preparing for a product launch and calling for synchronized contributions from different parts of the organization. To be successful in their own role, Level 2 managers have to learn how to get things done through colleagues to whom they cannot issue commands. They are likely to need to keep in touch with peers in other areas of the business in order to share knowledge – particularly if problems must be tackled by means of various kinds of specialist know-how (some of which they might not possess themselves).

6. External interaction

In some functions, such as sales, external interaction at Level 2 is characterized by the management of a Level 1 team working within a designated territory, usually with regular customers. There are limits to the scope of the Level 1 sales people's work. Level 2 leaders will operate as the first point of reference, helping (if there is no supervisor) in the resolution of issues for specific customers. They might also do some selling where more flexibility and negotiation beyond Level 1 guidelines is called for.

There are also cases where the sales force front line is at Level 2. An example of how selling accountability can migrate from Level 1 to Level 2 is the concentration of the grocery trade in many countries. The number of customers has shrunk substantially, and the complexity and scale of the selling transaction has changed enormously as a result. More skill and experience are now required to match the sales offering to the customer opportunity. This calls for a higher degree of diagnosis and judgement than in the past, when hundreds of salesmen at Level 1 sold a set range of products from a standard price list in which variable discounts were standardized based on volumes sold.

If an individual has particular external duties at Level 2, they will generally involve acting as a first point of contact with bodies that the organization must cooperate with or serve, such as customers, suppliers, trade unions and so on. The shape of that interaction is likely to be largely influenced at the next level of accountability – Level 3. Typically job-holders at Level 3 will have a variable number of customers or suppliers across more than one location or territory.

7. Task horizon

My research suggests that the average impact of decisions taken at this level can vary dramatically depending on the industry involved. In some cases (in retail stores and bank branches, for example) the time frame for the impact of major decisions to become apparent is generally from about three to six months. In other industries, such as consumer goods and biosciences, the decisions of managers at Level 2 can generally be assessed within a year. The annual budget is the common overall framework for work at this level.

In the desire to appear fast-moving and responsive to customers, some companies can become over-reactive and prone to panic. There can be confusion over providing prompt customer satisfaction and the substantial demands of managerial accountability. An emphasis on speed may be used to justify constant readjustment to plans and demands for immediate action, with the consequent and predictable short-term disruption, which then makes the organization inefficient in the short term.

Implications for management

Jobs can be at Level 2 for different reasons. First, roles can be at Level 2 because they are accountable for the performance of others reporting to them, who are at Level 1. People in these roles are managerial leaders and are held to account for the 10 components of management accountability, although many organizations are unclear where to draw the line between supervision at Level 1 and managerial leadership at Level 2.

An even more complex issue is identifying when the front line should be higher than Level 1. When many organizations undertake an organization design exercise they assume a standard front line in terms of accountability. But this is a major organization design failing, as it inevitably leads to too many layers of hierarchy. The job-holder may not have subordinates, and may not be accountable for an expense budget of any significance. However, to identify whether the role in question is Level 2 or higher, the other six DMA Elements must be taken into consideration.

Know your front line

One of the most common unresolved conundrums in organizations is where the correct location for the front line lies. Most organizations seem to assume that the front line is invariably at Level 1, but there are certain situations where this is not the case.

It is wrong to assume that simply because someone does not have a budget or direct subordinates, then they must be at Level 1. The front line can be at Level 2, 3 or (very occasionally) even higher. Many small start-ups may have a front line above Level 1.

The problem with professionals

The most frequent example of a front line at Level 2 is where a professional entry requirement calls for Level 2 know-how and experience, and a competence to deal with recognized problems and to apply solutions in a manner requiring specific kinds of expertise – expertise that is often gained through study, training and experience. This entry process calls for more than 'years in the job', as there are objective standards that have to be met before a person can practise their profession.

A profession in the 21st century – what is it?

It is not always an easy question to determine what is and isn't a profession. Lawyers, doctors, architects; these are commonly acknowledged as professional occupations, but the term 'professional' has also been appropriated by a host of other occupations from journalists to HR managers.

So what exactly constitutes a profession in the 21st century? Fortunately, some academics have helpfully detailed certain conditions that they believe distinguish a profession from other forms of work:[1]

- Professions tend to be built on high ideals and values that should override self-interest. Many professionals, but not all, are motivated by aims such as service to others, and are often idealists for whom the nature of the task or work – its inherent worth and meaning – can be more motivating than purely material rewards.
- There Is a recognized objective body of knowledge based on reasoning that underpins the profession. Sometimes the reasoning is driven by analysis of data (accounting), precedent (law), or case history (medicine).
- Professionals have to master their profession, which typically takes many years of study, often strictly prescribed, and experience. (There may also be recognized paths to acquiring the relevant experience, before the individual is accredited to practice.)
- A profession has its own entry standards and requirements and usually runs a form of self-regulation to ensure potential members meet the recognized standards of the profession. This process also takes into account the personal qualities and values of the individual,

preserving softer, more ethical requirements of the profession along-side those pertaining to competence and performance.

In some cases – such as the Hippocratic Oath – individuals may be called on to commit themselves explicitly to the underlying values and ideals of the profession. In short, the profession expects its members to respect both the spirit and the letter of laws that govern their chosen work.

- It typically takes between four and seven years, following school or university, to become a recognized professional – endorsed by those obliged and authorized to maintain the standards of the profession.

Working at the wrong level

Sometimes the importance of professional accountability is devalued. This occurs when a professional, who should be working at Level 2 at the front line, is forced to do too much mundane administrative work at Level 1. It is another case of poor organizational architecture stultifying the performance of people and the organization. Talent is being wasted.

It is important to note that the key to Level 2 accountability depends on the decisions a person is held accountable for, not simply the degree of formal knowledge or education they might possess. I have seen PhDs doing Level 1 work in research laboratories who are clearly capable of operating at a higher level.

By now a number of things should be clear. First, the requirements of membership in the traditional professions do not resemble those of a Level 1 job. The front line of a profession is likely to be more aligned to the second level of accountability. If there can be only one layer of management per level above Work Level 1, then it is clear that organizations that contain a high proportion of professionals should be flatter than those of non-professionals.

Secondly, it is clear that not all the functions in a 21st century organization meet the requirements of a profession. Activities such as HR, the supply chain, IT, marketing or sales most frequently have a front line at Level 1. Although efforts are often made to establish more professional credentials for those working in these areas of the organization, they are not yet as rigorous, consistent and universally recognized as those in place for the ancient and traditional professions. This can make assessment of an organization's true front line very difficult.

Thirdly, this situation is often complicated by the tendency to place an overqualified individual at the Work Level 1 front line. A chartered accountant, for example, is probably ready to work in Level 2, but I have seen many individuals with this qualification given Work Level 1 assignments for too long. It may come from the desire of some organizations to employ 'God for sixpence'. Thus PhD students are put on the bench in the laboratory and assigned to routine experiments. Qualified lawyers are given straightforward correspondence to carry out. And so on. This is a false economy; this talent is usually marketable and can vote with its feet.

This misuse of talent is often compounded by the market rates for some recognizable qualifications. The job evaluation system becomes snarled by the need to award grades to individuals who have a market value not aligned to their job grade. The grading system is effectively disregarded. Individuals are, in a sense, compensated for the work they are not given to do; or paid for the work that they could do, but are not doing.

A fourth point emerges from the consideration of professions and work levels. If management is a profession, then Work Level 2 is the front line of management. The first layer in the hierarchy calls for a number of objective, recognized standards of management accountability that can be consistently and rigorously applied around the world. These requirements are clear, and the need for technical competence in IT, HR, etc can be aligned to this definition. But the problem is that these latter-day professions have not clearly defined their minimal requirements for the front line.

The HR Business Partner (HRBP) is a role that has become fashionable recently. The HR Business Partner is supposed to work at a 'strategic' level. In reality, however, it seems that the majority of HRBPs work at Level 2 (at best). They have often degenerated into 'yes-roles', which are aimed at serving the business but which do not maintain the values and standards of their profession.[2] If these roles were subject to more rigorous accountability definitions, then that would rule out such misalignments and at the same time sharpen the rigour of the standards within the function.

The front line at Level 2

It is clear that because of the requirements of a number of well-established professions, regarding both education and experience, the front line of a profession may be at Level 2. This indicates that there can be two paths to Level 2. The processes by which Level 2 managers are formed may be less rigorously organized than those involved in the training of the acknowledged professionals. In each case, however, there is a gradual acquisition of knowledge and experience, over a number of years, allowing the individuals exposed to this process to acquire knowledge enabling them to address an array of recognized problems.

It is not simply a matter of age, either. The tertiary education system takes longer in different countries (although attempts to harmonize education systems via the Bologna Accord may change this), or is coupled with military training, which means that people starting at Level 1 may be of significantly different ages. This can impact on how quickly an individual might traverse Level 1, or whether they might have enough knowledge and experience to move directly to Level 2.

Whatever the case, many organizations still might insist on such entrants spending a very short time at Level 1 – say a matter of months – to gain a rapid induction into the type of business they have joined.

Attention: spans

How many Level 1 team members can a leader at Level 2 manage?

This leads to consideration of the span of management, or the span of control. How many people at one level of accountability can be successfully managed at the next level? Unfortunately, at least for those looking for certainty, the real answer is: 'It depends.'

The answer depends on a number of factors, such as the nature of the work undertaken by the team members, the work of the manager, their respective locations, the technology used, the coordination required, and the direction and control required. The answer also varies according to the level of accountability of the team members. So, there is plenty of scope to get things wrong, and in most cases that is exactly what happens.

Why are spans invariably still too conservative?

Given all the hype about semi-autonomous teams and empowerment in recent years, thinking regarding spans of control remains remarkably conservative. In my experience the average management span of control in most companies has moved very little over the last 30 years – from about four, to about five or six.

The problem is largely with middle management. Most organizations demonstrate an hourglass figure-like structure. (This is set out in Figure 6.1, which

Layer of management

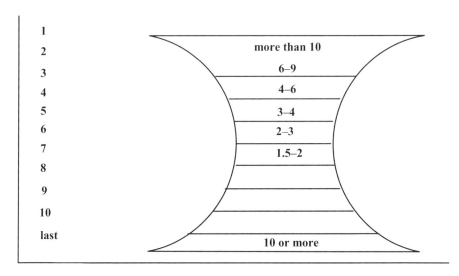

Average spans of control

Figure 6.1 Cross-section of spans by layer

is a cross-section of spans in a global organization.) Both the CEO and the managers at the front line have a large span, but in middle management spans are often limited to only one or two people. This correlates with organizational 'bulge' – too many layers of management in one level of accountability.

Narrow spans of control have been the most enduring cause of over-layered and unhealthy organizations in the 20th century, and this trend looks set to continue into the 21st century. One reason appears to be that without a good understanding of how many layers of management are required, CEOs are unable to resolve the problem of conservative average spans of control.

An enduring myth

One of the most enduring myths relating to spans of control dates back to the assertion by mathematician Graicunas in 1937 that a leader could not directly manage more than six subordinates 'whose work interlocked'. This is commonly known as 'the rule of six'; noone can manage more than six direct reports.

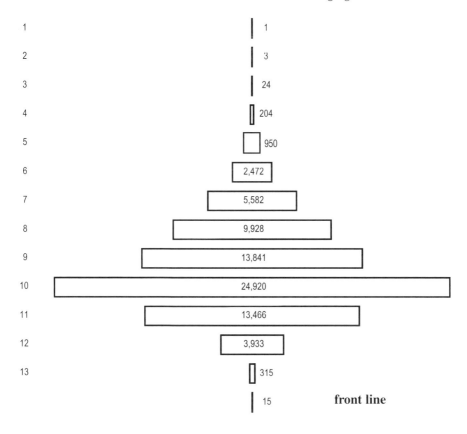

Figure 6.2 Over-layered with narrow spans

Some simple calculations, however, reveal how this thinking, which has taken hold among the world's corporations, is flawed. Accepting an average span of six together with seven layers of management, the maximum number of employees in an organization could be about 275,000. But there are only 39 companies on the Forbes Global 500 2006 list with 250,000 employees or more, and it seems very rare for those to be limited to seven layers of management. An organization with only 6 layers and an average span of 10 would total 1 million employees. Evidently, spans remain conservative.

This conservative approach is illustrated in Figure 6.2: an analysis of an organization with narrow spans and too many layers. This was a growing international business that justified six layers of management at that time.

The 'rule of 10'

The reason why so many modern organizations' structures are ineffective, over-managed and under-led is an inability to identify their levels of accountability. Back in the 6th century BC, however, the Persian king, Darius, appeared to have a good understanding of the concept of spans. Darius used a 'rule of 10' for his army. The Greeks and Romans copied this configuration: a 10-man squad in the Roman Army was known as a maniple, with about 8 maniples making up a century – thus the centurion usually led about 80 men.

Today, on more than one occasion I have come across situations where the span at the front line of an organization is comfortably up to 150. In some agricultural operations, such as tea estates, the number could be even higher. The Level 2 managers will typically have 3 to 10 support supervisors who help them manage these numbers. The contribution of the support roles, with the relevant authority, is critical to the management of the labour and shift-intensive operations. Generally, top management is shocked by the thought of spans in excess of 100, but in fact that is what they have, even though it is usually masked by multiple layers of supervision and murky accountabilities.

In today's organizations it is not necessary to have line of sight to sub-ordinates. Many operations in call centres, factories, distribution centres, super-markets and the like run on a 24-hour basis, 364 days a year. The manager of a call centre, for example, will not be present on every shift. Each shift will have supervisors. The numbers on a shift can vary from 30 to 100 per shift, depending on the nature of the work involved.

Better technology is another factor influencing the numbers that can be reliably managed. In many situations people are dependent on technology to do their work: the till that works out change at the checkout desk in the supermarket; or the IT screen in the call centre or factory control room. Not only does this technology help the person working with it, but invariably it also provides instant feedback on the progress and performance of a given operation, such as number of calls answered, time per call, etc in a call centre.

Much of the information generated by technology can also be accessed online from different locations in different time zones. Thus it would seem that many well-organized units of up to about 1,000 employees can be effectively managed at Level 3, and I would expect this number to increase over time.

Cultural considerations

My experience suggests that cultural conditions and history can help to cause and to preserve unhealthy management structures in many organizations.

Europe v United States

It is interesting to compare how cultural developments have influenced the effectiveness and competitiveness of the United States and Europe. Their respective experiences over the last 60 years are intriguing. There is incontrovertible evidence that Europe has lost out economically to the United States during this time. Has it also lost out in terms of organizational efficiency and effectiveness?

Culturally the United States is seen as more flexible, adaptable, fast-moving and prepared to take risks than its counterparts in (especially Western) Europe, given the latter's continuing obsession with protectionism following the Second World War. I well remember the frustration of some Brazilian colleagues years ago trying to share the reasons for a great marketing success with their European colleagues. The general response of the Europeans was an underwhelmed mix of: 'It probably would not work here', 'I think we have tried that before', 'Of course, you have a much younger population,' 'The French (or the Germans or the English, etc) would not like it', and so on. The frustrated Brazilian marketing director finally summed things up as follows: 'You know, in Brazil when we are confronted with a challenge, we say "it is possible". In Europe the mindset seems to start with "it is not possible". I am sorry but we don't understand that sort of negative thinking.' It was hard to disagree with him.

I have worked in two organizations, one in the United States and one in Europe, operating through into the 21st century in the same industry. They had identical business profiles of products in the same type of markets, and ostensibly the same top structure. Both organizations were multi-billion dollar businesses with similar revenues, both operated work levels and both had over 1,000 managers at Work Level 2 or above.

Although neither organization was as efficient as it could or should have been, there were significant differences. These differences seemed to be influenced by history, geography and, perhaps most of all, mindset and culture.

The total number of managers above Level 2 in the US company was treated as an index of 100. The corresponding index for the European company was 168. This meant the European company had an excess of 800 managers in Work Level 2+. At level 4+, when the US company's index was 100, the European company's was 277.

One of the problems was that the European organization was a new pan-European organization, previously comprised of 15 different national organizations. Thus the new organization was much more effective in relative terms but not in absolute terms. That is a predictable outcome of cultural blindness.

Company culture

It is common to hear people explain how their organization, market or industry is inherently more difficult, challenging and complex than any other. And this attitude is often used to justify overlooking the importance of work levels and effective organization design. I have heard people in a telecommunications company say: 'Levels can't be for us if they come from retail. Our business is much more complex.' Or research scientists saying: 'You can't apply a factory system to us.' The reality is, however, that accountability is a universal principle that applies across organizations and sectors.

But it is interesting to see how company cultures embed structures. In one grocery business that I have worked with, for example, there was a tendency to have about 10 Level 2 managers across the foods section of a hypermarket, and this was an echo of historical organizational structures in their stores. On the other hand, another retailer, also selling food in its hypermarkets but with a history and culture of general merchandise, tended to have two or three Level 2 managers in its stores of comparable size and complexity.

It was intriguing to see the company with a history of non-foods possibly oversimplifying the demands of running a very large foods operation, while the retailer that began in grocery possibly over-elaborated the accountability of running the foods side of its hypermarkets.

The spectres of finance and IT

Sometimes the culture within a function or part of an organization can be equally resilient and resistant to change. In my experience, often the worst-organized functions are finance and IT. They seem to have developed over-managed and narrow spans of management into a form of black art. An average span of more than three in these functions is a rarity.

In finance, the rationale for this state of affairs is usually dressed up in terms of compliance, with narrow spans deemed necessary for control purposes. There is also a strong tendency to add layers of management just to check the numbers going to the stock market or into the annual accounts.

A real and related problem is the fact that many of today's CFOs are themselves products of these conservatively organized departments and are not always open to new approaches. My most frustrating discussion in 2006 was with a CFO of a multibillion dollar international business who believed that he could not manage more than two direct reports, while at the same time expressing a wish to tackle the endemic over-management and consequent staff churn within the finance department.

In IT the problem seems to stem from the rapid pace of change in technology. This seems to be a combination of an inability to manage the technology effectively, coupled with the fact that IT departments often have a front line at Level 2 or above and are organized on a project basis. These latter two factors are invariably sources of great confusion and a lack of true accountability in the design of the organizational architecture.

Managers of IT departments invariably assume their front line is the equivalent of Level 1. But frequently the front line is really at Level 2 given the 'professional' nature of the work. The result is a structure with too many layers of management. This in turn leads to duplication and inefficiency, which is further compounded by haphazard project organizations.[3]

Finance and IT functions are support activities to the main line of the business. One of the reasons they tend to be over-managed is because the key criterion about the need for specialist knowledge is not applied with sufficient rigour. A support role, particularly at head office, must add specialist knowledge that is not otherwise available in the team. If this is not the case then duplication and the fudging of accountability is inevitable.

Span of control guidelines

To build an effective organization, where individuals can flourish and make an optimal contribution while also being fulfilled in their work, it is essential that management get to grips with spans of control.[4] This is a significant challenge. In fact when the Conference Board tried to replicate some international studies about spans of control in Europe in the early 1990s, the European companies approached (in the Conference Board's European Council on Organization) did not even recognize the term and were unable to collect the necessary data.

It is a good rule of thumb that any organization of at least 500 people with an average span of five or less is over-managed, and any organization in a country with a GDP of up to US$100 billion with more than five layers of management is unhealthy.

The span dilemma

The challenge is to decide the appropriate spans for each department at different levels in a complex organization, knowing that while there is no 'one size fits all' solution, nevertheless an average span of less than eight suggests that the structure is ineffective.[5] This might be less in the corporate head office with small specialist departments. Even so, it should not average less than five.

A problem with comparing span data from around the world is ensuring that the approach is reliable and valid. Very wide spans are possible for the first true layer of management at Level 2. But companies universally draw organization charts with those at the front line reporting to their supervisors. When there are multiple layers of supervision at Level 1, this complicates the issue and inevitably drives the number of spans downwards on average.

As Head of Organizational Development at Barclays, my colleague Adam Pearce carried out important work on tackling shortcomings in spans and layers. His approach was to treat the supervisory roles in Level 1 as hierarchical tiers, along with the managerial leaders from Level 2 and above, even though strictly speaking there are no layers of management in the first level of accountability. It is also another reason why, arguably, spans are statistically conservative.

A simplistic focus on spans?

This is a classic example of the mistakes that occur when organizations just focus on spans of control. It is a recipe for disaster to consider spans of control in isolation from the organization's vertical dimension – the number of layers.

In the example below, the consultant analysis suggested this company in the US could save over US $7 million by 'extending its average span of control from 4.6 to 5.3'. Even 5.3 is a low average, but that is not the key point here. The consultants felt the problem was in 'Levels 5 to 7' (ie layers 5 to 7, as they were counting down from the CEO despite the claim of a 'bottom-up analysis'), since that is where most of the management were.

Projecting span of control benefit applies the benchmark to individual levels of each organization considered in a 'bottom-up' fashion.

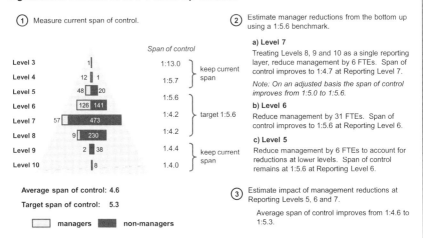

Figure 6.3 Example: span of control benefit estimating approach

But they missed the critical point. The company was heavily over-layered. The low average span of control was an outcome, not the cause, of the basic design flaw. The recommendation to tinker with average spans in layers 5 to 7 was not going to solve that fundamental problem as it left the excess layers intact.

In order to be effective, the company in question had to remove more than one layer and the savings were well in excess of the consultants' estimate. But they had not even recognized the real problem (and the many others that stemmed from it) and had no way of identifying the non-value-adding layers of management.

A simplistic focus on spans of control in isolation is guaranteed to traumatize people and wreck the fabric of even a moderately successful organization.

Key steps to define the optimum span of control

During my extensive work on control spans, across a number of different industries, I developed and refined the following approach to finding the optimal span of control:

1. Ensure that you have a clear understanding of the nature of the roles involved.
2. It is easiest to analyse a structure where a work level system has already been implemented. Leadership levels establish the layers of management that add value to the business.
3. Start applying the span of control questions listed later in the chapter to Level 1 roles reporting to Level 2 roles. Then continue with Level 2 roles reporting to Level 3 roles, and so on. Repeat this process for each spine.
    By doing this you will be in a better position to:
    ● find the spans that are good for your people, customers and suppliers;
    ● establish the right number of management jobs;
    ● ensure alignment with the work levelled structure.
4. If current spans emerge as too narrow, consider the following changes to improve them:
    ● Change reporting lines, grouping roles under one manager based on these criteria:
        – Role tasks are interdependent or have a significant impact on each other.
        – Information and knowledge will be shared because of higher interaction of these roles and this adds value to the customer or the business.
        – People need to use their capabilities more, and becoming part of a wider span will enable this.
    ● Evaluate to see if there is compression – too many layers within a work level – based on the analysis of levels. If there is, then identify the role that is not adding sufficient value and re-allocate accountabilities and responsibilities to obtain a reporting line that follows the work level principles.
5. If spans are too wide, then consider the opposite steps to those referred to in point 4 above.

The optimum span depends on the:

- nature of work of the lower level roles involved;
- nature of work of the leader's role;
- geographical spread or contiguity of the various roles;
- the level of coordination and integration required of the leader;
- the level of competence and experience of the unit or team.

The span of control questions

If the answer to the following questions is 'yes', then it suggests that a wide span is both possible and appropriate:

- Are the tasks performed relatively simple?
- Is the role supported by documented policies and routines?
- Are the roles in the team similar or even identical in nature?
- Are problems rare, usually repetitive and covered in guidelines?
- Are most roles in the team independent from other roles?
- Are jobs located near each other?
- Is the unit/team mature and experienced, providing stability and know-how?
- Do people have considerable discretion to prioritize tasks, to track their performance, and to manage their time?
- Typically, does the training and development of a new starter take less than a month?
- Is the manager not expected to perform many non-managerial duties?
- Is the unit organized into teams with considerable autonomy that don't require close management?

If the answers are more 'no' than 'yes', then a narrower span is called for. These various questions can be weighted to provide more detailed guidance to management as appropriate.

The advantages and shortcomings of narrow and wide spans

Generally, as already indicated, managers are more likely to design structures with spans that are too narrow rather than too wide.

Benchmarks

Global companies have a median average span of control of eight across their entire business, although I have also worked with a number of businesses where, once the correct number of management layers has been established, the average has moved up to 10.

Experience indicates that average spans in head offices tend to be lower, partly because there has been a major drive in recent years towards smaller or centreless head offices. The specialist head office departments are generally small groups of specialists and not the mass numbers associated with call centres, factories and hypermarkets. Consequently, their average spans are lower.

Companies do not normally require huge teams of patent lawyers, tax experts, PR managers and the like. Nevertheless, a target head office average span of five is both realistic and achievable. At present, most head offices seem to average closer to three, which usually means many unnecessary layers of management.

Layers: redressing the balance

Earlier in this chapter I outlined an example of an organization with far too many layers (see Figure 6.2). The good news is that situations like this can be redressed.

Once it was aware of the extent of the problem, top management ensured this company dramatically improved over an intervening two-year period. The improved situation is summarized in Figure 6.4.

The 'after' scenario is some 18 months after the data presented in Figure 6.2, and much closer to the optimal situation. One-third of the roles have been removed or reallocated, and the number of hierarchical layers reduced by three, with a total saving of more than US$50 million.

A lot of tidying up remains to be done, as the figures in layers 11, 10 and 9 (still close to 16,000) clearly indicate, but the company has already achieved a substantial improvement on the 41,000 people in layers 9 to 13 in the first scenario.

In my experience, companies cannot cope with more than a 20 to 25 per cent change in jobs, processes and structure at a time. Also, they tend to have problems facing up to the fact that their existing situation, which they may

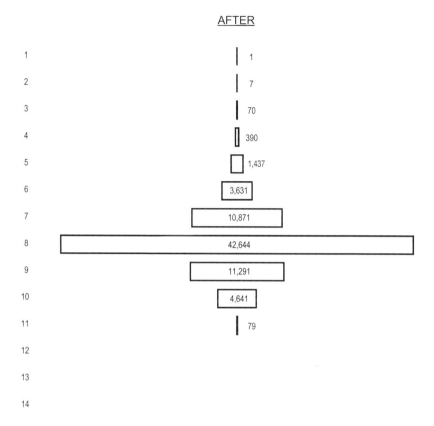

Figure 6.4 Positions by hierarchical layer for the group overall – after delayering

have purposefully constructed, can be so bad. Therefore, heavily over-managed organizations may have to undertake two or even three change programmes to reach an optimal situation.

Without the rigour of accountability levels, it is not easy to know what the optimal target organization should be. The twin dangers are that in the end the organization either goes too far or not far enough.

The Accountable Leader Chapter 6: Key points

This chapter illustrated how the root of most organizations' faulty structures stems from the way they organize work, first for those working at the front line and secondly for those held accountable for the performance of front-line teams.

The following key points are important:

1. It is best to design an organization by beginning with the perceptions of those at the bottom rather than the top. Consideration should be given to the work that they undertake, and the point at which an additional layer of management can make a genuine contribution to that work.
2. The front line can be at Level 2, 3 or (very occasionally) even higher. The most frequent example of a front line at Level 2 is where a professional entry requirement calls for Level 2 know-how and experience, and a competence to deal with recognized problems and to apply solutions in a manner requiring specific kinds of expertise – expertise that is often gained through study, training and experience.
3. Talent should not be wasted by devaluing professional accountability through forcing professionals to do too much mundane administrative work at Level 1.
4. The average management span of control in most companies has moved very little over the last 30 years – from about four, to about five or six. Narrow spans of control have been the most enduring cause of over-layered and unhealthy organizations in the 20th century, and this trend looks set to continue into the 21st century.
5. The commonly held 'rule of 6', that is, noone can manage more than six direct reports, is deeply flawed. Well-organized units of up to about 1,000 employees can be effectively managed at Level 3, and I would expect this number to increase over time.
6. In my experience often the worst-organized functions are finance and IT. An average span of more than three in these functions is a rarity.
7. It is a good rule of thumb that any organization of at least 500 people with an average span of five or less is over-managed, and any organization in a country with a GDP of up to US$100 billion with more than five layers of management is unhealthy.

Notes

1. Hilmer, F G and Donaldson, L (1996) *Management Redeemed: Debunking the fads that undermine corporate performance*, The Free Press, New York
2. The UK's Chartered Institute of Personnel and Development (CIPD) has produced a detailed and rigorous examination of the pros and cons of

the Michigan tripod model for HR, in Tannen *et al* (2007) *HR Coping with Change.*

3. For a fuller treatment of how to build an effective organization based on projects at different levels of accountability, see chapter 10 of *The Healthy Organization.*

4. Whether you prefer the term span of control, span of management or span of support (the latter makes the most sense today) the first of these terms is historically the most well established, so it is the one used in this context.

5. This finding was initially based on Allen Janger's 1989 survey of international companies, which found a median average span of eight.

7 Managing the managers

'I run an operating unit and/or process, juggling competing steering wheel requirements to deliver a balanced set of results or services.'[1]

Strapline for the third level of accountability in Tesco Work Level Workbook

Leaders at the third level of accountability are the backbone of a successful organization. They are the operational general managers who make sure things happen. They work with given assets, resources and people, ensuring that current objectives are met, improving performance and raising productivity. The Level 3 leader is the lynchpin between operational and strategic work, held to account for delivering short-term work while contributing to the longer term.

Work at Level 3 moves beyond leading one situation at a time, or diagnosing a single case, to balancing the needs and outcomes for a number of different individuals and sets of circumstances. In its more advanced form, it requires the managing of a flow of activities – across different departments, for example – to decide what the best outcome would be at a given time. This may call for short-term trade-offs while still focusing on longer-term objectives.

The essence of work at this level is being held to account for running a discrete unit and integrating the work of departments that sometimes have conflicting objectives. The managerial leader at Level 3 must balance and optimize their work and performance to achieve the best overall result for the unit.

Take the situation in a factory where two subordinate managers at Level 2 are leading production and engineering. The engineering manager wants long runs without any down-time, to ensure engineering performance ratios are optimal. The production manager's workforce, however, wants more variety and product changes on the line, and enjoys the down-time as it provides an opportunity to work on other tasks. The factory manager has to optimize the production output, efficiency and morale in the plant to ensure the critical objectives, or key performance indicators (KPIs), for the complete unit are met.[2]

The quotation at the beginning of chapter refers to the Tesco 'steering wheel' – a balanced scorecard comprised of four segments: finance, operations, people and customers. Objectives and targets that should reflect the values of the organization are set in each of the quadrants.

Tesco's steering wheel has its greatest initial impact at Level 3, as this is the level at which a manager owns all four segments of the wheel, rather than just one of them (individually these would be owned by Level 2 managers). A hypermarket manager, for example, has to juggle competing steering wheel requirements in order to deliver a balanced set of results. The longer term – typically a year or so in this case – has to be kept in focus while short-term, tactical needs are actively managed. Dealing with these immediate requirements may call for minor deviations and adjustments to the original production plan.

The essence of Level 3 accountability

Managerial leaders at this level are held to account for delivering operational excellence and continuous improvement in the performance of existing operations, while maintaining good morale in their teams. They are also expected to make a significant contribution to the formulation of policy and strategy. This is the first level at which managers are expected to lead other managers and talent-spot future managers.

1. Nature of work

The key aspect of work at this level is the delivery of planned performance, while at the same time continuing to get better performance from the assets and resources year on year.

The key performance indicators or targets are tangible and measurable and typically focus on what (quantity), how (quality) and by when (time).

The attention is on things such as better service, greater output, more sales, less cost, less waste – all directed, for the most part, towards achieving greater productivity.

Individuals working at Level 3 must move beyond dealing with a sequence of individual situations, case studies or independent events and episodes. The essence of Level 3 accountability is managing a sequence or flow of work tasks and events, which have to be managed as a whole, not as a series of unconnected events. Level 3 roles are typically carried out by individuals working in operating units or head office departments, supported by an infrastructure of people in Level 1 and 2 roles. The different sections or parts of the unit may have potentially conflicting objectives; these must be balanced, prioritized and integrated for the good of the whole operation.

Individuals working at this level pull together the work of people, processes and systems, juggling competing requirements while constantly adapting priorities as necessary in order to deliver a balanced service or set of results.

2. Resource complexity

Managers at Level 3 are not yet accountable for changing the fundamental disposition of the resources at their disposal. If someone at this level is running a call centre it is not their job to decide to relocate it, although they might recommend relocating. Resources have to be managed in the context of an integrated system, unit or head office department. Level 3 managers are expected to improve performance within the unit, but cannot change the purpose or fundamental activity of the unit. Thus if the factory in question makes ice cream, it is not the job of the factory manager to decide to make chocolate instead, but to aim to be the best ice cream factory in the world.

Financial targets are important. Level 3 managers are assessed on the performance of the variety of assets for which they are accountable and in relation to the formulation and on-time delivery of capital expenditure projects. Continuous improvement, often resulting in increased productivity, is expected at this level, and project leadership – involving the integration of a number of disciplines and teams – also becomes significant.[3]

Working at Level 3 often requires authoritative specialist knowledge. The manager might be expected to be a knowledge leader in certain areas. Scientists working at this level, however, might be producing new solutions or applications, but would not be producing new science; they would be introducing refinements to existing knowledge. They would be in the realm of development – improving an existing product, system, or pharmaceutical delivery process. Discovery or invention occurs at Level 4.

Finally, the Level 3 manager is accountable for the identification of potential managers and their appointment to Level 2.

3. Problem-solving

The thinking process at this level is still predominantly about the actual and the tangible, rather than dominated by abstract analysis and the need to find a solution that does not yet exist, as it is at Level 4. For the Level 3 manager, problem-solving involves identifying patterns in the actual performance of existing products, technology platforms and systems. This requires the scanning of a series of activities, establishing and evaluating linkages between them, and identifying and analysing significant trends.

The Level 3 manager may not need to be physically present at every stage of the flow of work in order to assess what needs to be done. Concrete and specific metrics are available, such as output per shift or department, sales per region, market share per product, clinical trial results, customer service assessment, and employee morale assessment, which signal implications for this year's, or even next year's plans.

Individuals at Level 3 manage a flow of interrelated problems that need to be prioritized and solved using the resources within the team. They are expected to make contributions to strategy and policy based on their knowledge and experience. They are not accountable for strategy and policy but should see the implications and shortcomings of current practice and the need to shape different approaches going forward. A skilful approach to making contributions to policy and strategy, and in seeing implications across a wider field, is a good indication of someone working at Level 3 who has the potential to move to Level 4.

4. Change

The Level 3 manager is accountable for ensuring that existing resources – such as products, systems and scientific platforms – continually attain new levels of performance. Likewise, subordinates should also be led to new stages of personal learning, development and achievement.

The essence of Level 3 change is continuous improvement. This contrasts with strategic change, which is expected to reach beyond continuous improvement to levels of breakthrough and discovery.

Operational scientific change culminates in Level 3 innovation. This level of scientific work generates the 'new and improved' formula. The crucial word is 'improved'. New science is not involved. There is no technological breakthrough. Clever refinement, adaptation, modification (possibly requiring patent protection) and improvement are the hallmarks of good development at this level and are key contributors to business success.

Change is often equated with innovation. It is important to distinguish between operational innovation, which occurs up to Level 3, and strategic innovation, which occurs at Level 4 and above. The essence of the marketing's 'new and improved' product or process is usually Level 3 innovation, or what is known as development. This activity creates excitement around the brand, product or process that justifies new promotions. It is the heartbeat of a good marketing manager's plans. But the innovative person in this example at Level 3 is still working with existing markets, products, processes, science or technology.

Strategic innovation, the type of innovation required at Level 4, is fundamentally different. At this level, the change is more than a matter of improving what already exists. It involves a move into research and new domains; the discovery, invention and delivery of breakthrough, 'first in the industry' solutions.

Strategic innovation is rare. Confusion over these two aspects of innovation is widespread and as a result some companies organize for operational change when what they actually intend is a strategic change outcome.

5. Internal collaboration

Managers at Level 3 normally work across group disciplines, functions within a business, and sometimes a number of countries, in order to improve the performance of their unit or department (by ensuring a product's critical path is met and launched on time, for example) or to improve the delivery of a process, operational system, study or project. The key point here is that the managerial leader is accountable for their effectiveness collaborating with peers. Collaboration in this sense is not just about contacts, liaison and the exchanging or the sharing of information. To be effective carrying out the job, the individual in question has to work with colleagues. Level 3 managers are expected to be able to collaborate, and cannot fulfil the requirements of work at this level without doing so effectively.

Managers at the same level cannot tell colleagues what to do. Instead they must persuade, convince and cajole cooperation and support from people who have their own priorities and objectives.

The higher the progression in an organization, the more important this ability becomes. Indeed, a common reason for faltering career progression is that an individual is seen to be arrogant, a loner or a poor team player.

Today's larger, more complex and generally flatter organizations depend upon competent managers who can collaborate effectively across the organization. In this sense the command and control ethos is dead.

The key contacts and peers of managers at this level are usually on different sites or – in the case of international companies – in different countries. These collaborative networks increasingly tend to be managed at a physical distance (not usually the case at Levels 1 and 2). The advent of internet online facilities and video-conferencing has enabled virtual teams to work together across time zones around the world.

6. External interaction

External contacts at Work Level 3 tend to be at a national level, in contrast to those at Level 2, which tend to be local or regional within a country. These interactions often involve negotiation of agreements – whether with customers, suppliers, national trade unionists or representatives of government departments.

The key thing to note about the external challenge at Level 3 is that the response to the external world outside the organization is reactive. The individual is endeavouring to get the best outcome for the organization, whether it is responding to a trade union demand, a customer or supplier's negotiation tactic or the request of a local or national politician. By contrast, at Level 4 the manager needs to be proactive: planning to influence and change something in the external environment that might otherwise have a negative impact on the organization. At Level 4 the need is to modify the external world. At Level 3 the need is to cope with what the outside world presses upon the organization.

These external contacts could also involve positive collaboration. In the case of a bioscience company, for example, the external network might involve universities, federal agencies such as the Food and Drug Administration in the United States, hospitals, central laboratories and civil servants in the health sectors, or those in the funding sectors related to medical well-being. In such a company, much of the work is centred on the successful execution of clinical trials or of studies that could involve: the investigation of the performance of new molecules; the discovery of new products in the health business; or the discovery of applications and platforms that could affect the markets that the company is targeting. In this type of business, positive external linkages are vital to its success.

7. Task horizon

Managers at Level 3 are very much involved in the delivery of the annual plan. It is important that a Level 3 manager does not simply replicate the work of Level 2 subordinates, who in most organizations are also held to account within the annual budget. A Level 3 manager adds value by looking across individual plans and budgets and ensuring that their contribution is such that the whole unit or department meets its time-related targets. It may be that it is necessary to flex and modify expenditure up or down, depending on emerging circumstances, to ensure the overall plan is met. In short the emphasis here should be on the integration of performance against the overall annual plan.

These managers are also expected to make a significant contribution to the plans and activities of the following year. This can involve the delivery of critical milestones in longer-term plans (such as research studies or projects that go well beyond a year, but that have critical phases to be delivered across periods of up to two years). Thus there is accountability for deliverables within the one-year time frame and an expectation for some contributions relating to the two-year horizon.

The crucial responsibilities are assessed in relation to the average time taken to complete the balance of tasks in the respective roles. The balance of tasks comprises more than fifty per cent of the burden of accountability.

Issues at Level 3

The skills crossover point

When someone joins an organization at Level 1 the key requirement is the level of skill they bring to bear on the job in question. And, as we have seen, professional skill can be important at the front line of some Level 2 jobs. Generally, skill requirements can be categorized as a triangle in relation to levels of accountability, as in Figure 7.1.

The skills requirement typically dominates the nature of the work at Level 1 and then becomes relatively less important at Levels 2 and 3. Thus in many functional areas of the business, the technical skill required to master a given job is the prime requirement – being a competent accountant, engineer or pharmacist and so on. The job requirements and the skills needed are technical.

But with promotion to Level 2, the job starts to involve general skills, such as the ability to lead others. Individuals are held to account for more than just the technical demands of IT, HR and so on. This becomes more pronounced

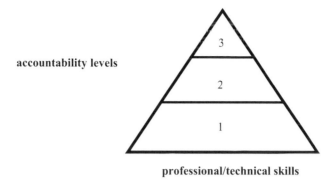

Figure 7.1 The professional/technical skills triangle

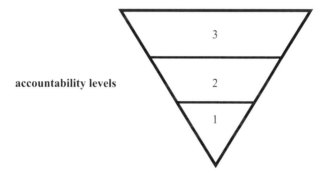

Figure 7.2 General management skills triangle

at Level 3, where the need for general leadership skills is even greater. This can be summarized as an inverted triangle (see Figure 7.2).

At Level 1, for example, workers are not required to have skills relating to managing others, other than might be required in a supervisory support role. The general skills required as one moves up from Level 1 would include people management, project management, planning and implementation, communication and general information management skills. Weaknesses in these areas may offset strengths in the technical area. We have all encountered the boffin who is not good at holding others to account. Deep technical skills do not guarantee that general management skill levels are equally strong.

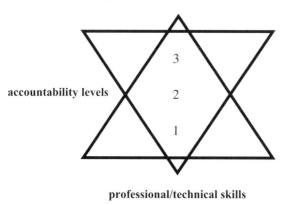

Figure 7.3 The skills crossover point

At Level 3 general skills start to become more important than technical proficiency alone. It is the skills crossover point, as indicated in Figure 7.3.

As Figure 7.3 illustrates, if you start in a factory, for example, as a certified engineer, and then become a factory engineer at Level 2, a promotion to factory manager at Level 3 will call upon fundamentally different abilities and will be a very different experience.

Moving through the accountability levels, the skill balance changes. Now different types of skill are needed to be successful. While knowledge of engineering would be useful, it would not be essential for the factory manager. It can in fact be a disadvantage for the ex-engineer factory manager to stay too close to the engineering department (working at the wrong level). Now the manager must deal with more than just technical engineering issues. General management skills are required and there may be a need for extra training and development. Managerial leaders at Level 3 have to learn how to run the ship, not just steer it.

The business unit

Another key issue emerges at Level 3; whether an organizational unit is too large or even too small and therefore inherently prone to sub-optimal architecture.

Some suggest that the business unit is the cornerstone of organization design, a useful insight for grouping work across the horizontal axis.[4] Unfortunately, noone has offered a way of determining the level of accountability of the business unit, or placed sufficient emphasis on the need for an appropriate vertical axis in an approach to organization design. A truly effective organization must have the vertical and horizontal aspects of their design in balance.

This is one of the great shortcomings of civil organizations: most do not have a clue where their critical levels of accountability reside. If you compared it to the military model, a business unit could be at the same level of accountability as a company, a battalion, a brigade. Who knows?

The business unit might well be the key to effective organization design, but only if it can be related to the level of accountability. It is not enough to focus only on the horizontal groupings of activities when designing an effective organization.

Business units defined

A business unit is a part of a larger organization because it is not totally self-sufficient. It may discharge a number of different activities, depending upon the size and complexity of the parent group. I have seen a variety of business units between Level 3 and Level 6, depending upon the size and complexity of the organization in question. The essential differences in business units at Levels 3 to 6 are briefly summarized in the following box.

Types of business unit

Level 3[5]: the operational BU
This is an operational business unit (OBU), which is externally or market focused, whether defined by customer, product/service or geography.

- It typically has top-line metrics, such as market share or sales by product, region or customer.
- It has control of some of its costs, but not its full profit and loss (P&L).

Level 4: the auxiliary BU
Although operating at a strategic level, the auxiliary business unit (ABU) does not have a full deck of functions or processes that underpin the product or service being sold or offered.

- It may receive products or services from another business unit, as it is not a self-sufficient unit in its market.
- It has control of significant own costs, but not all of them. It is likely to have an arm's length relationship with internal clients elsewhere within the group.
- It does not have control of all its operating costs, nor therefore its full P&L.[6]

Level 5: the unitary (or lead) BU

The unitary business unit (UBU) is a fully fledged BU, which would normally have:

- a full range of functions or processes;
- complex technology sufficient for its market;
- presence in a key market – eg a significant country;
- a significant record of ongoing growth;
- self-sufficiency in its strategic resources, ie a Level 4 infrastructure;
- a lead role in relation to ABUs and OBUs;
- full operating P&L;
- allocated group overheads.

Level 6: the network BU

A network business unit (NBU) is a large, complex business unit leading an infrastructure of Level 5 UBUs in a very large country, or across a number of countries. Strategy shifts to a seamless network of markets. Customers are increasingly likely to be international. Markets and associated supply chains are likely to be interlinked and therefore more complex and interdependent.

An NBU is likely to be self-sufficient in its key resources, such as research and development, capital expenditure and talent development, for:

- a significant region such as a continent;
- a portfolio of businesses or markets;
- a global line of business.

It would set investment priorities and allocate resources such as capital and overheads to business units within the network, based on group policies and strategy.

The NBU's results would directly impact the performance and reputation of the group.[7]

Is the business unit too large?

Many business units are at Level 3. As this level, at the top of operational management, is often responsible for managing about 98 per cent of the employees in a given organization, it can also provide a critical clue about the optimal size of a branch, call centre, factory or store. This is because it can be shown that a managerial leader at Level 3 can cope quite comfortably with about 1,000 people in the unit. Any more and the unit starts to creak as compression – more than one layer of management in a level of accountability when only one is required – is designed into the unit. It results in the opposite of empowerment.

If there are too many people in an organization, there seems to be a tendency for more managerial roles to be brought in just to cope with them all. Faulty ideas on accountability and spans of control merely seem to aggravate the situation.

I have already referred to the widespread tendency to build in unnecessary tiers of supervisors. This is based on faulty assumptions about how many people can be managed. It is then complicated by unclear accountabilities or poorly designed roles.

One company was running a large call centre business unit consisting of nearly 1,000 full-time equivalent staff (FTEs) – the actual number of individuals on the payroll was over 1,000, since a number of them were part-time or had job-sharing arrangements. The company assumed that only a small number of individuals could be effectively supervised by any one supervisor. This was largely due to a recently introduced appraisal system, adapted from the system used for their Level 2 and above management. However, it was unduly complicated for Level 1.

As a result, the company felt obliged to build too many tiers of supervision because of the number of people in the call centre. But each of these tiers – a point of escalation in the customer complaints process – had no more accountability to get things done. The result was a bureaucracy of busy people, snowed under with paperwork, driven by an irrelevant and poorly designed appraisal system. This in turn generated too many managers to 'manage' the tiers of supervisors.

This example demonstrates how the mere existence of large numbers of workers can lead directly to too many layers of non-value-adding management.

But there is another issue about the number of people who can be held to account in Level 3. There comes a point when an operational unit is too large to be run with only two layers of management. My experience suggests a need to be very careful about designing units in excess of 1,000 at Level 3, unless the work is very routine and only needs minimal supervision or interference.

When it comes to the ideal size of a business unit, a good rule of thumb seems to be that organizations should not build operational units such as hyper-markets, factories, call centres and the like with more than 1,200 employees, as they are apt to be unmanageable. One problem, however, is that the size of stores, distribution centres and the like tends to be determined by accountants and engineers seeking economies of scale, and not by organizational design professionals.

Is the business unit too small?

Sometimes business units are designed with two layers of management as if there were three levels of accountability, when in fact there are only two. In that case only one layer of management is required for the business unit. This may raise the question of whether the business unit is too small and sub-optimal. In developed countries with smaller populations, such as Scandinavia, New Zealand, Singapore or Eire, business units might be small, and Level 2 would then be appropriate. But in countries with larger populations, such as the United Kingdom, Japan or the United States, there is sometimes a tendency to build sub-optimally small units.

I recently worked in a financial services company in one of these large countries that had four call centres, each with about 200 employees. Managing 200 people is usually too much for a single Level 2 manager, but it hardly warrants a full-time Level 3 manager. In this case the units were too small and generated more management infrastructure than necessary.

The appropriate solution for this company was to move to two call centres or even one. The ultimate decision was influenced by issues such as backup and criticality of service in a key national activity. In the end, the decision was made to move to two.

It is now clear that an analysis of Level 3 accountabilities can be vital in helping to identify whether a business unit is actually too large or too small. New technology is constantly redrawing these demarcation lines. A practical guideline in the 21st century would be that 1,000 people in a Level 3 business unit (assuming work at both Levels 1 and 2) is appropriate.

Automation

Since accountability at Level 1 is prescribed work, it is often capable of automation. The issue of whether it is automated or not is down to cost of technology (and the capabilities and impact on quality of service) versus cost of labour.

In the developed world there are many examples of Level 1 work being progressively automated. The Japanese car factories pioneered the use of robotics at the front line. In a number of countries airport managers are finding the number of their subordinates decreasing as both the check-in and cargo handling processes become more automated. In New Zealand there were about 200 cooperatives in the mid-1980s producing dairy products. Today the total is about 2 per cent of that number, and those that remain are highly automated. In many countries supermarket customers check themselves out via new scanning technology. And so on.

The number of employees is not a rigid indicator of levels of accountability. Sophistication of technology is a key factor. There is also the impact of the front line being at Level 1 or higher to be considered. But in those types of operations that involve large numbers of similar, unskilled to semi-skilled jobs from Level 1, then up to 150 for Level 2 and up to 1,000 for Level 3 seem to be tipping points in many labour-intensive units.

Organization design problems at Level 3

Many companies seem to have organization design problems at Level 3. This is particularly the case with corporate office jobs, whether at national or international level.

A corporate office should not have many jobs below Level 3. Otherwise it is tending to duplicate the work in the field and not add value to it. The effective front line of key jobs in a corporate office should be at Level 3, contributing to policy and strategy.

The importance of the third type of value-adding authority that underpins support roles is critical here: one of the key reasons for a support role is the 'provision of expertise that does not reside elsewhere in the team'.[8]

We have already established a number of reasons for the Level 3 bulge in many corporate offices (two or more layers in one level of accountability):

- No framework for identifying levels of accountability.
- No specialist knowledge required for the job that is not already present in the corporate office team.
- Very narrow spans of control (four or less) at Levels 4+ above the job.
- Job grade and cost creep from the job evaluation scheme leading to administrative promotions.
- Confusion of line and support roles.

How it works in practice: a Work Level 3 case study

Recently I was asked to examine an organization's buying function. The director responsible for this function was concerned as he was picking up a lot of indications of frustration, de-motivation and unhappiness in the department, mostly from the buyers.

The structure of the department was as follows (read from bottom to top):

- the vice president of the division
- category directors, to
- senior buyers, to
- buyers, to
- junior buyers, to
- buying assistants, who reported to

The vice president felt the problem might be that the directors were not adding value to the role of the senior buyers. He was concerned that the directors might be compressing the senior buyers, who in turn were making the jobs of the buyers increasingly difficult. He felt the role of buyer was becoming undoable as a result, hence the complaints coming from many of the buyers.

The key questions were, in brief, as follows:

- Is the buyer's role becoming undoable?
- Is the horizontal reach too broad?
- Do the buyers have the requisite skills?
- Are the accountabilities clear?
- Are the roles inherently too stressful?
- Are the directors adding value to the senior buyers?

The approach was to conduct a number of Accountability Probes, during which interviews were conducted covering roles from the front line along a reporting chain up to the CEO, to determine the levels of accountability that existed in the organization.

The investigations started with the front line (buying assistants), through the key categories, up to and including the vice president. This established how many levels of accountability there were in total. It was then possible to work out whether there were any structural anomalies in the function.

The findings about the levels of accountability and the current layers of management are summarized in Figure 7.4.

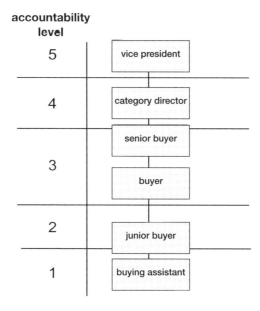

**accountability
level**

5	vice president
4	category director
3	senior buyer
	buyer
2	junior buyer
1	buying assistant

Figure 7.4 Compression in a buying department?

The investigations showed that, while the function consisted of five levels of accountability – inclusive of the vice president – there were major issues at Levels 2 and 3. The junior buyers were not fully empowered. They were not fully accountable for the assistants and often had no budget.

This was because both buyers and senior buyers were at Level 3, causing a compression of the two roles. Key buying decisions had up to two, and sometimes three, identical inputs as a result of overlap and duplication, which generated work but not job satisfaction. The three levels of buying did not all have discrete decisions for which they were held to account.

While the vice president had anticipated problems at Level 4, the investigations showed that the real bulge was caused by an unnecessary layer of management at Level 3. It was at this stage that the president told us that, over a period of about a dozen years, the role of director had been removed, reinserted and was about to be removed again. As it happens that would have been a disastrous decision, which would have seriously hampered the performance of the business.

This company, like many, knew it had an organizational problem. But as it had no reference frame of principles to guide its organization design, the wheels had been spinning with little to show for it for over a decade. This was because of a totally incorrect assumption as to the cause of the problem.

It further emerged that the company had constructed its buying structure by using the buying structure of another company in the industry as a guide. But in replicating the other, highly successful company's buying structure, this company merely cemented its faulty structure and continued to de-motivate its buying staff. In fact, because of its greater size and complexity (eight times sales, six times as many categories and so on) the comparator company actually needed another level of accountability.

The optimal organization suggested following the investigations was as set out in Figure 7.5.

Summary of recommendations:

- Establish category teams under the leadership of a dedicated Work Level 4 director.
- Fully empower the buyer and junior buyer at Levels 3 and 2 respectively.
- Strengthen team targets but with clear individual accountability, such as margin for buyers.
- Ensure effective functional support through the implementation and measurement of consistent processes.
- Define team-focused accountabilities for each key category team member at Level 3.

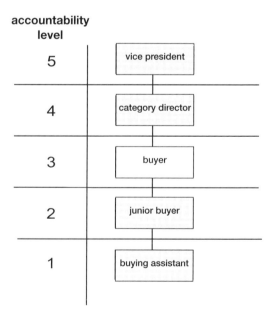

Figure 7.5 The optimal buying department structure

- Identify skill and competency profiles for each role and clarify career development paths.
- Identify and meet priority training and development needs for job-holders.

In turn this led to focus on the 'horizontal reach' and the relationships of the buyers with other functions. Previously, because of the lack of clarity about the spine of accountability, there was a lot of confusion in the working relationships with other functions. Objectives were unclear and overlapped. For example, the buyers felt that they were accountable for sales and profits, whereas in reality all they could directly influence was the margin on the products they purchased.

There were countless meetings with vague agendas that agreed on few decisions. At times, up to four layers of management could be present. Product promotions lurched towards launch dates. Behaviour under pressure was erratic as priorities changed at short notice. It was little wonder that the buyers recognized they were trapped in a vice of pressures that made their job impossible. The problem had been rooting out the cause.

The category structure detailed in Figure 7.6 was proposed to improve the accountability for the category structure across the business.

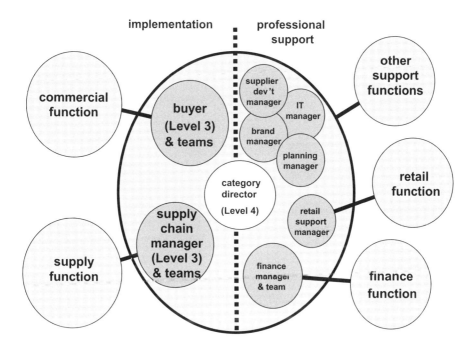

Figure 7.6 Proposed category team structure

This case study is a good example of how important it is to get the Level 3 accountabilities correctly defined. It also illustrates the power of focusing on the vertical axis of organization design.

Once it became clear that the compression problems were at Level 3, it was possible to improve the horizontal connections across the organization, which until that time had not been working very well. It emerged that there was need to identify which roles in the other key functions – such as supply chain, marketing and finance – were also at Level 3. Prior to this, meetings chaired by the senior buyers were attended by a mishmash of managers at different levels. Buyers felt that much of their work was needlessly duplicated by the senior buyers, who created both work and pressure.

In the new organization, meeting agendas could be aligned to the work levels, so that the managers present had the relevant information available to make the appropriate decisions. The agendas for junior buyers and their peers at Level 2 were quite different to those for the buyers at Level 3. There were no more delays due to someone at the meeting not having access to the required information (since they operated at the wrong level in the organization and therefore had to go away and ask 'the boss'). Authorization levels for expenditure and budget accountability were more sharply defined and allocated.

Category metrics were also more focused. Buyers were held to account for margin, marketers for share, supply chain for working capital, retail for sales and costs, and finance for provision of profitability. The team as a whole, led by a category director, could be jointly targeted on all of the above, in line with the annual and medium term plan, so that an individual had his or her bonus influenced by two sets of objectives: individual and shared.

A key finding: the view from the bottom

One of the key findings set out above relates to the buyers' view of the job of the senior buyers. One of the advantages of interviewing people at the front line, on the spine of accountability, is discovering which jobs are viewed as interesting and worthwhile by the people 'underneath'. People lower in the organization can see who makes decisions, who helps them and moves work forward. It is also abundantly clear who is not adding value, who is merely duplicating work, checking it, or generating superfluous work because they cannot or will not take decisions.

This awareness tends to be shown in two ways during interviews. Sometimes the person whose position is compressed in the same level of accountability simply bypasses the supposedly senior person to get to the real decision-maker (usually in the next level of accountability). People don't necessarily use those terms, but when interviewed they are usually quite clear about which person is able to take the decisions. The problem with this type of bypassing, going straight to the decision-maker, is that it is not acceptable in some hierarchically minded cultures. This merely builds up frustration among the people who need a decision quickly to get their job done, as the decision-making process becomes snarled-up with social ritual.

The other telling response is an answer to the question: 'Which job would you like to do next?' People tend not to want to do a job that they can see is lacking authority or accountability, and not adding value. So look out for answers that steer clear of a particular job, especially if it is the job to which the person currently reports.

Although in this case the buying function was badly organized, people were still dedicated – working very hard and for very long hours in many cases. There was evidence of considerable pressure, with people being on more stress-related medication than their colleagues. This pattern is not uncommon in unhealthy structures; they generate unhealthy outcomes.

And yet, as we have seen, top management in this organization had misdiagnosed the problem for about a decade. They also wondered whether they had a talent problem, as they could see that people were working hard but results were starting to stagnate and slip.

The real problem had not occurred to them: a lack of empowerment at Levels 2 and 3. Understandably, they did not think in those terms. Worse than that, they were in great danger of applying the wrong solution. They were about to strip out the strategic level of accountability (the category directors at Level 4), leaving the original set of problems in place. This would have led to a gap in accountability and the inevitable overloading of the vice president. The net result would have been that strategic work would have suffered, as the urgent tends to drive out the important.

Dwell-time at Level 3

Given the importance of Level 3 jobs as the backbone of a successful organization, it is not surprising that the amount of time spent at Level 3 ('dwell-time') has emerged as a critical factor in the development of leaders who successfully reach Level 5 and above.

Levels 3 and 5 have emerged as being particularly significant. This is because they are both forms of general management; one is operational, the other strategic. Jobs at these levels are accountable for a 'whole cake', whereas those in Levels 2 and 4 invariably have only a 'slice of the cake'.

How many people can be managed at each level?

In answer to this critical question, Table 7.1 sets out some guidelines that appear most appropriate to today's workforce.

Table 7.1 Guidelines for the numbers of people that can be led at different levels of accountability

Level 1	Up to 30, for a supervisor. Although 15 to 20 would be more common.
Level 2	Up to 150 for the first layer of management. For example in a call centre, factory or hypermarket.
Level 3	Up to 1,000. 750 seems to be a sound total in many situations, but this could go up to 1,250 if many staff are full-time equivalents (FTEs), giving a higher head count than the number of roles.
Level 4	Up to 5,000.
Level 5	Up to 25,000.
Level 6	Up to 100,000.

These numbers are based on leadership demands in a developed country. The operation could be on a 24 × 7 × 52 weeks per year basis. Numbers in the developing world, eg on a tea estate, where the front line is not highly skilled or the work interrelated, could be higher.

For companies dependent on advanced or intricate technology or those in industries such as media or closely linked to the internet, where many of the front-line roles could be at Level 2 or even higher, these numbers would be too high. Therefore, discretion has to be used.

But it remains true to say that many organizations are still too conservative in estimating how many people can be led at different levels of accountability.

Some people, such as professionals, can pass through Level 1 very quickly. There is also evidence that they can move through Level 2 quite quickly – averaging about four years.[9] But those who are successful at Level 5 spend around six years or more at Level 3. This does not mean that they are doing the same job all the time. In fact, 'boundary moves' within a level are vital contributions to leadership development.

There is also solid evidence that shows excessive acceleration through Level 3 leads to burnout and even failure at the strategic levels. This is important to bear in mind when dealing with rapid growth. There is a strong temptation to crash them through the promotion levels. Unfortunately, 'crash' seems to be the operative word.

I have seen this happen in emerging economies in Latin America and Africa. I believe there are signs of it happening in China at the moment, and as a result many of the young generation of Chinese managers may not be so successful when they reach the tops of their organization.

Age is not a determinant of career development. It is merely that, given some clear assumptions about when a person enters an organization and the level of that entry, the demands of dwell-time per level mean that age tends to correlate broadly with level of accountability or level of achievement. This is a very important consideration when grooming future managerial leaders.

The Accountable Leader Chapter 7: Key points

Level 3 is hugely important as it is at the apex of operational management. This is the first layer in an organization that manages managers.

The following key points are important:

1. Leaders at the third level of accountability are the backbone of a successful organization. They are the operational general managers who make sure things happen.
2. The essence of work at this level is being held to account for running a discrete unit and integrating the work of departments that sometimes have conflicting objectives. The managerial leader at Level 3 must balance and optimize their work and performance to achieve the best overall result for the unit. Managerial leaders at Level 3 have to learn how to run the ship, not just steer it.
3. Work at Level 3 moves beyond leading one situation at a time, or diagnosing a single case, to balancing the needs and outcomes for a number of different individuals and sets of circumstances.

4. At Level 3 general skills start to become more important than technical proficiency alone. It is the skill crossover point.

5. If the business unit is to contribute to effective organization design, it must relate to the level of accountability. It is not enough to focus only on the horizontal groupings of activities when designing an effective organization.

6. Types of business unit are as follows (business units are not justified below Level 3): Level 3: the operational BU; Level 4: the auxiliary BU; Level 5: the unitary (or lead) BU; Level 6: the network BU.

7. Regarding optimal business unit size, organizations should not build operational units such as hypermarkets, factories, call centres and the like with more than 1,200 employees, as they are apt to be unmanageable.

8. A corporate office, national or international, should not have many jobs below Level 3. Otherwise it is tending to duplicate the work in the field and not add value to it. The effective front line of key jobs in a corporate office should be at Level 3, contributing to policy and strategy.

9. The amount of time spent at Level 3 ('dwell-time') has emerged as a critical factor in the development of leaders who successfully reach Level 5 and above.

Notes

1. Tesco's 'steering wheel' is what other organizations would recognize as a balanced scorecard.

2. The factory manager in this example is Level 3. This would be the most common example. But it is possible for a bank branch, call centre, factory, distribution centre or supermarket to be at Level 2. This would be a small, more straightforward operation, which does not require an infrastructure of Level 2 roles. Indeed in some very small branches or stores, the top job might be only at Level 1; effectively a supervisor.

3. Meaningful projects really only start at Level 3. There are no true projects led at Level 1, and Level 2-led projects are really subsets of Level 3 projects, which themselves are often parts of strategic programmes at Level 4. The issue and organization of projects is discussed at more length in Chapter 10 of *The Healthy Organization*.

4. Goold, M and Campbell, A (2002) *Designing Effective Organisations*, Jossey-Bass, San Francisco, California

5. Business units cannot be justified below Level 3. As described earlier in the chapter, the need to integrate a flow of work across and within a unit, with potentially conflicting sub-objectives, commences at Level 3.

6. The issue of balance sheet compliance is not included here, as this is a legal rather than an operating requirement of the business unit. It therefore does not impact directly on its organizational architecture.

7. Although not part of this analysis, a Level 7 BU would be a pan-network business unit, and the Level 8 variant the mega business unit. Thus the abbreviations from Level 3 to Level 8 would be: OBU, ABU, UBU, NBU, PBU and MBU.

8. See Chapter 5. One of the key reasons for a support role is the 'provision of expertise that does not reside elsewhere in the team'. This principle is frequently fudged in head office roles, which then compress other Level 3 jobs.

9. See chapter 8 of *The Healthy Organization* on the concept of 'tracking' for a more detailed treatment of this issue.

8 Managing on a global stage

'Nothing should be done by a larger and more complex organization which can be done as well by a smaller and more simple organization.'

Pius XI, Quadragesimo Anno

So far, the discussion has focused on an individual being held to account for operational work within a single country. Now, however, we need to consider international accountability, which takes us well into the strategic strata of accountability. The divide between operational and strategic work is fundamentally different to that between the first three levels of accountability.

Strategic work involves the realignment of assets, based on an assessment of resource gaps and market opportunities, to ensure that future plans will be met. This is difficult enough in one country. It is even more challenging when a manager is held to account for several countries around the world. Many international companies get confused when aligning accountabilities across regions of countries and continents. Regional headquarters (RHQs) and corporate headquarters (CHQs) are notoriously prone to non-value-added work, and they carry the most expensive jobs in the organization.

In short, organizing 'above the country' is a major challenge.

Strategic accountability

While there are many organizations that only operate in one country and have a number of strategic layers of managerial leadership, the focus of this chapter is on international strategic accountability. At the level of strategic work, the constraints and restraints on resource configurations are lifted. The international dimension adds an additional facet of complexity. But international accountability *per se* does not guarantee that the work is necessarily strategic. That is clarified by assessing the Seven Elements of a given role. The following is a definition in relation to Level 4.

1. Nature of work

Jobs at this level are accountable for work that is more strategic than operational. It is not just a matter of ensuring existing assets continue to perform better. That is the thrust of accountabilities up to and including Level 3. The job-holder must make authoritative recommendations for change to overall policy and direction based upon an analysis of gaps in the availability and performance of resources, product portfolio and systems.[1]

This is the key difference from Level 3, where an individual has accountability for a flow of activities whose overall performance needs to be optimized and continuously better levels of delivery attained. Now, at Level 4, the challenge is to identify resource gaps and constraints that adversely impact on performance and have them redressed. A gap in the market, for example, could be an opportunity leading to new products or services. These gaps could stem from lack of resource capacity or current scientific knowledge, or an unfilled need in the market-place. The authoritative recommendations for change might entail the addition or removal of existing assets, systems or services.

The person at Level 4 is accountable for the technical and professional input of the gap-assessment and suggested solution(s), and for their quality and accuracy. That person would not usually be accountable for the decision to close the identified resource gap or business opportunity.

2. Resource complexity

As indicated above, Level 4 managers are increasingly accountable for identifying new opportunities and resolving gaps in know-how, technology, the application of systems, the delivery of services and the meeting of untapped or new needs. They have to think beyond the product, system, unit or service being managed in Levels 1 to 3.

Level 3 managers ensure excellent performance from the unit and make sure that agreed objectives are met. The supply chain vice president at Level 4 decides what those objectives should be. The factory manager making cosmetics cannot decide to make chocolate, or to close the factory and move it to another location. Those are strategic decisions.

When I was working on an assignment at Amersham, an international bioscience company (taken over by GE in 2003), scientists there were striving to find treatments for Alzheimer's and Parkinson's diseases. The need was clear. The potential rewards were clear. But the means was not at all clear. In fact the knowledge to treat either disease did not exist – it had to be discovered, and at the time of writing has still to be discovered. This was the rationale for the company's extensive research programme. Finding these answers will require huge investment, wide-ranging research and dedication from top medical scientists.

3. Problem-solving

The strategic ability to truly think outside the box, beyond what is known or exists, is essential. (Unfortunately the word 'strategic' is now totally overworked and devalued. I would be a wealthy man if I had received a dollar every time some brand manager in Level 2 told me: 'I am accountable for the strategy of brand A or product B.') Strategic responsibilities represent a qualitative leap forward. This is why promotion on the basis of good performance at Level 3 is not a guarantee of success.

Abstract and conceptual analysis is required to identify problems and assess potential solutions involving new formulae, products, technology, systems or policies. This mental modelling process entails identifying the causes of patterns and linkages, perhaps first identified at Level 3, and devising the right solutions.

4. Change

The quality of change needed to align with this more extensive form of problem-solving moves beyond superficial trend analysis, fads and the changing of labels. The change now called for involves fundamental realignment of assets and resources. It is not just a modification of what exists, it is taking leadership in an industry, science or profession based on breakthrough, first in the industry, best in class, trend setting change.

The application of this sort of change is potentially unlimited, until factors such as money, politics and religion come into the mix. This kind of technical and scientific Level 5 change, based on blue sky research, is probably getting into the realm of Nobel Prize winners. The scientist who finds the cure for AIDS, Alzheimer's disease or Parkinson's disease will warrant that sort of recognition.

5. Internal collaboration

In an international company the network of peers is likely to span a number of different countries. In the 21st century this collaboration is facilitated by technologies such as the internet, video-conferencing and teleconferencing. Thus it is possible to set up a seamless innovation network of scientists or marketing executives across many countries.

The same is increasingly the case with buying networks and trading configurations in the retail industry, for example. This is a very cost-effective way of harnessing the strategic potential of these networks if their respective accountabilities are clear. My experience suggests that there is still a tendency for companies to add additional layers if they are working across national boundaries. When this is done in areas such as research, the debilitating effect on the creative process is far reaching.

Internal networks in large international companies can be fraught with internal politics such as the dominance of the home nationality of the CHQ, and lack of clear accountability for expenditure and allocation of additional resources. These shortcomings can disrupt international networks even within an organization.

Some years ago, Philips (the electrical products company) was admired for its technological innovation but not for its marketing innovation. Marketing was called the 'commercial function', which is an insight into the company's attitude to marketing at that time.

Collaboration is never easy. International, strategic collaboration is one of the most challenging types of collaboration of all.

6. External interaction

The nature of the interaction with the environment is the key difference between work at operational and strategic levels. In the first three levels of accountability the response is reactive. The manager is responding to an initiative coming from the external market, such as a negotiation with an international supplier.

At the strategic levels managers are expected to be proactive. Increasingly, they are expected to influence and shape the external environment to the advantage of the organization, or at least mitigate the damage that might otherwise be done.

Consider the example of an international CEO visiting the head of state of a country to discuss the implications of their company moving into or leaving that country. This would be a case where the CEO's agenda is to influence the head of state, who is judged to be a key potential enabler of the planned portfolio development.

Or a Level 4 HR vice president, representing the retail sector, might be co-opted onto a government committee drafting a green paper on overtime working practices. This individual would be expected to lobby other companies in the industry to arrive at a consensus view. This in turn might entail more work with other constituencies such as customers, civil servants, trade unions and politicians to ensure the retail industry's concerns are taken into account and legislated for appropriately.

The aim of strategic external interaction is to influence agencies outside the organization to change their behaviour, plans and actions. For example, there are many international bodies, such as the IMF, World Bank or Greenpeace, that require proactive relationship management by multinational corporations. The fact that most of these are unwieldy bureaucracies makes these interactions increasingly challenging and time-consuming for top international managerial leaders.

7. Task horizon

Generally, the time frame for operational work seems to be up to two years. For strategic levels of accountability, it seems to be up to about 15 years. It is important that longer time frames, beyond 15 years, include clear milestones as part of that journey.

I recall the head of an international research network describing the challenge of managing long research time frames – those demanded by the FDA, for example, often last about seven years. He said: 'If I asked someone to translate the Bible, I would not simply leave them to it. I would set targets for the completion of Genesis, then the Pentateuch and so on. So I could question whether a certain book had been completed, was running into problems, needed more resources, time and so on. In this way I would have no surprises and would be on top of the overall project, but not doing the work of my scientists. My job is to ensure the brief is clear, select the right scientist for the task in question and that they have the ongoing resources they need to complete the assignment.'

One of the challenges of designing RHQs and CHQs is factoring in jobs with a clear delineation of accountable time frames. Too often the RHQ overlaps a country or countries and the CHQ overlaps and duplicates the work of the RHQ. A rigorous review of the respective time frames can identify this problem. It can also help to identify situations when there is not enough total accountability across the organization to justify the existence of an RHQ.

When is a regional headquarters justified?

A key issue for large organizations when considering the optimal organizational structure is deciding when a regional headquarters is required.

In my experience there are four questions that need to be asked before setting up an RHQ:

1.   Why is an RHQ needed?
2.   How will the RHQ differ from the country operations?
3.   How will the RHQ differ from the CHQ?
4.   What will the RHQ do?

1. Why is an RHQ needed?

The guiding principle is to build up the structure from the front line, and in this case the key building block is the individual country. First decide what is best for the country, and then consider what support and parenting it needs.[2]

Designing what is appropriate for a country links back to the CHQ. The design of the country organization will be driven by a number of factors, including size, complexity, and the interplay of design variables such as market, product, technology, function and geography. These in turn will be influenced by the company's strategy, and whether or not the country is a lead country, eg in Europe or North America, with a geography that encourages cross-country structures. Consideration of these factors will help define the appropriate country business unit.

The country business unit can be anything from Level 3 to Level 6. Once the country structure is clear, then the country business unit should report to someone who is at least one level of accountability above. If not, there is no value added by the next layer.

Beware the cluster organization

One major trap that organizations can fall into here is called a 'cluster organization', where one country chaperones a number of others. Too often the cluster country manager is at the same level of accountability as the other countries. In effect it is a span breaker, one that US and European companies are apt to use in Asia, for example, where their logic is overly influenced by travel times and distances, rather than issues of accountability.

One of the worst situations I have seen occurred in Asia, where one country was moving into Level 6 while the so-called cluster manager for the region was at level 5. In this case the cluster manager was the manager of one country in the region. The other national managers were all Level 5. While the cluster manager was expected to lead all the other countries, he was no more than a 'first among equals'. The problem was that the cluster manager was not accountable for the other countries.

This is not a recipe for success. The region ran meaningless meetings. Nothing was done by the cluster manager that could not be decided by the respective country managers themselves. Anything above their level would have to be decided by the executive vice president in the CHQ, and not by the cluster manager.

In other words there was no accountability space for the cluster manager. He was operating at the same level (at best) as his colleagues. This resulted in great frustration, and a substantial waste of money, time and effort. Status was the only real difference between the country managers in this configuration. Overlay this situation with emotional factors, such as the cluster manager's nationality being the same as the home country CHQ, and you have a mess.

In very large multinationals, featuring decentralized, geographically based structures, most country organizations have historically been Level 5. This is because the CEO has been accountable for a single, cohesive, fully fledged, stand-alone organization. A fully fledged stand-alone company like this would usually possess the following features:

- a full range of functions or processes, with its own manufacturing, selling and development activities;
- complex (relative to the industry) technology warranting a Level 4 infrastructure;
- presence in key markets;
- the ability to have a material impact on the performance and reputation of the region.

Stand-alone features would include:

- a significant record of ongoing growth;
- self-sufficiency in key resources, such as sales and manufacturing, requiring an infrastructure of jobs up to Level 4.

There are situations where one country can meaningfully manage neighbours. In this context they might be seen as sub-regions within a potential RHQ. A financial services company in Kenya, for example, was responsible for activities in Tanzania and Uganda. At the time, the operations in the neighbouring countries were smaller and less complex. The country units in Uganda and Tanzania were one or two levels below that in Kenya. Thus the CEO in Kenya could add value to the units in the other two countries, which nevertheless kept discrete and separate organizations.

Other configurations might involve a more seamless organization. This is often true when countries have trade agreements, such as in Australia and New Zealand, where many companies operate across both countries with one structure. This is possible because both countries operate a Closer Economic Relations (CER) agreement – effectively a free trade policy.

Larger neighbouring countries operating a trade agreement, such as the NAFTA agreement, might warrant an infrastructure more akin to an RHQ. It would depend on the role and location of the CHQ.

Changing nature of the country manager role

The emerging challenge for anyone involved in designing international organizations today is the fact that the fully fledged, stand-alone country manager role is disappearing. That is, some country management roles are moving from Level 5 to Level 4. This move is being driven by economic-political changes such as those in the EEC and NAFTA, and those now mooted for MERCOSUL and SEATO nations. This makes the answer to our second question more difficult.

2. & 3. How will the RHQ differ from the country operations and the CHQ?

The two key questions to answer when designing the RHQ are:

- How does it add value to the subordinate business units?
- How does it differ from the CHQ?

In other words, the regional headquarters must add value to the country or business units under its hegemony and the corporate headquarters must in turn add value to the regional headquarters. If care is not taken then RHQs can easily end up duplicating the work of the business units, or the CHQ can end up duplicating the work of the RHQ. In the worst-case scenario, both shortcomings are evident.

This is because for most CEOs of global companies, the design of an RHQ is largely a matter of guesswork. They invariably do not have a set of tried and tested principles or a framework to guide their deliberations. The outcome is often an RHQ that is there for the comfort of the CHQ but that does not add value to the subordinate business units.

For example, there have been instances of RHQs that existed 'to support country operations'. This does not sound like sufficient rationale for the added cost of an RHQ. Does it pass the accountability test, or is it merely a beguiling way of describing 'control from above', rather than 'empowerment from below'? Empowerment will not exist if accountability is compromised.

Managing a large, complex business, operating on every continent,[3] is difficult. Top executives know that they need to spend time on the ground in order to assess the performance of the business. But while the internet may enable real-time connectivity with every part of the globe, keeping in touch with what is happening in individual countries cannot all be done via e-correspondence, teleconferencing and video contacts. For organizations that span at least 50 countries, however, the CEO cannot always be in the field. There has to be a middle way.

A number of factors can influence the choice and location of an RHQ. These include:[4]

- the evolving, at times contradictory, nature of global–local developments;
- increases in customer power;
- skill shortages;
- downsizing of national operations;
- the impact of technology, especially in communications and logistics.

Equally important are internal questions, such as:

- What is the corporate strategy?
- How does the RHQ support and help that strategy?
- Would the RHQ enhance or impede the pursuit of local and corporate goals?
- Are there sufficient skills and resources to ensure the RHQ can deliver?
- What are the pluses and minuses of the RHQ?
- Does industry practice provide any clues?
- Does it fit the company's life cycle, such as:
    - to help entry;
    - to help expand regional activity;
    - to exploit consolidation in the region?

It will now be shown that the principles set out in Chapters 1–3 help provide the answer to how this problem can be approached and solved.

The RHQ and Decision Making Accountability (DMA)

The essence of this approach is that the RHQ must make only those decisions that the business units cannot make, not because the business units are not allowed to, but because they are unable to as they don't have the necessary know-how, resources or experience. Similarly, the RHQ must make decisions that the CHQ need not and therefore should not take. This is because the RHQ knows better for the region under its control than either the individual business units or the CHQ. It works to achieve synergies and opportunities for the region as a whole, which individual units could not achieve on their own.

In the same way, the CHQ is accountable for the total international or global picture, and is expected to set regional priorities and objectives against that backdrop and allocate resources accordingly. The DMA approach defines the respective accountabilities to ensure there is no overlap, duplication or missed opportunities.

The DMA approach to identifying different levels of accountability complements the principle of subsidiarity: namely, that only those things should be decided at the RHQ that cannot be decided just as well in the business units. Furthermore, the CHQ should decide only that which cannot be better decided at the RHQ or in the country organizations.

The key ideas of the DMA Solution Set, therefore, drive organization design even at RHQ and CHQ level. They also tackle the issues of individual development, career planning and reward management.

The rationale for an RHQ must be strategic. This means that only the very largest, global companies can comfortably meet this requirement, and then only if they have a number of country business units that are at least at Level 4. This tends to suggest an organization with at least six levels of accountability, and probably seven or more. Otherwise, the RHQ is only a span breaker in the overall scheme of things – an unnecessary cost and a guaranteed source of frustration and stress, which slows down decision-making and potentially threatens the quality of decisions being taken.

Caught in the vacuum between an RHQ and the CHQ

George was the HR Director of a major regional strategic business unit operating outside the home country across a number of different countries. He reported into the managing director of the business unit, which covered a couple of continents, who in turn reported to a member of the group executive board, who reported to the group CEO. The regional HR role was clearly at a strategic level.

George's role was important, involving a transformational change agenda with a timescale focus looking forward up to three years, but with a considerable amount to be achieved within 18 to 24 months. As a member of the business unit executive, George had accountability for the direction and performance of the human resource function, with about 100 staff.

After a successful and satisfying four years in the role, during which time the performance of the business was turned around and it became a significant contributor to group profits, George accepted another senior executive role in the central Group HR function. The new role was to head a specialist area within an HR centre of excellence. This role reported to the head of the centre of excellence, who reported to the group HR director, who in turn reported to the chief administration officer, who reported to the group CEO. This meant that the accountability of George's new job had been diluted by an extra layer in a more complex reporting chain.

The role was perceived as a step up from the regional business unit role ('because it was at head office') and involved an increase in salary and grade. The reality, however, was that this was not matched in terms of the accountability. At best the new role was Level 3.

The impact from a motivation and personal development perspective was profound. In George's own assessment, it resulted in feelings of frustration, as his opportunity to lead the strategic agenda was restricted, stifled by the hierarchy above. As his frustration grew, from the organization's perspective it seemed that there was a belief that George was now a 'square peg in a round hole', as it was expected the job-holder would only input into strategy and be operationally focused.

The classic capability question now arose in the minds of the managers above him. George, who had not heard of accountability levels at this stage, nevertheless recognized that his career had taken a step backwards and decided to take his talent elsewhere.[5]

This is a classic example of a job that appeared to be a more senior job (by virtue of title and salary) turning out to be a less senior job after all. The reason that this type of situation occurs so frequently is that the true value of a job in terms of challenge, motivation and job satisfaction comes from its accountability, and its position in the work levels within the organization.

Often, promotion from an RHQ to the corporate centre is not quite what it seems to be. Like many other similar types of organization, the large, international company in this case was burdened with too many layers of hierarchy and confused lines of accountability, most notably at senior management and executive levels.

The lesson to be learnt is clear. It is important to understand the accountability that a role offers and not to be seduced by an apparent move up the hierarchy, expressed in external trappings such as a new grade and salary, when the job actually amounts only to an administrative promotion. (An administrative promotion is an upward change in grade, but without a concomitant change in accountability. It can even involve a drop in accountability, as in George's case.)

In real terms George had actually been demoted in his 'promotion' to the corporate centre. And although he could not explain this clearly, he felt it, which is why he left his former employer. So it is critically important to ensure that the corporate centre really does add value to the decisions of the various countries' operations and to the regional business units. That was not the case in this instance.

4. What should the RHQs do?

In explaining what RHQs should do in a particular organization, the following assumptions will be made about that organization.

That it has:

- implemented levels of accountability;
- a number of national business units at Levels 4 and 5;
- operations in every continent around the world;
- RHQs at Level 6 in more than one business line or continent;
- the top executive role at Level 8.

It is likely that such a company will have in excess of US$50 billion in sales or assets, and will operate in at least 50 countries.

Organization of RHQs

Based on the five assumptions above, I have found that most fully fledged, stand-alone national business units tend to be headed at Level 5. This in turn calls for an RHQ with a top job at Level 6.

The RHQs tend to have regional roles covering finance, HR, marketing, supply chain, innovation and customer service or sales. These positions are invariably at Level 5 and have a dual role. First, they help to ensure that the job objectives of the Level 6 regional president are met. This also entails the regional managers delivering the group strategy and policy in their functional areas and proactively feeding back into global policy development. Secondly, these regional managers are expected to lead the relevant regional network in finance, HR and so on. Their colleagues in different countries tend to be at

Levels 3 and 4, depending on the size and complexity of the national business unit. These RHQ roles were responsible for regional excellence and best practice.

Sometimes, depending on the type of business, there are subsidiary regional roles at Level 4 in areas such as IT, property, market research and operations support. Given the geographical spread of global companies, audit roles are also carried out at regional levels. These jobs may also link back into corresponding corporate roles at Level 5, which are the group custodians of best practice in their specific areas.

Understand your environment

Once global strategy has been finalized, one of the main determinants driving the design of RHQs is the local environment. Dividing the world into its six continents (ignoring Antarctica), the local business conditions are very different.

Integrated RHQ

Europe and North America (Canada, Mexico and the United States) favour seamless regional organizations. This is because the geography is increasingly being run as one cohesive economic, political and legal entity. Goods, services and to a certain extent labour can be moved freely across national boundaries. There are pressures to harmonize currencies, tax regimes and legal approaches to business.

India and China are interesting variations. They have the size, plus the cultural and language complexities of Europe or North America, but as single countries are viewed as national organizations.

In these regions it is possible to build an integrated RHQ.

Aggregated RHQ

Most other regions in the world do not have these external factors helping to drive lean, efficient RHQs. Latin America and South East Asia are heading in that direction but are not there yet. They have pockets of sub-regionalization that can be taken advantage of. But in general the potential regional synergies are limited.

The Middle East, Central Asia and Africa are all a long way from this ideal. It would seem that political and religious considerations will constrain their regional cooperation for some time yet.

In these regions it is possible to build only an aggregated RHQ. The organization synergies feasible are limited by the regional environment.

A European RHQ:
an integrated model

Within the European Union it is increasingly possible to organize as one seamless organization, with the bottom line being managed on a regional basis and not on a national basis as had previously been the case. It is no longer necessary to have fully fledged subsidiaries all producing, marketing, innovating and selling products in each European nation.

Thus European operations can be set up as an RHQ. The advent of a single currency, the Euro, used by about a dozen countries, means that it is easier to run finance, treasury and tax on a pan-European basis. In theory this should lead to lower administration and overhead costs.

A European RHQ can be organized to manage a single supply chain and orchestrate the most effective production and distribution across the continent. The legacy of factories in every country can be abolished. Many existing factories are no longer needed. Supply can be similarly centralized. Buying can be done on an international basis from a handful of mostly international suppliers. Commercials for TV can now be made once, not 15 or more times in different formats and languages.

Innovation can be more concentrated. One consumer goods company, for example, concentrated innovation in four countries only, each of which focused on a specific category of products.

IT can be more centralized. By 1999, Unilever had already organized its IT infrastructure on a global basis with four regional centres, one of which was in Europe.

For the first time, some elements of the same organization could be centralized, while others were decentralized. This was a new challenge though, and one that was not always dealt with very effectively. Previously, organization design choice had been bipolar: centralization or decentralization. Many companies continued to limit themselves to this design choice, even though it was superseded by the opportunities of the new environment. This led to confusion and extra cost.

The sales function, for example, was initially organized on a decentralized basis retaining a national focus, because at the time the trade was still national. Grocery chains, for example, tended to be limited to one country. HR was also organized on a strong national basis, as unions and collective agreements were national and even management pay was linked to national, not regional, markets.

But by the beginning of the 21st century, the process of regional centralization was accelerating. The European Union was expanding. The retail trade continued to expand internationally. About seven of Nestlé's major grocery customers now operate across a variety of countries, although none are yet truly global. The Wal-Marts of this world do not want to deal with a myriad of national sales forces. They seek regional and international interfaces with their suppliers.

Similarly, HR in Europe is moving towards a more regional centre of gravity. Large organizations require a European works council. There is a constant stream of common employment legislation flowing out of Brussels. Some companies, such as IBM, have or are setting up pan-European HR call centres or service centres, to better cope with the creeping regionalization.

The European RHQ model is integrated because the region has political, legal and economic structures (the EEC) driving it in that direction. European companies are being encouraged by these developments to organize across many countries to become more cost-effective and competitive. Initiatives in the areas of taxation, sales levies and social security are all moving in the same direction, albeit at a different pace.

But not all continents have those enabling environmental structures in place, and therefore a different model is appropriate for their RHQs.

An East Asia Pacific RHQ: an aggregated model

At present it is not possible to organize a pan-Asian company along the same lines as pan-European companies. The economic conditions in Asia mean that it is not a serious competitive option at present. Most international companies organize in East Asia with a profit-accountable general manager leading each business unit or country operation.

An East Asian RHQ is an aggregate of these national organizations, which are not fused into one overall seamless organization. Instead their individual results are aggregated to become the regional result.

The objectives of the RHQ are optimizing regional synergies, sharing innovation effort while minimizing cost, driving technological and supply chain efficiencies, and establishing regional priorities and best practice, which may differ from those in other parts of the world. While contributing to global strategy, the RHQ must also determine the feasibility and pace of that strategy's implementation in the region. The national operations are accountable to the head of the RHQ, who is supported by direct reports in accomplishing the regional plans and objectives.

Although the region has various sub-regional agreements, eg CER in Australia and New Zealand or SEATO, these do not have the tight overall regional economic and political bonds of NAFTA or the EEC. Thus for an RHQ in, say, Singapore, covering countries as diverse as China, Japan, Indonesia, Thailand, maybe the Indian subcontinent, Vietnam, Australia and New Zealand, the possible regional synergies are much more limited.

In these countries the profit-accountable national managers tend to be at Level 5. Some movement towards integration has started, eg in Australasia, where one organization would cover both countries. But the region is a long way from the integrated model of Western Europe, where the country organizations have been seamlessly absorbed into the regional organization. In the European integrated model there are no longer profit-accountable national managers in Germany, France, etc controlling all aspects of their P&L.

The East Asia Pacific RHQ is still briefed to maximize common systems to best exploit the region's resources. It drives regional initiatives where feasible, which lead to improved performance. Thus much of the innovation is now shared. Unilever, for example, set up an innovation centre in Thailand to lead key product development across the region. This is important, as some aspects of its product range, eg hair products, need different features, as Asian hair is not the same as Caucasian or African hair.

IT infrastructure can also be centralized in a regional IT office, such as Singapore, as can purchasing, financial systems and reporting. There can be many regional initiatives in the supply chain to provide more cost effective products, but the continuing existence of national tariff and duty boundaries remains a major regional constraint.

Some regional sharing is feasible in HR, such as in training and management development. However, this presupposes that the management speaks English, which is not always the case in China, Indonesia and Japan, for example.

The drive is towards regionalization, but at the pace that is relevant and advantageous for the businesses in the region. Informal groupings and virtual team networks can cooperate across the region. The RHQ president would be at Level 6, as in Western Europe, but for different reasons. The infrastructural configuration and cost base of the business is very different.

The total number of Level 5 and Level 4 jobs will be much greater in the aggregated model than in the integrated model, all other things being equal. Country managers in East Asia will continue to be at Level 5, whereas in the integrated model most were Level 4. The consequence is that there are very many more Level 4 jobs in East Asia than in Europe, where most infrastructures go up to only Level 3, under the country manager. This is one reason why a comparison between Europe and the United States in terms of efficiency currently favours the United States. Europe's history in terms of political and economic integration is very recent. The United States has treated its similarly sized geography as one country for a couple of hundred years. It has a head start in that regard. Europe is playing catch-up, and Asia is further behind.

What does the CHQ do?

Once the various country and RHQ accountabilities are clear, then the CHQ must be designed to take decisions that cannot be taken at national or regional level.

What the CHQ is not

The corporate office must meet two pressures. One, we have established, is from below. The other is from above. The CHQ must support and ensure delivery of the corporate strategy. It must also meet regulatory and governance requirements. Depending on the nature of the business, these pressures will impact on the design of the corporate centre in a number of ways.

There are three business models that call for very different corporate office configurations. The three types are:

- The holding company.
  In this case the CHQ is very limited, interested only in portfolio management and the management of their value. Hanson Trust would be an example.
- The aggregated global conglomerate.
  In this case the centre ensures the portfolio is balanced and broadly manages for value and growth. Its key concerns are strategy, capital allocation and leadership across the business. GE would be an example.
- The integrated global company.
  In this case the centre also manages for value and growth, but with a more interventionist drive for synergies across the company. There will be a conscious effort to leverage operational costs, marketing, brands, finance and people. A major difference from the first two models is the central focus on research and development across the business. Resource allocation such as capital and people will be a critical role. General Motors, Procter & Gamble and Nestlé are examples.

The first two of these three business models do not concern us. The following comments relate to the integrated global business model only. The two former models are less likely to warrant RHQs, as they are not about driving and maximizing synergies across the global organization.

The integrated global model

In this case the CHQ will typically need to meet demands in the following areas:

- governance;
- compliance;
- strategy and business performance;
- merger and acquisitions;
- functional excellence;
- research-led innovation;
- shared services – although this has been heavily impacted by outsourcing and now offshoring.

The obvious demarcation is that the CHQ should focus only on global or group issues, and those stemming from the statutory requirements of doing business on an international scale.

This is very important in areas such as innovation. If there is a central approach to research, then the establishment of regional innovation centres can be a source of duplication, excessive cost, confusion and inefficiency, if the respective contributions are not thought through. Technology can aid the effectiveness of virtual teams, but if accountabilities are not well defined, it can be a major cause of rampant time-wasting and inefficiency. People can 'meet' anywhere in the world, at all times of the day and night and decide nothing.

We have established that tasks break down into those that are operational and those that are strategic. But generally, the top two layers of accountability in an organization relate to governance. Governance decisions cover the following questions:

- What business are we in and why?
- What is the appropriate strategy for the group?
- What are the appropriate values for the group?
- What markets, businesses and countries should we be in?
- How should the business portfolio be managed?
- Do we need RHQs?
- How should RHQs be organized?
- How should the group be organized?
- What are our people policies on succession, career planning and reward across the group?
- How do we ensure that the group meets its corporate, environmental, legal and social responsibilities?
- What is our business approach to research and development?
- What are our policies and approaches to stakeholder constituencies such as consumers, customers, suppliers, shareholders, trade unions and international pressure groups?

These all relate to the corporate office accountability, when country and regional structures are in play. The CHQ is then held to account for policy guidance and leadership in these 12 key areas of governance.

So, the basic rationale for the CHQ is accountability for governance. Otherwise it will be encroaching upon the accountabilities of either the RHQ or the country or even both.

What is the value added by the corporate head office?

A fifth question not posed at the outset of the chapter is now relevant. Namely, what is the value of the CHQ (in an integrated global company)? What should it do?

The DMA logic helps clarify the accountabilities of the corporate office. Two key questions need to be asked constantly:

- Why should a national issue be decided in the RHQ?
- Why should a regional issue be decided in the CHQ?

The CHQ should drive the strategy, values, synergies and performance of the total organization. It should be the only part of the group that has a global remit, not merely a regional or local focus. It has a longer task horizon to consider, more fundamental research and investment concerns, and a wider range of stakeholders to satisfy. It defines the regions.

In global consumer goods companies, such as Coca Cola and Procter & Gamble, the global brand equities are devised and established in the corporate centre. Guidelines are agreed and set for regional and national application. In the area of innovation, the regions may drive development, as in Unilever, but research is a corporate accountability.

In companies with a global reach, treasury and taxation can be more effectively managed with a global remit. Other key financial functions in the CHQ would include statutory reporting, internal group audit, mergers and acquisitions activity and sometimes strategy, although less so these days.

Recent technological developments favour a more centralized approach to IT, including both hardware and software. There is a swing away from the shared IT services models that were a feature of some CHQs not so long ago. The centralization process tends to incorporate the more strategic work, with great swathes of transactional work now outsourced and offshored. This trend is also affecting some of the transactional work in other functions, such as HR and finance.

HR and pension policy and priority setting for people across the whole organization can be appropriately run from the corporate head office. The legal function is also likely to be required in the CHQ, but the size of the legal department can vary enormously depending on the home country, from a large department in litigious countries such as India and the United States, to a much smaller department in Japan. The range of brand names and patents owned by a company could also impact on the size of the legal resource needed to guard and defend intellectual property and trademarks.

The management of shareholder issues and the stock market is an increasingly high profile corporate accountability. The interface with the stock market is typically managed by the CEO and the CFO.

The corporate office will probably be called upon to proactively manage the group's image, reputation and corporate brand. This can be quite different for a company like BP, Ford or Nokia, where the company is the brand, than for ones like Colgate Palmolive or Diageo, which have many different brands. For the former, PR would be more critical and hence the corporate resources in that area might be greater. The latter would have larger marketing networks, driven but not staffed by the CHQ. To help ensure that these networks run smoothly, with local and regional input, a number of forums should be arranged to orchestrate this.

At the top of the business there should be a working group that pulls together the top CHQ executives and those in the RHQs. This helps lock together those responsible for the strategy and governance of the business. It is the ultimate dovetailing of the value added roles of the regional headquarters and the corporate office.

Impact of governance and compliance initiatives

The favoured organization design for corporate head office seems to ebb and flow. Ten to fifteen years ago the centreless centre was in vogue. Corporate headquarters favoured a federated option with a small centre. ABB was often cited in this context. But the pendulum is swinging back.

Some of the less savoury events of recent times, such as the tangled compensation excesses of Home Depot, plus the scandals of Enron, WorldCom, Merrill Lynch, Ahold and the like, have led to strident calls for transparency, compliance and control by shareholders. But they do not guarantee accountability.

More recent governance initiatives, mostly in Europe, have led to the establishment of a new raft of committees, which tend to generate pressure to create more roles in the corporate centre. These developments have helped spawn a burgeoning compliance bureaucracy that is adding pressure to the size and cost of corporate head offices. This has been fuelled by well-intentioned legislation, such as the Sarbanes–Oxley Act in the United States. The essence of this legislation is aimed at ensuring the accuracy of reported financial data.

The additional work involved is largely about efficiency. Efficiency means extra cost, not greater effectiveness.[6] This new work increasingly tends to be locked into Level 1. It is very debatable whether this bulging administrative workload is, on balance, improving organizational performance.

Sarbanes–Oxley is based on a false premise. Law and organizational design cannot offset collusion. Many audits have failed to discover a fraud because of criminal collusion between a treasurer and a cashier, for example.

Minimalist v activist corporate centre

So, in recent times we have moved from the ideal of a minimalist corporate office to the current fashion of an activist CHQ. Generally, the minimalist model would be most appropriate for the holding company, and to a lesser extent the aggregated global company. The activist CHQ would be more appropriate for the integrated global company. Both types of CHQ are prone to extremes that contribute to failure.

Take the increases in the auditing function evident at the majority of large companies. It is important to recall the key question of the DMA Solution Set: 'Are the new audit roles taking decisions that cannot be taken elsewhere in the checking and verification process?' Audit teams are project teams and therefore should be organized according to the same principles of accountability.[7]

Multiple layers of auditors in one level of accountability do not improve the quality and reliability of an audit. One company in Nigeria that I worked with was aiming to tighten its purchasing process following a serious fraud that cost the company millions. The new improved process had some 70 check points built into it by the auditors. In fact, it was so complicated that the potential for fraud was made easier; the exact opposite of the outcome intended.

The current increase in compliance measures is in danger of achieving a similar outcome. It is certainly affecting the design of CHQs.

Reporting links

One question that needs some consideration is: 'To whom should the enabling functions, such as finance, HR and IT, report?' Some favour the reporting line through the national and regional organizations, while others prefer reporting directly to the corporate office, often through a span breaking COO.

While most companies would favour the former approach, it does depend on the group's strategy and priorities. And if these change over time, then these reporting lines could also change. Unilever is a case in point. In 2006 it centralized its finance and HR functions through to the corporate centre. This was partly to increase control at a time when the business performance was below target, and partly to emphasize the thrust of innovation and marketing, which were also centralized at the same time.

In a more decentralized structure these functions would variously report to the national and regional offices, bearing in mind the logic of the integrated and aggregated regional options discussed earlier in the chapter. Lightly staffed relevant functions in the corporate office would then exercise thought leadership of the appropriate networks. Work levels can greatly facilitate this process by identifying the relevant accountabilities.

A tale of two HR networks

Consider the HR networks of two global companies.

In the first company, which implemented work levels, the HR function was accountable for the people function in each country. In a Level 5 country, prime accountability for people in Levels 1 to 3 was decided in-country. In those situations the top HR role in the country was Level 4. Recommendations affecting Level 4 issues were forwarded to the RHQs, which then took a decision. Issues for Levels 5+ went to the CHQ.

This worked most effectively across the main areas of HR. The accountability lines were clear. HR managers at the different levels in the network were accountable for the assessment of those in the levels below them, jointly with the respective line managers. Thus a regional HR manager would assess national HR managers, who in turn assessed and developed those managers in the country organization. People within the HR network across the world knew who was responsible for their development and rewards. Career paths were clear. Line management understood the process.

By way of contrast, in the other company (of almost identical size and complexity), the HR network was not organized according to levels of accountability. A major external review of the function in 2005 revealed a number of issues. Accountabilities were not clear. Decisions were slow and based on a 'consensus of least offence'. Top management had major concerns about capability and the network was far more extensive in numbers than it needed to be.

There was widespread overlap of activities, duplication of work via many meetings and an undue focus on process. Many individuals described their role as 'contributing to this or that process'. There was little or no customer or business focus. The path to the better HR roles was not straightforward or easily understood. Given the blurred accountability and overlap of jobs, individuals' appraisals tended to cluster around the mean. The function was not held in high esteem by line management.

It is hard to make an impact in an accountability blancmange.

What about large national organizations?

The assumptions outlined so far applied to large international companies. But some international companies might be as small as Level 5, and some national (probably governmental) organizations can be very large. Does the approach still apply to regional offices within a country?

The answer is: yes. Some national organizations employ millions of people – for example, the British National Health Service employs 1.09 million people and China National Petroleum employs 1.34 million. This begs an intriguing design question about whether they are too large to be effective, but given that they exist, it is likely that they will require some regional infrastructure.[8] Provided the principles of value-added accountability are followed rigorously, RHQs might be appropriate in a large, complex national organization.

However, as can be deduced from the material outlined so far, if the RHQ is at Level 5 or even less, then the front-line units would be small (Level 4 or 3). But if, as outlined in this book, the intention should be to empower roles from the front line, then this works against the idea of having many RHQs. It is therefore apparent that not many organizations can justify value-adding regional headquarters between their front-line units and the corporate headquarters. Thus the number of managerial leaders who can be held to account for many countries is not great.

> Not many organizations can justify value-adding regional headquarters between their front-line units and the corporate headquarters.

The Accountable Leader Chapter 8: Key points

This chapter shows how leaders can be held to account for more than one country. It also illustrates the differences in accountabilities needed within a country, compared to a regional headquarters, compared in turn to the corporate head office. Applying DMA concepts ensures that both RHQs and CHQs really do add value to front-line business units.

The following key points are important:

1. Organizing 'above the country' is a major challenge. Many international companies get confused when aligning accountabilities across regions of countries and continents. Regional headquarters (RHQs) and corporate

headquarters (CHQs) are notoriously prone to non-value-added work, and they carry the most expensive jobs in the organization.

2. There are four questions that need to be asked before setting up an RHQ: Why is an RHQ needed? How will the RHQ differ from the country operations? How will the RHQ differ from the corporate headquarters (CHQ)? What will the RHQ do?

3. A major trap that organizations fall into is creating a 'cluster organization', where one country chaperones a number of others.

4. The RHQ must make only those decisions that the business units cannot make, not because the business units are not allowed to, but because they are unable to as they don't have the necessary know-how, resources or experience.

5. The RHQ must make decisions that the CHQ need not and therefore should not make.

6. The most fully fledged, stand-alone national business units tend to be headed at Level 5. This in turn calls for an RHQ with a top job at Level 6.

7. The CHQ should drive the strategy, values, synergies and performance of the total organization. It should be the only part of the group that has a global remit, not merely a regional or local focus. It has a longer task horizon to consider, more fundamental research and investment concerns, and a wider range of stakeholders to satisfy. It defines the regions.

8. Not many organizations can justify value-adding regional headquarters between their front-line units and the corporate headquarters.

Notes

1. Authoritative recommendations are based on specific experience and/or specialist expertise. For example, a Level 5 CEO might call for specific input to a long-term plan from an HR vice president at Level 4. The recommendations would be assessed, prioritized and accepted or rejected by the CEO, but the CEO would not expect to have to second guess or correct the professional content of the HR plan. It should be robust, based upon the authoritative expertise and experience of the HR vice president. Otherwise that vice president is in the wrong job, which then might become a resource decision for the Level 5 executive.

2. Campbell, A, Goold, M and Alexander, M (1995) The Value of the Parent Company, *California Management Review*, **38** (1), Fall

3. Antarctica can be ignored for the purposes of this book.

4. Kramer, R J (2003) *Regional Headquarters Roles and Organization*, The Conference Board, New York
5. Time and time again it is the most talented who are first to be frustrated in a poorly designed organization. As they are very marketable they leave and the mediocre remain, comfortable in their non-jobs.
6. According to Peter Drucker (1967), efficient is doing things right, and effective is doing right things. Thus efficiency adds to cost but not to value-added activities.
7. See chapter 10 of *The Healthy Organization*.
8. It is not clear what organization design principles govern the structures of the United Kingdom's public sector organizations. For example, why should the NHS be centralized, while the police are decentralized into 52 independent forces, when the total number of police is about 10 per cent of the number of NHS employees?

Part 3

9 Organizational design accountability and leadership in practice

'For men improve with the years,
And yet, and yet,
Is this my dream, or the truth?'

W B Yeats, Men Improve With The Years

Leadership development schemes and why they fail

In the global knowledge economy, talented people are a key competitive differentiator. Talented individuals are also necessary in public life, leading public institutions and inter-governmental bodies to meet the challenges of 21st-century society.

But the evidence suggests that talent is in short supply. It is a situation unlikely to improve in the near future. The US Bureau of Labor Statistics, for example, forecasts a labour shortfall in the United States of 10 million workers by 2010, with the 500 largest US companies losing 50 per cent of senior management in the next five years.

Global demographic trends are not encouraging. By 2025, the number of people aged 15–64 is projected to fall by 7 per cent in Germany, 9 per cent in

Italy and 14 per cent in Japan. Over the next 25 years there will be 75 million fewer Europeans and 65 million fewer Japanese.

If talented individuals prove to be in short supply in the employment market, they will cost increasingly more to acquire. It makes good sense therefore to ensure that besides diverse and innovative recruitment strategies, organizations operate effective leadership development programmes, growing their own talent whenever possible rather than purchasing it externally.

Sadly, many leadership development schemes are no more successful than a random process of chance. There are a number of reasons for this, and they will be outlined in this chapter.

Inordinate amounts of money are wasted in the name of leadership development. The cause is noble, but the campaigns are notoriously profligate. This is because there can be no effective leadership development without an effectively designed organization.

Three variables are critical for the successful development of leaders throughout an organization:

- a role with clear accountabilities;
- an organization structure with the right number of layers;
- an individual with the right degree of competence for the job.

Unfortunately, the first two factors are invariably ignored.

Organization design is critical to leadership development

Talented individuals cannot contribute to their full capacity and potential in a cluttered, top-heavy organization that blurs accountability and stifles initiative. Yet, for some reason, the critical link between effective organization design and successful leadership development is often ignored. Leaders cannot be held to account in a vacuum.

The contribution of organization design is ignored

It is still widely accepted that organization design and strategy are very closely linked. Yet the critical link between effective organization design and successful leadership development is less well appreciated. Organization design is typically seen as a means of improving strategic performance, with cutting costs as a by-product. It is not really seen as a way of creating a leadership development platform.

Many organizations totally neglect the role of structure in leadership development. They fall prey to what I like to call the 'Salmon Fallacy'. If 100 salmon are swimming upstream and you cull the slowest 10, then the other 90 will swim faster. The trouble is that the Salmon Fallacy ignores the environment or setting in which work or activity takes place. The problem of the prevailing current is ignored. The focus is only on the abilities of the salmon. The context is neglected.

Forced ranking, or 'yank and rank', was popularized by Jack Welch at General Electric. But, as Art Kleiner, author and editor of *Strategy+Business* magazine once noted: 'All too many Welchist efforts threw the human creativity out with the bureaucracy-water.'

Companies will admit to spending enormous amounts of effort, money and time aiming to recruit the very best people. And yet, apparently their recruitment efforts are so bad that they have to spend the next few years getting rid of the worst people. Taking into account conservative 'normal annual wastage' or staff turnover suggests the organization will have jettisoned the 'class of 2000' by 2007.

Although people are more important than jobs, processes or structures, the logic that works best when developing talent is: define the work and its accountabilities first, and only then assess who has the appropriate talent to meet the job requirements. Most organizations invest heavily in the latter but neglect the former.

The aim is not to create an unnecessarily flat organization though, because an organization where the structure is too flat is equally damaging to good leadership development. The managerial leader who is overloaded owing to a missing layer of management is as ineffective as the micro-managed or compressed manager in a cluttered hierarchy of diffuse accountability. No amount of training to improve performance and enhance potential will overcome these structural shortcomings.

If a role does not add value to the work of others, it is unlikely to enable an individual to grow and learn. A surplus job in the organizational structure does not add value and challenge. It cannot be the basis for the development of high-flying individuals.

Hollow jobs lead to hollow development

This tendency to neglect structure is not helped by the fact that writers on organization design have not explored the link to leadership development to any great extent. This was one reason I created the Seven DMA Elements.

At the outset of this book I highlighted the plight of a financial services company. The company was keen to improve its leadership development scheme, but did not realize that the shortage of talent it assumed was contributing to its problems was exacerbated by organizational design structure defects that both blocked the development of talent and made it very difficult to identify talent. So when vacancies occurred, the company tended to recruit externally.

Following a series of Accountability Probes, the real levels of accountability were revealed, identifying both where the problems resided in the structure and what could be done about it. There were two unnecessary tiers of supervision in Level 1, and three unnecessary layers of management, two in Level 3 and one in Level 4. In summary, the company could move from 12 hierarchical layers to 7. This is set out in Figure 9.1.

Figure 9.1 illustrates how this organization had nine layers of management but only needed six, and it also had three tiers of supervision but only needed one. The company was spending a lot of money and effort on leadership development but with disappointing results, so it was felt that a transfusion of new talent was required. The company was guilty of flawed thinking. It was focusing on the 'salmon' but ignoring the 'prevailing current'.

The company's development programme and career planning process would never be successful as long as it tolerated such a totally ineffective organizational structure. It was impossible to reliably assess the talent in terms of performance and potential across the severely compressed Levels 1, 3 and 4.

The multiple tiers of supervisors in Level 1 were essentially all doing the same work. Budget accountability was missing from Level 2 (where it should have cut in) and from the first two layers in Level 3. It eventually emerged in the job stacked on top of two others in Level 3 – the fourth layer of management, although only two layers were necessary. This job had taken over the role of cost centre from the more junior managers, 'Otherwise', as the person doing the job said, 'I would not have enough to do!'

Reliance on administrative promotions

As we have already shown in Chapter 3, most large organizations have a grading or rank system based on some form of job evaluation. These systems tend to be quantitatively based and do not assess the quality of decisions taken and whether they add value to the mission of the organization and the work of others. Job evaluation schemes take the job that exists and 'measure' it. They are typically based on budgets and numbers of people managed, and the route to another grade is merely the acquisition of more resources. They do not ask, as the DMA approach does, 'Should the job exist? What is its added value?'

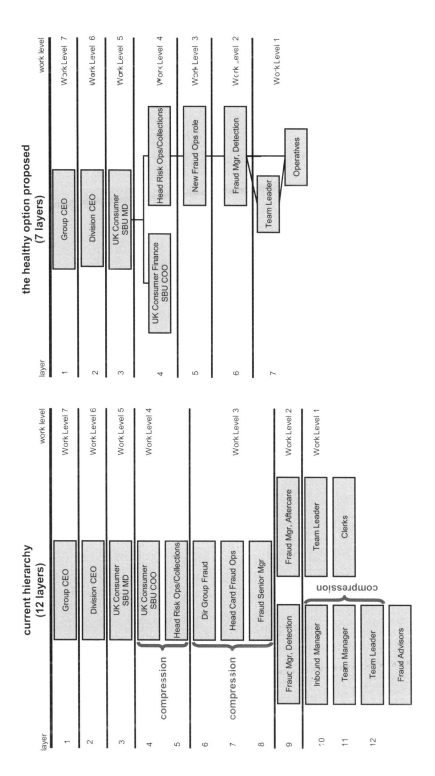

Figure 9.1 Financial services company Accountability Probe findings

The new resources are invariably obtained by inserting another layer in the management structure. Thus job evaluation ends up driving organization design, when organization design should drive job evaluation.

We have seen that the ensuing promotion is often a move to a higher grade, but not necessarily to another level of accountability that calls for a different quality of decisions. The promoted individual is invariably given a new grade, a salary increase and perhaps a significant change in the fringe benefits and perquisites attached to the role. This is of course why so-called administrative promotions are very popular and strongly entrenched in many large organizations. Furthermore, we have seen that even the same grade might be spread across different levels of accountability.

This means that moves to new grades or job classes are often not true promotions. They are administrative promotions. The move is dressed up in new trappings, but the substance of what needs to be decided and done in the role has not fundamentally changed. The person promoted does not move into an area or zone where they are called upon to make different types of decisions. The move is upwards in the administrative system, which then masquerades as leadership development.

Many global companies have correlated their administrative grades for remuneration purposes, thereby sharing and spreading the disease of over-layered structures and administrative promotions. It is little wonder they find it difficult to challenge and develop their managers.

Administrative promotions are hollow promotions leading to hollow personal development.

Returning to the company in Figure 9.1, it is clear from the figure that the company is suffering from more hierarchy than is needed. It is also clear where the damaging blockages occur. These are decision-making and leadership development blockages.

The company had a promotion and reward system based on grades. Assuming that the grading system starts at A, it ranges potentially from grade A up to grade M. So someone in grade A would be keen to be promoted to grade B, and so on up the tree. The existing system in the company assumed that the progression of responsibilities was linear. Thus a promotion from grade A to B was considered similar in type and nature to that of a move from B to C, and so on.

The analysis revealed, however, that a move from one grade to another was not always a real promotion. Often the two roles in question were in the same level. A move from grade B to C, both stacked supervisory jobs, meant that the person being promoted had no enhancement in accountability.

Grades B and C were compressed roles in Level 1. The key development steps would have been from grade A to grade B and then to grade E, but nothing in the administrative grading logic made that clear.

The situation, as Figure 9.1 illustrates, became even more tortuous. The equivalent of grades F, G and H were all in the third level of accountability. And yet, according to the grading system, moving through them would entail a further three promotions.

Not surprisingly, the interviews with individuals at these grades revealed a high degree of frustration. They could not really decide anything. Some were remarkably clear in diagnosing the cause of their hollow jobs though, and even accurately identified which jobs did not add any value on the spine of accountability: 'They do not make any decisions. They can't move anything forward. The wheels spin, while they have to wait to see their boss and maybe the boss's boss before anything can be decided.' This inevitably adds to decision gridlock and frustration for those concerned.

This company felt it had a system of identifying people for promotion combined with careful career development that compared with the best. It invested heavily in its appraisal system. A lot of time was spent by senior managers on people matters. It was puzzled by the evident poor quality of its managers, who seemed unable to lead effectively.

But the managers in this company were unable to lead because they were not truly held to account. The organizational structure was working against them. They did not have true leadership roles.

Operational and strategic work: identifying the dividing line

The difference between operational work and strategic work and the implications for leadership development is critical. Identifying where this difference occurs in an organization is even more critical. But most leadership approaches do not focus on this vital division, largely because the clarity of the demarcating line is blurred by administrative grading systems.

Kenneth Brousseau, an expert on organizational behaviour, studied the decision-making style of 180,000 managers from around the world.[1]

He concluded: 'Somewhere between the manager and the director levels, executives hit a point where approaches [in decision-making style] that used to work are no longer so effective.'[2]

The keyword in that statement is 'somewhere'. The research shows that the type of decisions taken in management change, but not how they change or why. Culture and use of status titles further muddy the water. In the United States, for example, it is not unusual to have managers reporting to directors, to vice presidents, to senior vice presidents, to executive vice presidents, to a COO and finally perhaps the CEO. It is rare for all these roles to align with separate levels of accountability.

This title inflation also makes it difficult to recognize where operational work ends and genuine strategic accountabilities begin. This is one of the reasons why the role of COO is so controversial. All too often it is merely at the same level as either the CEO or the layers of management below, as was the case in Figure 9.1.[3]

The use of identical titles around the world can complicate matters further in international organizations. For example, in one global company, jobs with the label 'director' in the United States are assessed at Level 3, while 'director' roles in Europe are at Level 4. This is because in Europe the directors report to a general manager, such as a managing director, not a vice president, as in the United States. But most companies use the same grade for the same title, even though accountabilities might not be the same.

Fortunately, leadership levels allow us to precisely identify the location of this vital area where the decision-making requirements change fundamentally.

It is the change in the substance of the accountability that drives the subsequent need for a change in 'decision-making style'. Knowing this and where it occurs is vital for the assessment and development of potential leaders.

So what are the major differences between the operational and the strategic?

Operational accountability is ensuring that existing assets or resources continue to perform better. The resources are given. Problem-solving remains related to actual events, rather than in the abstract. The essence of Level 3 accountability is the delivering of continuous improvement in performance and productivity. The response to the external environment is essentially reactive, principally responding to initiatives by others. Progress of an individual through the operational levels is linear, even when accurately aligned to levels of accountability. The quality of decision-making is, in essence, more of the same.

The move up to strategic accountability is a qualitative step change. Resource gaps and constraints have to be identified and solutions provided. A gap in the market, for example, is an opportunity to be exploited. This may call for the cutting or addition of resources, products or services. Problem-solving moves into the abstract domain. The type of thinking called for is fundamentally different. Solutions have to be found that require mental modelling, as they do not yet physically exist. The governance echelons have to be convinced to allocate resources to a new project at the idea stage, before it can be seen, touched and tested. Changes have to move beyond merely improvement to include breakthroughs, discovery and invention. The environment has to be managed in a proactive manner.

Grading systems and job evaluation models are unable to highlight this critical difference in accountability.[4] This is because their focus is on quantitative measures, but the jump from operational to strategic accountability is a qualitative change in the decision-making required, not simply a quantitative change.

Consider Figure 9.1 again. In that example it was revealed that grades F to H were in Level 3. Budget accountability finally cut in at grade H, and yet sometimes key people decisions on recruitment, changes of duties and the like might be decided by jobs in grades F, G or H.

Now we come to the interesting job at grade I. According to the company this was just another linear promotion. Wrong. The job at grade I was in Level 4. It entailed strategic accountability. In this example, the move from grade H to grade I was a real promotion. Furthermore, it entailed a move across the key development dividing line. But the company had no idea of this, or what it should entail in terms of preparation or leadership development; it did not know what to look for in potential leaders at this level. In fact, our sample company further compounded this problem by putting all those from Level 3 and above into a common senior management grade.

No wonder this company suspected it had a capability problem. But it was not necessarily the quality of the employees that was the real problem.

Performance is no guarantee of promotion

Good performance at the top operational level does not guarantee the potential to move into the lower rungs of strategic accountability. A good factory manager does not necessarily make a good supply chain vice president. Thus grading systems and status developments, such as using titles in a particular way, feed the administrative promotion syndrome that undermines leadership development in a great number of organizations. This makes it virtually impossible to build reliable and valid competencies to identify who might have the potential for a particular managerial leadership role.

Models that ignore, or cannot identify, this critical dividing line between operational and strategic accountability make leadership development more subjective and unreliable, and needlessly increase the element of chance.

The importance of boundary moves

As there are only four or five levels of accountability in most organizations, the first concern is predictably: 'But how will I motivate my people if I can't promote them?'

A healthy, optimal organization is one that meets its purpose, while those in it are doing work that adds value to the work of others and simultaneously enables them to learn and grow as individuals. Personal growth and development does not just come from moving up through the levels of accountability, even though administrative grading systems and their related reward systems constantly refer to promotions. The pace and type of development is crucial. This is invariably neglected as organizations strive for accelerated development of key individuals or the minority of the moment. But true accelerated development is based upon boundary moves.

A boundary move takes an individual outside their comfort zone but not outside their learning zone. The aim is to stretch and broaden the learning of the incumbent.

My research indicates that comfort zones are within the same level of accountability, while the most demanding change in learning zones involves an increase in accountability by one level.[5] But important learning phases can be structured within a level of accountability too. My research also demonstrates that certain accountability levels (eg Level 3) are critically important in consolidating the learning and development of leaders.

Five types of boundary move

Boundary moves occur when job moves entail:

1. A change in accountability level

These are the most challenging and fundamental types of development. They are also arguably the most important for an organization to get right. But they presuppose a clearly identified platform of accountabilities, which most organizations do not have.

This type of boundary move would be a major promotion. However, it is important to note that accelerated movement across levels of account- ability is a major cause of burnout.

2. A change to another function

This would be a move from an activity such as sales to another such as finance. It represents a significant move and it is suggested that it should normally take place within an accountability level. This is because some key functions require various degrees of professional accreditation, so it can entail an unrealistically steep learning curve for the person on the move.

3. Changes in the type of experience for roles with the same title

This would typically be a move to a job in the same level but with a different type of challenge. An example would be a hypermarket manager who has successfully run their first hypermarket for 18 months, at say Level 3. Results are good, but this was a successful store prior to the manager's arrival. They are not yet ready for promotion to the next level of accountability. (In fact, we now know that insufficient time at Level 3 is a recipe for disaster.)

The next logical challenge would be a turnaround situation. Send the manager to the next role with a salary increase and an explanation of why this is a good development move for them. They now have to prove that they can improve sales, lower costs, improve customer service and increase morale in a comparable business situation. Once the manager has succeeded again, after two years say, it is time for another boundary move within Level 3.

This time the challenge could be a start-up role. This would involve running a new hypermarket where the manager chooses the staff for the first time, and sets the standards, objectives, priorities, values and targets expected in the new unit. They then have to train and develop the team. It could take about another two years to prove they can master this assignment.

Now, after about six years or so at Level 3 (sufficient dwell-time), our young star has proven their ability in a variety of different situations. They may well be ready for promotion to Level 4, where they may have accountability for 8 to 12 hypermarkets, which are all likely to be in one of the three phases they have experienced.

This series of boundary moves through a series of different types of assignment helps reduce the risk factors in promoting the manager to Level 4. (This will also depend on a competency assessment, which will be covered later.)

This type of boundary move could include changes in product types – established versus new – brands, markets, technology and so on.

4. Change from line to support

This is one of the most critical learning moves in the development of top leaders. The manager is moved from a position where they are in control, accountable for others and able to tell them what to do, to a position where they can only persuade, cajole and influence. It is crucial to master these influencing skills in order to be successful in the upper echelons of large, complex organizations.

This type of boundary move is often done in conjunction with a move to the corporate centre or an assignment to a project or strategic corporate programme. The value of such a project move is that the individual now has to learn how to obtain results from others working in the main business lines of the organization, people who have their own line management objectives and consider themselves quite busy enough without being involved in additional work from 'the centre'. To begin with, managers that are well used to the power of working in the line find this the most frustrating type of move, and many successful managerial leaders in Level 5+ report that a head office project was their toughest assignment to complete successfully.

> A move to the corporate office to work on or lead a strategic programme affecting most or all of the group is excellent exposure and development for someone assessed as having strategic leadership potential.

> A change from support to line is equally challenging and developmental but is often more difficult to orchestrate, especially at the strategic levels.

5. Change of country

Recently I worked with a company planning to expand into more countries. It needed to be sure it had enough potential Level 5 national managers in the internal pipeline. The policy was to promote the national managers from within the company, not to buy them on the international market.

The company has a very strong culture and set of values, and the leaders from Level 4 and above are vital for establishing and maintaining these. This company believes that the right leaders at Levels 4 and 5 can train and influence more junior local managers, many of whom might be recruited externally, but then acculturated by the key leaders.

The change of country move is most important in an international organization where cross-cultural experience and an understanding of other cultures, religions and socio-political systems are vital for genuine success. It is the most important boundary move for an international organization that believes in the importance of internal promotions.

Many organizations balk at the cost involved in moving people to international assignments. Then they tend to do it haphazardly or half-heartedly, paying lip service to promotion from within, which is a waste of time and money.

The fact is: competitors can copy everything a company does. They can replicate processes, products, structures and training programmes. But competitors cannot copy the way that a company works together. That is the ultimate business justification for building seamless cadres of international management.

I have observed many powerful examples of how this can work. A multinational company based in the developed world, for instance, had a truly international management development programme. As part of this programme a local manager was transferred from India to a key marketing role in Indonesia. Following that successful assignment he was transferred to the head office, where he undertook an important international marketing role in the same product area. He was then promoted to run the Argentinean business.

No sooner had he arrived, than the major competitor made a huge multimillion dollar investment in new plant and capacity. The competitor's market share was well under 30 per cent but with a stated ambition to double its share. The new managing director needed to do a very rapid market review to block any gaps in the market. This, in a sense, any good marketer could do. But, and this is the value of the internationalization process, a good local would not have his international contacts and leverage in the organization. Once he knew what was required for the Argentinean market, he knew the key players in the organization who could deliver new products and material quickly.

The result was that the competitor's share was halved during his tenure, and the manager in question was promoted to run a larger company elsewhere in the world.

Now if this company had ignored the local manager's potential, and balked at the further costs of expatriating him during the first move to Indonesia, then this company would have incurred great cost but not achieved commensurate value and return on its investment. This is what happens when companies have half-baked internationalization programmes, or tend to move abroad only those, or very predominantly those, from the home country nationality base.

The lack of a robust platform of accountabilities, and a culture of internal, grade-based promotions, can lead to the calcification of an organization.

How many boundary moves in one go?

Clearly some boundary moves are more important and more difficult than others. Perhaps the most important, and increasingly difficult, is crossing a level of accountability. Similarly challenging is a move to another country, or even a move to another function.

If it is felt that a certain individual has the potential to become a country manager, it makes sense to move them abroad while at Level 3. The demands of operational general management are an excellent indicator of how someone deals with and leads people from another culture. If they are not very good at it, then it is better to know that before they are appointed to the role of country manager.

The same tends to apply to cross-functional moves. These can become difficult beyond Level 2 in truly professional leadership roles, such as in law, accounting and engineering, for example. It depends on the nature of the organization's business and the central criticality of these functions. In other respects it is important to bear in mind the skills crossover point, illustrated in Chapter 7 (Figure 7.3), which could help decide when a functional move might be appropriate.

Most high-fliers can cope with one boundary move at a time. Two is highly risky, as it assumes the individual concerned can definitely reach Level 5 and above. Three boundary moves at once, eg a move to another function, to the next level of accountability and to another country, would be courting failure, unless the individual had the capability to reach Level 7+. But it is virtually impossible to reliably predict that kind of potential at Levels 3 or 4 if that company has no record of tracking previous success.[6]

Remember, even successful transition to Level 7 is facilitated by considerable 'dwell-time' at Levels 3 and 5. High-fliers that crash through Level 3 in the name of accelerated promotion have a disappointing record of burnout and failure at Level 5.

With the company that wished to identify and produce country managers from within its own ranks, once we had identified that these were invariably Level 5 roles, then it was possible to draw up a list of 10 possible boundary moves that would better prepare individuals for this role. This included information about when to move out of a function, which blend of functions would provide the best business background, when to move to a new country and so on. It was also clear that this could be a 15-year programme for someone who had just moved to Level 2.

In Chapter 10 we will see these ideas applied to the role of secondary school principal, demonstrating how the leadership development principles work in practice, and that they are universal in application, regardless of sector.

Faulty organization design masks the identification of talent

We have seen that many job evaluation and competency models are unable to pinpoint the vital changes in learning zones that drive the development of an individual. They are also not often able to indicate when a boundary move or set of moves stretches beyond the learning zone, and is therefore likely to destroy rather than build an individual.

It is tough (if not impossible) to identify performance, good or bad, in a cluttered, top-heavy organization. Over-layering blurs accountability, making it difficult to identify objectively who is doing a good job and who is not. Poor performance leads to finger pointing. Success has many parents, with everyone claiming to be the cause of the good performance.

This inability to judge performance inevitably leads to politics over who gets promoted, administratively or otherwise. Reliance on the home nationalities or tribes in some parts of the world as the source of candidates for key jobs seems to correlate with this inability to reliably and fairly identify real talent. Most companies preach 'promotion on merit' these days. But not many practice what they preach. Worse than that, many don't even understand why they can't practice what they preach.

Behavioural scientists have made it clear for over 50 years that talented people want a challenging job, which offers meaning, recognition, a sense of achievement and a chance to make a difference or an improvement. The one thing they do not want is close, heavy supervision or micro-management.

Some organizations seem to recognize this and do something about it – one large bank I have been working with wisely refers to its organizational restructuring project as designing 'Clear space to lead'. However, a disturbing number cast the problem into the basket marked 'too difficult'. The classic response being: 'We have other priorities at the moment.' (This was the response in 2005 from a UK HR director in a FTSE company that was underperforming compared with its peers.) That attitude has generally returned to haunt those organizations later on.

Orange, part of the telecommunications giant, France Telecom, introduced levels of accountability ('work levels' in their case) to build an organization that was:[7]

- agile;
- lean;
- noted for good, rapid decisions;
- fast to market;
- cost-efficient.

Cost was a factor but not the driver. Orange knew that if it was agile, lean and quick to react to customers and to get products and services to the market ahead of its competitors, it would be cost-effective and work would be more interesting for its employees. Work levels helped identify the organizational obstacles in the way of that vision and the action that was needed to redress them.

Most of us have received poor service at the hands of public service organizations around the world. They, along with the international political bureaucracies such as the UN, continue to be among the most over-layered and stultifying organizations, frustrating both their employees and their customers. Governments exacerbate this situation by confusing top-down control with accountability. Worse still, they call it 'accountability'.[8] One national government service with hundreds of thousands of employees saw its senior service grow 21 per cent in the five years up to 2007. This was because it was controlled top-down and had no idea how to assess accountability appropriately.

At the end of 2006, a major organization in New York was criticized in the press for its inability to collect its outstanding debts. Apparently some individuals were in debt to this organization to the tune of seven figures, and yet these debts were not being collected. When my colleague Adam Pearce and I examined their structure and organization, we discovered they had far more layers than needed, the average spans of control were only five, and staff were confused and demoralized by the bad publicity coupled with the lack of clear internal accountability.

Many financial institutions continue to be among the most over-managed companies in the private sector. They have recognized the importance of leadership development, yet they continue to wonder why many of their leadership development initiatives are ineffective. The reason lies in the fact that they are apt to have nine or more layers of management, which turns their leadership development programmes into a lottery. Throw in a myriad of politically correct initiatives and the result is a mess.

Confusion about values, skills and competencies

Without a clear idea of what is being measured, success is apt to remain elusive. What then are organizations supposed to be measuring as part of their leadership development programmes? Values, skills and competencies are all part of the leadership development mix. Unfortunately, even though they might have a sound organization design, many organizations still confuse values, skills and competencies; it is one of the main reasons why so many leadership development programmes fail.

Unsurprisingly, given the appalling failure of accountability at the top of Enron and WorldCom, many organizations are now emphasizing the importance of ethics and values. What is more surprising is how many companies are trying to use values as a vehicle for leadership development.

A flawed approach

Although values and skills, especially technical skills, play an important role in who should work in an organization – who should belong and on what terms, and who should be rewarded for competent performance – they are not reliable guides for assessment of potential and who should be promoted.

Most companies mix up values, skills and behaviours in what are labelled 'competencies'. Some are known to spend disproportionate amounts of time trying to assess innate qualities (referred to as 'talent' in Figure 9.2) without taking into account the total picture, especially the differentiating behaviours. Figure 9.2 is an illustration of how values, skills and competencies fit together.

The importance of the concept of potential, as distinct from performance and factors such as personality, is critical to the process of predicting and identifying future leaders to be held to account for strategic work.

1. Values

An international company that I worked with recently spent almost a year trying to build a leadership development programme for promotion based solely on values.

Values are important and are indeed the building blocks of a successful organizational culture. For example, most if not all retail companies espouse the value of customer service. At a company like Tesco, customer service really means something and is demonstrably practised and believed in by the CEO, Sir Terry Leahy. Not all organizations are so committed to the values that they espouse, however. Many companies talk about their values, frame them, hang them on the wall, and that is as far as living the values goes.

Values are badges of belonging. They should send the message: 'If you do not share our values, you cannot be a member of our family.' But you do not promote people for demonstrating the organization's values. If integrity, for example, is a value, you do not promote people because they have more integrity. You do, however, fire those people who do not have integrity; they do not deserve to belong. The person at the front line should have as much integrity as the CEO, otherwise neither should be in the organization.

You do not promote someone solely on the basis of their commitment to the organization's values, because values do not differentiate between levels of accountability and indicate who has leadership potential.

Components of Outstanding Leadership		
Values	Skills	Competencies
personal beliefs/attitudes (derailers/constraints)	transferable abilities (job requirements)	level-based behaviours (context-dependent practices)
Value-based Behaviours • integrity • commitment • respect for others • customer focus	Technical, Professional and General Skills • manufacturing • marketing • selling • buying • logistics • IT • HR • accounting • engineering • law • project management • time management	Differentiating Competencies* • setting direction • harnessing resources • analysing and deciding • managing change • influencing colleagues • managing the external environment
'Must-haves' membership	*'Can-dos'* performance	*'Could-haves'* potential
Talent innate qualities IQ EQ energy personality		

* Used in the example in Chapter 10 to predict leadership potential for Level 4.

Figure 9.2 Components of outstanding leadership

2. Skills

The same argument that applies to values also applies to skills. Skills influence performance. They should not be confused with the concept of potential to lead at the next level of accountability. Technical and professional skills increasingly give way to the importance of general skills, with a crossover point at Level 3. But performance in one level of accountability is no guarantee that the individual should move to a higher level. The best maths teacher in a school is not necessarily the best candidate for the role of school principal.

The clearest example of this over-reliance on skill assessment as the basis for promotion occurs at the top of Level 3, when an organization is planning to promote across the dividing line between operational and strategic decision-making and accountability. Just because a manager can run a call centre, a factory or a hypermarket efficiently does not guarantee effectiveness at the next level of accountability. This is because the fundamental nature of the work has changed. Accountability at Level 4 is not more of the same, more productivity, or even merely continuous improvement. It entails a fundamental step change in the quality of decision rights that have to be mastered.

Yet it is surprising how many organizations view skills and performance as the gateway to leadership development. Skill mastery is a critical part of success up to the top of Level 3. From Level 4 and above, the picture becomes more complex. The fact that the country manager who is on the list for promotion to regional CEO might have started his or her career in the accounts department now has little or no bearing on whether they have the capability to be held to account for the region. Skills influence performance, but they do not reliably differentiate who can perform at the next level of accountability.

3. Behaviours as competencies

As already indicated, the assessment of potential to move to a higher level of leadership is often muddied by the issues of values and skills. This is because at best they refer to performance in the current level of accountability, not the next level. And it is the next level that is, or should be, the focus of any leadership development programme.

This is the great conundrum of any assessment of potential – that it is an assessment of whether an individual can perform at the next level of management. So it is no surprise that there is such a strong tendency to rely on an evaluation of current performance, given that the aim is to predict future performance.

But performance is about current leadership. Potential is about future leadership. This is a key distinction.

The higher the progression into the upper reaches of an organization, the less relevant professional skills and performance become as predictors of future performance. It is necessary to assess behaviours to gauge how an individual might perform at a future higher level. But, as with any recruitment process, the outcome is still no more than a sophisticated guesstimate. The challenge is to make the process as reliable as possible.

If there is not a valid accountability platform, then the assessment of leadership is unreliable. It is critical that the behaviours are linked to accountabilities. This is because different levels call for different qualities of decisions. It is important to identify the appropriate behaviours that align to these. These aligned behaviours are called competencies in this context. They indicate who has potential to move to a higher level and perform successfully. This is the basis of true leadership development.

Competencies consisting of behaviours, aligned to levels of accountability, are the most reliable indicators of potential. Competencies are the differentiators that indicate those managerial leaders who are most likely to be successfully held to account in the future.

A definition of competencies?

At the Third International Competencies Conference in Rome in the mid-1990s, Richard Boyatzis, one of the leading experts in the field, admitted that competencies are a 'definitional quagmire'. In short they are a mishmash of attitudes, habits, skills and capabilities. They involve much of what goes to make up a person – a lot of which eludes definition.

Currently, most competency models are a mixture of behaviours and skills. This is a difficult area, as one implies the other in certain circumstances – ie a skill implies a certain behaviour that manifests it.

But skills relate to how the job is done in a technical sense. They are operational, describing an ability to perform a task, and are limited to assessing performance at a particular level of accountability. As one moves up to higher levels, the need for technical skills starts to wane. Thus it is not important whether a CEO started out as an accountant or an engineer.

Behaviours, on the other hand, relate to what is required to execute accountabilities or make decisions; they include skills, but more is involved. Behaviours are more psychological, vary by level, and can be more reliably used to indicate the potential to perform at a higher level. They reflect the way a task is tackled: for example, is abstract or concrete thinking being employed?

This is why it is not sufficient to promote on the basis of skills and performance alone. But if there is no agreement about the nature of competencies, how can there be any agreement about what they measure? This problem means that competencies are also frequently an unsound basis for leadership development.

Too many competencies

Various competency models exist. However, often the number of competencies being assessed is too many.

A global company that I once worked with implemented the Hay McBer model of 11 competencies. In a review, about a year or so after it had been implemented, managers were unequivocal in stating that they wanted to assess no more than five competencies. They felt that they were becoming buried in a bureaucracy of little value. And they were right.

The consultants suggested condensing their model into five clusters. They missed the point, and a year or so later the company threw out the 11-competency model.

My own experience would suggest six differentiating competencies is the maximum for line managers to assess.[9] Some non-differentiating factors relating to psychological stability and energy will also be important. But most companies still have too many competencies, further undermined by unclear thinking about values, performance and potential.

Lack of context

Around the world, the most common failing for competency models is lack of context. For example, many competency models talk about 'seeing the big picture'. But the 'big picture' for a lowly brand manager in France is totally different to the 'big picture' for the global vice president of the category in New York.

Competency models ignore this vital component. They are unable to confront the problem if they do not have a way of assessing the different accountabilities of the brand manager in France and the global category vice president.

It is not enough to focus only on an individual's values, skills and behaviours. An individual's performance and potential must be assessed in the context of the role being discharged, and bearing in mind the next role.

In order to assess potential for the next, higher level of accountability, it is necessary to have a way of assessing the context of the two levels in question. Behaviours assessed out of context are meaningless. Yet that is precisely what most competency and leadership models do.

The way forward?

To move forward, two things are required. First, there must be a way of identifying different levels of management accountability. Secondly, there must be a set of differentiating competencies that identify the behaviours needed to be successful at each level.

Decision Making Accountability Solution Set

The Decision Making Accountability Solution Set meets the first requirement. It sets the context for each management layer.

It also provides a key to assessing the behaviours relevant to each of the levels. As described in Chapter 4, it is not a rigid model, but a set of universal principles that are sufficiently flexible to take account of the context in which either the organization or the individual finds themselves. In short, a solution to any set of organizational circumstances.

A job that is not adding value to the organization's mission or the work of others is superfluous. It is an unnecessary cost. It lacks true accountability, and therefore it does not add to the learning and development of a talented individual.

Differentiating competencies

It is important to design competencies that differentiate the behaviours needed at different levels of accountability. The six level-based behaviours listed in Figure 9.2 earlier in this chapter have been aligned to the Seven Elements at each level.[10] These form the basis for individual assessment.

Differentiating competencies are defined according to the levels of accountability (context). Each one is on a spectrum of increasing complexity. Since they describe the behaviours for effective performance at each level, they can be used as the benchmark against which current behaviour can be assessed. This can be for the current work level or the next work level. The latter enables these competencies to be used as a means of assessing potential, or leadership at the next level of accountability.

There are both positive definitions (desired behaviours indicating readiness for promotion) and negative definitions (behaviours that will not lead to promotion). The gaps between the actual and the desired levels of readiness indicate possible areas for development, provided that the appropriate underlying talent exists. This can be assessed by management observing their team members, as long as they know what to look for. The competencies can also be used as part of an external assessment process, for example in a merger and acquisition situation.

Assessment based on differentiating competencies

My colleagues, Lisa Cramp and Helen Roberts, have done pioneering work in this area. They point out, in Table 9.1, that all assessment approaches have common characteristics.

Table 9.1 Leadership frameworks incorporating the DMA Competencies

Leadership Capability	Behaviour Domain	'Big Four/Five'	Junglan Type	DMA Competency model
defining the strategy and vision	intellectual	openness	S–N	setting direction
inspiration and communication	social	extroversion	E–I	harnessing resources
managing relationships	emotional	neuroticism/ agreeableness	T–F	internal and external networks
execution to deliver results	operational	conscientiousness	J–P	problem-solving, change

They, along with Adam Pearce and myself, have developed a powerful model for the assessment of individuals, taking into account their current and future career aspirations assessed in relation to the relevant leadership levels.

The Seven Elements drive what decisions have to be taken. The DMA Competencies identify the behaviours that correspond to each Element. 'If this is what I have to decide, then this is how I need to behave to be effective at this level.'

It is not enough to simply assess the potential of a general manager. Remember, context is king. It is critical to know whether that person is in a Level 3, 4, 5 or 6 general management role, and whether they are being assessed for Levels 4, 5, 6 or 7. I have developed an approach that does precisely this. It has been used successfully with a number of clients and a significant database is being built up, against which individual general managers, for example, can be uniquely benchmarked.

The seven steps for building an effective leadership development programme

The typical leadership development shortcomings outlined in this chapter can be overcome by introducing the following seven steps.

1. Identify the levels of accountability. This is the step that establishes the context of a job. It is done by conducting Accountability Probes from the front line to establish the platform for leadership development.
2. Identify and define line and support jobs. Decide upon the jobs that are either on the spine of accountability, or that add value to the spine. In other words, which jobs hold the leader to account for people and which for know-how and expertise?
3. Plan the move to a healthy organization if necessary. If the Accountability Probe reveals the organization's architecture is ineffective, then a plan is needed to orchestrate the relevant change programme.[11]
4. Identify and establish a set of differentiating behaviours or competencies. These need to be aligned to the Seven Elements underpinning the levels of accountability.
5. Construct a reliable and valid method for assessing individuals against their level of accountability. This may focus only on performance and/or potential, depending on the current need.
6. Fill the value-adding roles with competent individuals. Identify key individuals based on assessment of their capability against the different levels of accountability, given the work in steps 1 to 5.
7. Identify key career and learning tracks. Once the value-adding management jobs have been identified, it is important to map how long a high flier needs to spend moving through the key levels of

> accountability. Identify key boundary moves. This should be done
> for specialist functions (eg finance) and general management.[12]
>
> Boundary moves are an integral part of this process.

The Accountable Leader Chapter 9: Key points

Top management has not paid sufficient attention to the importance of organization design as the necessary platform for effective leadership development. This in turn has undermined competency models.

These have failed because they neglect the context in which individuals are working. They have not highlighted the critical differences in levels of accountability and the importance of these for learning and development. They have focused unduly on skills, values and performance, neglecting the behaviours that are the markers of potential assessment. There are invariably too many competencies and they are not clearly defined.

The following key points are important:

1. There can be no effective leadership development without an effectively designed organization. Three variables are critical for the successful development of leaders throughout an organization: a role with clear accountabilities; an organizational structure with the right number of layers; and an individual with the right degree of competence for the job.
2. Talented individuals cannot contribute to their full capacity and potential in a cluttered, top-heavy organization that blurs accountability and stifles initiative.
3. If a role does not add value to the work of others, it is unlikely to enable an individual to grow and learn. A surplus job in the organization structure does not add value and challenge. It cannot be the basis for the development of high-flying individuals.
4. Administrative promotions are hollow promotions leading to hollow personal development.
5. The difference between operational work and strategic work and the implications for leadership development is critical. So is knowing where this difference occurs. Identifying where this difference occurs in an organization is vital for the assessment and development of potential leaders. But most leadership approaches do not focus on this vital division, largely because the clarity of the demarcating line is blurred by administrative grading systems.

6. A boundary move takes an individual outside their comfort zone but not outside their learning zone. The aim is to stretch and broaden the learning of the incumbent. Boundary moves include: a change in an accountability level; a change to another function; changes in the type of experience for roles with the same title; a change from line to support; a change of country.

7. Most high-fliers can cope with one boundary move at a time. Two is highly risky, as it assumes the individual concerned can definitely reach Level 5 and above. Three boundary moves at once, eg to another function, to the next level of accountability and to another country, would be courting failure, unless the individual had the capability to reach Level 7+.

8. You do not promote solely on the basis of a person's commitment to the organization's values, because values do not differentiate between levels of accountability and indicate who has leadership potential.

9. The same argument applies to skills. Skills influence performance. They should not be confused with the concept of potential to lead at the next level of accountability.

10. Competencies consisting of behaviours, aligned to levels of accountability, are the most reliable indicators of potential. Competencies are the differentiators that indicate those managerial leaders who are most likely to be successfully held to account in the future.

Notes

1. Brousseau, K R *et al* (2006) The Seasoned Executive's Decision Making Style, *Harvard Business Review*, February

2. They are not referring to levels of accountability in this sentence as defined in the DMA Solution Set.

3. See Robert Kramer's excellent report on COOs, *The Role of COOs* (2006).

4. Grades do not align accurately with levels of accountability. This has been the case in every organization in which I have worked that had a grading system, whether bespoke or that of a consultancy, such as Hay, Watson Wyatt, etc. Grading systems do not guarantee the organizational architecture has the right number of layers. This seriously hampers the identification of potential leaders.

5. See chapter 8 of *The Healthy Organization*.

6. See chapter 8 of *The Healthy Organization*.

7. See Shaunagh Dawes' outline in 'e-reward case study no 47' (2006).

8. For a revealing analysis of this phenomenon, read Baroness O'Neill's five Reith lectures (2002) on the theme of loss of trust in public services.

9. Research highlighted by Boam and Sparrow (1992) confirms this.

10. These competencies are explained in more detail in chapter 7 of *The Healthy Organization*. An application relating to their use to predict potential to cross from Level 3 to Level 4 is set out in Chapter 10 of this book.

11. A healthy organization is fit for purpose and optimally organized with its management layers effectively aligned to levels of accountability, such that individuals can perform, learn, grow and develop when discharging their work.

12. For example, some years ago Unilever plotted career path options for its finance function. It illustrated what key experiences were needed to reach Level 5 and at which level these could be obtained.

10 Leadership development schemes: how can they succeed?

'Sing in me, Muse, and through me tell the story of that man skilled in all ways of contending.'

Homer, The Odyssey

It is all very well explaining the theory of accountability and work levels, and how that relates to leadership development, but how are these theories applied to real world examples?

This chapter provides an example of how the ideas in this book can be put into practice. It shows how leaders can be identified and developed for future jobs in which they will be held to account.

The ideas in this book apply equally to both private and public sector organizations. Although the case study described in detail here relates to the identification of potential secondary school principals, it is presented in a way that should make its relevance for the private sector obvious.

The challenge

There is strong anecdotal evidence that there is an acute shortage of school principals[1] in a number of countries at present. This is certainly the case in

Australia, New Zealand and the United Kingdom, and also seems to be the case in Eire and North America.

Unlike private sector organizations, educational bodies are not noted for identifying leaders with potential and preparing them for leadership roles, such as principal of a school. One reason may be that many teachers are not inclined to pursue such roles, at least at first. Teaching is a different kind of activity to managing, and those attracted to the former may be less interested in the latter. Moreover, those best placed to assess the potential of teachers to take up leadership roles – their immediate superiors – may have little incentive to do so.

The problem was neatly summed up by one principal in Australia who said recently: 'There is no incentive for me to develop my best teachers to become my successor. First, where am I going, as I am already leading one of the best schools in the country, and secondly, why should I create more problems for myself encouraging my best staff support to move on?'

Given these factors, altruism remains the only motivation; not really a sufficient basis for sound leadership development. And there are no reliable sets of competencies designed to identify potential leaders, despite well-meaning claims to the contrary.

This situation is aggravated, in many countries, by the fact that principals are selected by school boards, which are more often than not untrained in the recruitment and selection process. During 2006, over 80 per cent of the principals running leading schools in one area of a country were removed from their posts, largely owing to poor recruitment and selection procedures.

Given the lack of manpower and career planning, there is also a tendency for principals to stay too long in their job. Since they do not know where they might go next they stay put. Consequently, many principals go stale from unduly long tenure in the same job.

The key steps to identifying and developing leaders

This case study shows how to identify potential secondary school principals, and the key steps involved in ensuring those leaders are identified, developed and held to account.

The procedure is as follows: first identify the key levels of accountability involved; then focus on identifying leaders who can cross the operational–strategic divide and become a school principal.

The key steps in the identification of potential principals are:

- Identifying the accountabilities within a school.
- The identification and design of the relevant boundary moves for leadership development.
- The adaptation and application of a differentiating competency model (the DMA model was used in this case).
- The design of the assessment process – what to assess, how and why.

This approach can be described as an assessment or a development programme. It can be either or both. For the organization it is primarily about assessment; deciding who can move to the next level of accountability. From the individual's perspective it is primarily about personal development. In ideal cases the assessment forms the basis of a series of development steps that ensure the identified potential is realized. Hence assessment and development will be used interchangeably in this chapter.

Step 1: identifying accountabilities (the leadership platform)

The first step was to establish the level of accountability of the different roles in a typical secondary school. Work began in a number of schools in New Zealand, and then progressed to Australia.[2]

The Accountability Probe process was followed. Interviewing started at the front line, assessing the Seven DMA Elements of the roles under review, and then moved up the reporting line until the role of principal was reached. This process was followed in a number of schools. The sizes of the secondary schools in terms of pupil population were generally between 600 and 2,000 pupils, with the mean around 1,000. None of the principals ran a campus of schools, although some had additional infrastructure such as farms, boarding establishments and the like, in addition to the standard curriculum-related activities.

Key findings

1. At a secondary school the front line is at Level 2. This is consistent with the discussion on professional jobs in Chapter 6 These teachers must undergo required training, usually about three years, and must have taken a degree in the subject in which they have chosen to teach.
2. The first promotion for many teachers is to become head of department. But these jobs are almost never at the next level of accountability. This is because the bulk of their weekly or monthly work is still in the classroom

– that is, still at Level 2 (see the second key principle of the DMA Solution Set in Chapter 4). Many other part-time roles, such as dean, pastoral advisor, sports coach and the like, were also still at Level 2.

In a very large school, particularly in a major subject such as sciences or languages, the head of department role might be organizing curricula and timetables for the current and following year almost full-time. In that case the role could be in Level 3.

3. Senior management, which usually consisted of a small team of key teachers, heads of departments and infrastructure managers, such as the bursar, consistently emerged at Level 3. But many jobs outside the classroom barely moved into Level 3. There seems to be a tendency in educational institutions to appoint a plethora of 'assistants' and 'deputies', often with the word 'principal' also in the title. Many of these jobs are overwhelmed with little more than low Level 2 or even Level 1 accountabilities, aimed at 'taking the load off the principal'. They are rarely the developmental opportunities that the titles might otherwise suggest.

4. The role of principal consistently emerged at Level 4.[3] This is because, although it might appear that a school principal is a general manager who could be at Level 5, in fact many aspects of the job are prescribed to a degree (bearing in mind the 10 management accountabilities set out in Chapter 1). Usually, the curriculum to be taught is laid down in advance. There is very little freedom to recruit beyond budgeted numbers, and invariably pay is fixed via some central governance or bargaining body. There is little real management of teachers' potential. Budgets are often set centrally, which limits input or discretion. Even the numbers of pupils and teachers in the school are usually set in large measure by a governance body above the principal.

The main findings on the analysis of accountabilities were:

- The front line of a secondary school is at Level 2.
- The role of principal is Level 4.
- Secondary schools are very flat, with only two layers of management.
- This set the platform for the leadership assessment and development process.

Features of a principal's role to be learned

Teachers need to have broadening experiences (in both Levels 2 and 3) that prepare them for a situation where they are:

- contributing effectively to the establishment of strategy in line with the moral purpose of the school;
- defining work, setting goals and targets with quantitative and qualitative measures, and changing them when appropriate;
- managing a financial portfolio;
- deciding who will do what by when;
- securing commitment;
- providing people with the authority and resources needed to achieve their designated assignments;
- ensuring the agreed obligations are met;
- giving feedback, training and development;
- deciding appropriate rewards;
- deciding who should leave the team, by promotion, demotion or whatever is appropriate.

These are not tasks learnt in a classroom. Wider experience and learning is needed.

Principals also need invigorating boundary moves. There is a tendency for principals to stay too long in the job, especially when the board is more than happy with their contribution and when – as is frequently the case at present – it has no clear approach to finding and developing potential successors. Moreover, the incumbent principal may have few employment options elsewhere in the network, given the current rigidities of time-in-job.

In those schools that are part of a larger world – for example, a school connected to a religious group with schools across a country, or indeed in other parts of the world – moving and developing principals is also important. Just as teachers learn from having a number of lateral moves within the same level of accountability, so principals appointed at a relatively young age into their first post should have a number of further moves; and these lateral moves may themselves follow a natural order. An experienced principal could take up the challenge of running a 'turnaround' or a 'start-up' school. A first-time principal might not be so well prepared for such a challenge. Thus an approach in the central educational office that meshes in appropriate experience would be beneficial.

The current development of principals is a lottery

Professions are not noted for fostering the personal development of their members in a very deliberate or structured way. After completing their training and entry requirements, professionals tend to develop new skills – outside the area of the core skills required for their profession – on their own initiative.

The teaching profession is no exception. And, unlike other professions, it is not easily able to build competence via the 'sitting by Ned or Nelly' tutoring and mentoring approach seen in the legal and medical professions.

In education circles there is often no clear overall picture of how many vacancies can be expected for secondary school principals in the next one to five years. There is little or no formal career planning, and scant effort to build up a supply of potential principals for future vacancies – to build up bench strength.

And yet career development in a very flat organization, such as a secondary school, is more challenging than in a larger organization with more layers of opportunity. Moves within levels are even more critical in a flat organization in order to broaden experience.

The break between operational and strategic work is also more critical, as there is a tendency to assume that the front line, the teacher, is only at Level 1. It seems there are rarely any valid and reliable approaches to the identification of potential. Furthermore school boards, who select these principals, are often not well enough equipped or prepared to select good calibre candidates.

In short, there is no certainty about how many vacancies exist or how many teachers have the capability to fill these roles. Not surprisingly there is anecdotal evidence that the quality of principals is becoming more variable, and this may explain the higher than acceptable rate of short-tenure principals, or of principals not surviving the first crucial years.

Step 2: identifying and designing the relevant boundary moves for the development of principals

Once the role of a secondary school principal was established at Level 4, it was clear that that was the level that needed focusing upon next. The appropriate boundary moves that would enable a teacher to get the best relevant experience in preparing for the role of principal needed to be identified.

Having interviewed a wide selection of roles throughout a school, we had a good idea of which roles were at which levels, and which might therefore provide appropriate grounding for a future job as principal.

Teachers do not traditionally seek out boundary move experiences. They join the profession to teach. It almost feels like a betrayal of their pupils to think of moving out of the classroom. But a newly appointed principal is likely to be more effective with a wide range of experiences in a school environment. The aim of these moves is to broaden the teacher's experience from merely managing in the classroom and prepare them to see the wider picture that exists across the school.

Types of boundary move

These development experiences are of five broad types, which were outlined in more detail in Chapter 9.

1. Change in accountability level
   These are the most challenging and fundamental type of development.

   But they presuppose a platform of accountabilities, which most schools do not have. Such a move would involve a major promotion.

2. Change in function
   This would entail a move from accountability for one subject to a role with a range of disciplines, with a wider impact in or across the school. It might also involve a move from the classroom into an administrative, pastoral or guidance role.

3. Change in environment
   This would entail a move from one school to another or from one sector (eg the state) to another. It could also include a move from the field to the national education head office. This works well if there is the possibility for principals to move on into 'the centre'.

4. Change to a support role
   This could occur if a teacher was moved from a command role where he or she is 'in charge', telling others what to do, to an advisory or a support role, such as a project. For potential principals it would be ideal if the project was of a strategic nature, affecting the whole school, and one where there was a known problem but no known solution as yet. The project manager would be expected to find, sell and even implement the new solution.

5. Change of country
   This type of move is important where cross-cultural experience would be an advantage for the potential principal. It tends to be rather rare in educational circles, given the national focus of state educational systems.

Since teachers can normally expect a total of two accountability moves to become a principal, most of their boundary moves take place within the same level.

Assuming a teacher commences their career in the 23–25 age range, those with high potential would probably spend about five years at Level 2, with a variety of boundary moves (two to three) and about seven years in Level 3, with three to four boundary moves. This would suggest high-fliers could be principals by the time they reached the 35–40 age range.

This would also suggest that they should have two to three principalships, assuming a 'dwell-time' for a principal in the range of six to eight years. Experience elsewhere would suggest that the refreshment of a new posting would be of benefit to both the individual principal and the respective schools.

Typical boundary moves at Level 2 might include:

- Moving a promising young teacher to take on extra work such as running a minor subject for a head of department.
- Taking on a role coaching a sports team or a debating team, or organizing the preparation of a school concert, event or outing, eg an annual camp or visit.
- Dean for a particular year, probably a junior year.
- Being assigned to a role in the Parent Teacher Association (PTA).

Thought should already be given to encouraging promising young teachers to take on additional formal education, such as:

- budgets and finance;
- time management;
- setting priorities;
- running meetings.

Changes across an accountability level

These are the two most critical boundary moves in a teacher's career.

The key difference for a teacher in moving from Level 2 to Level 3 is the taking on of management accountabilities. These should consist of the following:

- Selecting the team of teachers in the department, or at least having a veto.
- Defining work and setting goals and targets with quantitative and qualitative measures.
- Deciding who will do what by when.
- Securing commitment.
- Providing authority and resources to achieve the above.

- Ensuring the agreed obligations are met.
- Changing work and goals as deemed appropriate.
- Providing feedback, training and development.
- Deciding appropriate rewards.
- Deciding who should leave the team, by promotion, demotion or whatever is appropriate.

The effective management of these accountabilities is the essential platform that will underpin a principal's performance in the future.

Key boundary moves within Level 3 would typically include:

- Moving to roles such as head of department, faculty leader, dean, director of religious studies or special character.
- Becoming a member of a school senior management team.
- A move to become an assistant principal.[4]
- Moving to the role of deputy principal.
- A period, such as a term, as acting principal – the temporary crossing of a level of accountability.
- Moving to another school, especially to or from the state sector.
- Carrying out a key local project affecting the whole school, for example preparing the annual plan or budget.
- Being assigned to a head office, regional or national project, which would expose the individual to other schools.
- An exchange move to another country.
- Formal training, for example in management, relationships with a board or selecting staff.

These moves should be orchestrated in conjunction with the assessment of DMA Differentiating Competencies. For example, say you have a good Level 3 senior team member whose 'influencing skills are weak and in need of improvement'. This person would be a prime candidate for a key project where success depends on the ability to convince others and win their cooperation – selling – without having the authority to tell them what and how to deliver.

This inability to influence key constituencies has been found to be a critical weakness in principals whose careers derailed.

Possible pitfalls

The foundation to successful boundary moves is a sound system of differentiating competencies, coupled with a platform of sound accountabilities, which together indicate the type of moves likely to be beneficial. It has been demonstrated that the DMA Solution Set can provide those two vital components.

Hence there are two potential pitfalls in the development of school leaders, either of which can lead to lack of success. The first is the lack of clearly identified levels of accountability, and the second is the lack of a reliable and valid instrument to measure the capability of individuals at those levels.

Step 3: adaptation and application of the DMA Leadership Competency model

The third important step was to adapt the DMA Competencies model to apply to teachers and principals; the definitions had to be modified to reflect the fact that the job of principal was at Level 4.

Thus the competency for 'setting direction' across a number of roles within a secondary school was summarized, as in Figure 10.1.

1. Setting direction

Definition:	The capacity to set the direction and deliver plans over time, which are aligned to the needs of a defined context of accountabilities.
Related DMA Elements:	Nature of work – stems from the purpose of the role and defines where it differs in accountability from those above and below.
	Task horizon – focuses on the time over which the impact of the majority of the decisions of the jobholder will be felt.
Range:	short-term long-term
	operational strategic
	low level high level

Figure 10.1 DMA Competencies model (for secondary school principals)

Positive differentiating behaviours:

Work Level 2	• Sets, communicates and holds pupils accountable for delivery of stretching, short-term (up to 12 months) objectives.
	• Continuously reviews and acts to remove obstacles to achieving their progress.
Work Level 3	• Balances potentially conflicting sub-goals or objectives to achieve an integrated set of results for the department and the school as a whole.
	• Identifies trends, patterns and priorities for performance improvement and contributes to policy and plans for both this and the following year.
Work Level 4	• Has a comprehensive view of the school and is able to anticipate future needs and opportunities and set new milestones up to three years ahead.
	• Able to establish specific objectives and direction for the school's teachers from strategic intentions of the board and establish concrete plans from identified but incompletely defined opportunities.

Negative differentiating behaviours

Work Level 2	• Spurs self and students to action without a clear sense of direction and well-conceived objectives.
	• Ignores or fails to identify and remove obstacles to progress.
Work Level 3	• Tolerates and does not resolve conflicting objectives within and/or between subordinate teachers at the expense of overall departmental or school performance.
	• Is overwhelmed by detail and fails to identify negative patterns and to act on the causes of poor unit or departmental performance.

Figure 10.1 *Continued*

The competencies only went up to Level 4 since that was the top role in the secondary schools under review. There were no jobs found above Level 4 in Australia or New Zealand. In fact most secondary schools in New Zealand had around 600 pupils on average, with a spread from 250 to just over 3,000. Some of the very small schools might have a top job at Level 3.[5]

The focus of the assessment, to be outlined in the following steps, was on the Level 4 definitions for all six DMA Leadership Competencies. Only the first Competency, setting direction, is shown in Figure 10.1.

The Level 3 definitions proved very helpful when considering candidates who fell short of Level 4 potential. Reference to the Level 3 definitions helped verify what quality of behaviour was being observed and why it was not appropriate for a potential Level 4 principal.

Consideration of the negative definitions also helped refine the accuracy of the assessment of the candidates' strengths and weaknesses.

Step 4: design the assessment process

The next key stage is the design of an effective assessment process.

The assessment of accountability in a given role is the critical first step, yet it is frequently neglected. People are inclined to jump into the assessment process without really knowing where the assessment benchmark is.

This platform of accountabilities is the basis for a meaningful design of career developing boundary moves. It illustrates why it is so important to spend time assessing the respective accountabilities. It also explains why so much leadership development work is a waste of time, energy and money.

Parochial reaction

The suggestion to identify levels of accountability as the first phase in the assessment and development of leaders often gets a predictable parochial reaction, such as: 'You can't use a system used for shopkeepers on us [laboratory scientists].' Sure enough, we got the same reaction from teachers: 'You can't use some business approach on us.'[6]

The principles of accountability are universal, though, and apply to the private, public, military and voluntary sectors equally well. Any organization that exists for a purpose needs someone to be held accountable for the delivery of that mission.

We now knew we had to assess people currently at Level 3, doing operational work, to see if we could detect any behavioural indications that they could operate successfully at Level 4. The assessment process we designed consisted of four key steps.

The Potential Principals' Leadership Programme

The programme is based on knowing the level of accountability of the job of a secondary school principal. Once that is known, then the six DMA Leadership Competencies come into play. They form the bedrock of the assessment process, which includes the following:

- Candidates are individually interviewed to identify any significant gaps (lack of boundary moves) in their career experience to date.
- They complete two internationally validated psychometric tests, designed to assess their personal style and motivational profile.
- Then material from 360 assessments, based on consulting work colleagues, is assessed and analysed. The questions used in the process were previously validated via the repertory grid process to ensure they differentiated the significant behaviours needed in a successful principal.
- Candidates then attend a one-day development programme. During this day they work on a number of exercises designed to provide further information on their strategic competencies, while being assessed by professional observers. One-to-one feedback is offered after each exercise.

Five requirements underpinned this process:

1. Make sure that the teachers currently have real Level 3 accountabilities, since many important-sounding titles were in fact a front for Level 2 work. And we have good evidence that people cannot jump from Level 2 to Level 4, missing Level 3. Indeed they need a good few years in Level 3, gaining wide experience ideally, prior to a move to Level 4.[7]

2. Conduct a career history interview with the candidate. The main purpose of this process was to plot the experience, and particularly the boundary moves (or missing boundary moves), in the candidate's experience to date.

   Interviews also reveal a wealth of other information, much of it linked to behavioural cues that can be referenced in other parts of the process. The key here is to look for trends across the different forms of assessment that are relevant and consistent. The missing boundary moves helped to form the basis of the individual development reports and recommendations for action drawn up at the end of the total process.

   The interviews tended to last up to an hour and a half and were conducted by two consultants, one a psychologist if possible.

3. Apply the relevant psychometric tests. The main purpose of this part of the process was to test the emotional stability and resilience of the candidate,

and to help identify whether there were any quirks of personality or emotional health that would suggest a move to Level 4 would be a significant risk. Eileen Henderson was the experienced psychologist in our team and she administered the tests, explained the interpretation and led the feedback to the individuals.

As indicated earlier, the key steps in the development of a leader are to ensure:

- the job has discrete and real accountabilities;
- the job-holder is technically competent;
- the job-holder has a style that could be aligned to a principal role;
- the individual has the capability to perform at the higher level of account-ability.

The purpose of the psychometric testing was to zero in specifically on point three, namely to ensure that the applicant's personality and motivation were a good fit for a principal role. There are a number of tests that one could use in this context and this is an issue that needs to be discussed and agreed with an accredited psychologist. It is important to know what is to be assessed and why. These teachers all had at least one degree, so there was no great need to assess numerical and verbal intelligence, for example. (This can vary according to the context. When working with a retail business recently, where many of the managers had joined the company at age 17 without any subsequent tertiary education, it was vital to assess their numerical, verbal and spatial intelligence in relation to possible promotion to strategic roles, where an ability to think from first principles was required.)

In this case we opted to use the California Psychological Inventory (CPI). It was felt that this test focused on the softer aspects of Emotional Intelligence (EQ) and empathy, which were very relevant to the job of secondary school principal. Although there were some concerns about the face validity of using a foreign test, it was felt that this test was more difficult to fake than others. And in any case, the final choice was a matter of judgement given the circumstances. The other test used focused on issues linked to motivation.

4. Use a 360 performance review process in the assessment (ie an assessment of the candidate by their boss, peers and a selection of subordinates where relevant).

The relevance and validity of the 360 review was established via the repertory grid process. This is a process aimed at identifying differentiating behaviours.

Repertory grid technique

Repertory grid can be used to help identify differentiating competencies: that is, competencies that identify the different forms of behaviour needed at different levels of accountability.

First, the 360 review had to be designed, since none of the material we looked at was felt to be suitable for principals. Each industry tends to have its favoured terminology and its own blind points. It is important to design material that will get a positive reaction in a particular setting. Thus the wording used for a 360 review in one company might not work so easily in another, where people have different biases and preferences.

The process was broadly as follows. A number of questions were drafted, which we felt would identify the DMA Competencies we were aiming to assess. These needed to be tested to check both their reliability and validity.

The approach taken was to gather a group of individuals who had a good knowledge and experience of the role of principal. They were then asked to think of three outstanding principals, three who were average and three who were poor performers. The identities of these subjects were never disclosed.

Behavioural statements were then elicited from consideration and comparison of these nine subjects. All nine were then rated against each behavioural construct on a 1–5 scale. They were also rated on this scale for their overall performance. Following that, a comparison of each rating with the overall performance rating showed which behaviours were good predictors of performance. For example, 'Working well as part of a team' was an excellent predictor of overall performance (see Figure 10.2).

The scores of each question were trialled and those that did not give a consistently reliable response were deleted. These were clearly too blunt and ineffective for the final document. A sample of some of the questions is set out in Figure 10.2 to show part of the process of designing a 360 review using the repertory grid method.

In this example, a score of one indicates close agreement with the statement on the left hand side, and a score of five indicates close agreement with the statement on the right hand side.

The overall scores were assessed to decide which questions worked as differentiators and which did not. Those that did formed the basis of the 360 review.

5. Design a one-day programme of four exercises designed to tap into the same behavioural areas targeted via the psychological tests, the 360 review, and, to some extent, the interview. Some exercises were structured and some were deliberately unstructured. As indicated previously, we were looking for

	Outstanding			Average			Poor				
	A	B	C	D	E	F	G	H	I		
Performance Rating o/all	1	1	1	2	3	4	4	5	5		
Works well as part of the team and is a good team builder	1	1	1	2	3	4	4	5	5	Remains aloof from the team and does not promote teamwork	0
Very good at developing others	1	1	1	2	4	4	4	5	5	Is not good at developing others	1
Persuasive and brings other people with them	1	2	1	3	3	4	4	5	5	Not persuasive and has trouble bringing others with them	2
Inspires and motivates others to go the extra mile	2	1	1	2	2	4	4	5	5	Fails to inspire and motivate others	2
Has credibility – seen as competent, up to date with issues, understands the profession	1	2	1	2	3	5	4	5	5	Lacks credibility	2
Well organized and has good planning skills	1	1	1	2	5	4	3	5	5	Disorganized and lacks planning skills	3

Figure 10.2 An example of pairs of behavioural statements and scores based on three examples: outstanding, average and poor

relevant, recurring patterns of behaviour, which consistently emerged from the different forms of assessment.

The day consisted of four exercises assessing the candidates against the six DMA Differentiating Competencies. The aim of the day was to look for further evidence of behaviour that would indicate whether the individual in question had the potential to operate successfully at Level 4, given that that was the level of the principal's job.

One of the key exercises, therefore, was aimed at the ability to think in a truly strategic manner, given the level of the principal's job. Many teachers are very operational, comfortable with detail, and find it difficult to lift their game to the strategic level. This came through very strongly with a number of the candidates on the programme.

The day was observed by the four consultants, who also gave each of the participants some feedback after each session. They then sat together to exchange notes and observations of the total process; from interview, through tests and 360 review to the assessment day. The psychological tests were summarized and interpreted by Eileen Henderson as part of the process. She was also involved in the individual feedback, once the overall individual reports were completed.

The individual reports were then written up on the basis of these overall discussions and then critiqued by each of the consultants so that a consensus view emerged.

The reports focused on the six DMA Differentiating Competencies needed to be successful at Level 4. The first page was a summary of the findings and an overall recommendation:

- Could be a principal within 12 months.
- Could be a principal within three years.
- Unlikely to be a principal within five years.

An anonymous example is shown in Figure 10.3.[8]

Each of the remaining six pages of the report covered one of the DMA Competencies.

Figure 10.4 gives an example, from the same Chris Johns report, of the summary for one competency, that of 'setting direction'.

As can be seen, the report first summarizes what the competency entails. These are the behaviours for Level 4. This is not mentioned in the report, as the candidates know nothing about the DMA Solution Set, other than to be told about it in broad terms. It is not necessary for them at this stage to know more (although in an organization that has implemented levels of accountability, this obviously would be known).

The positive and negative behaviours are summarized. This is because although the positive behaviours are good, sometimes they can be undermined by negative shortcomings that can prove to be the more significant on balance. Most competency models do not take negative behaviour into the reckoning.

The competency report then consists of three very important components that make up the core findings. These consist of:

Summary of the Leadership Development for Potential Principal of a Secondary School

Chris Johns was nominated by his Principal to take part in a pilot project to assess his potential as a future Principal of a secondary school.

The process comprised an interview with Chris to learn of his career to date; two psychometric profiles; a 360° survey completed by Chris, his Principal and selected colleagues and a one-day development workshop.

A consistent picture emerged from the profiles, the survey and the development workshop, which are drawn together in this report and are documented in the Summary of Competencies.

Chris entered into the process with great enthusiasm and an obvious commitment to Catholic education. We are grateful to Chris and his Principal for their support and participation in the project.

Our overall findings lead us to make the following recommendation –
RECOMMENDATION
Chris Johns has the potential to be a Principal in the next 18 months to two years. No further boundary moves are needed at this stage.

Figure 10.3 Example summary of findings

- strengths;
- areas for development;
- actions.

The strengths rarely require further action. The areas for development are in reality weaknesses. However, as teachers (and others) are not too keen on being assessed, these are given a development theme. These then tend to form the basis of the actions needed to help ensure the individual is better prepared for the job of principal in the future, as indicated in the report.

This process has worked well. It has identified individuals in all of the above three categories, 'ready within one year', etc. In fact, the 'not within five years' category also covers cases of those who are considered most unlikely to become successful principals.

This report is then discussed with the individual and later with the principal who nominated the candidate. This is often because the suggested actions require the input and support of the teacher's current principal.

Those rated favourably have gained promotion and those assessed as 'not within five years' have been turned down when applying for the post of principal.

Summary of Leadership Competencies

Chris Johns

1. Competency – Setting Direction

DEFINITION: The capacity to set the direction and deliver plans over time, which are aligned to the needs of a defined context of accountabilities.

Positive

- Has a comprehensive view of the school and is able to anticipate future needs and opportunities and set new milestones up to three years ahead.
- Able to establish specific objectives and direction for the school's teachers from strategic intentions of the Board and establish concrete plans from identified but incompletely defined opportunities.

Negative

- Concentrates on short-term issues and immediate results to the detriment of longer-term objectives.
- Unable to work up a concrete plan of action from an idea or produce a solution to a new problem.

Strengths

Chris has a good short-term focus and is very organized, thorough and follows through on assignments. He is widely recognized as a completer.

He also shows some evidence of being able to see the larger picture and think about issues in the wider context.

Development needs

His primary development need is to learn how to effectively delegate and keep away from irrelevant detail. He needs to learn to say 'No'. He is well aware of this shortcoming but he has not yet been able to take appropriate action and is not always clear on priorities.

He is good at making things happen better, but can he identify gaps in resources and constraints in their delivery? He may not have had assignments that have provided this opportunity.

Action (priority)

To help him let go of the minutiae, it is suggested that he logs his activity for three months. He should set out how he intends to behave and plan a campaign of work. He should then log work priorities and time management and then compare what is actually done against the original plan. This should be tackled one month at a time to build in scope for improvement.

Suggest a project of about six months to create a strategic plan for the brightest students in the school, setting out how their performance could be lifted and sustained from year seven. It is suggested a mentor should work with him.

Figure 10.4 Example summary of Competencies

Feedback from nominating principals, participants and the boards of those involved has been very supportive of the process:

- Participants:
  'Enormously helpful, I can really see now where I am heading.'
  'A great experience, it really focused me.'
- Principal:
  'You found out all of that about Chris by doing that? It is spot on.'
- Board:
  'This should be really helpful.'

Pulling the threads together

This four-step process was designed to look for consistent trends in the individuals' leadership behaviour.

A full psychometric report, based on the two tests taken by candidates, was prepared by an experienced psychologist as part of the feedback.

In addition an overall personal summary report, based on the DMA Competencies, was prepared for each of the participants. This made use of the findings and trends emerging from the four main sources of information listed above. It is a consensus opinion of those who have done the interviewing, administered the tests and observed the development day. The individual's perceived strengths and weaknesses were summarized. A suggested personal development programme was outlined. Each candidate received a full feedback interview and discussion.

A summary judgement indicated whether the individual demonstrated potential to be a principal within 'one, three or five years'. Detailed comments are provided that could form the basis of an individual's development programme, aimed at better equipping the person in question to become a principal.

The Accountable Leader Chapter 10: Key points

This case study centred upon the need to identify school teachers with the potential to become principals. This entailed a move from Level 3 to Level 4, across the operational to strategic divide. Four key steps were outlined.

These steps can of course be applied in any organization with an accountable hierarchy, which needs or wishes to identify potential leaders.

The four key steps in the leadership development programme process are:

- Identify the accountabilities.
- Identify and design the relevant boundary moves for leadership development.
- Adapt and apply a differentiating competency model (the DMA model).
- Design the assessment process – what to assess, how and why.

Notes

1. The words 'principal' and 'head' are used variously in many different countries to describe the same role. I have used the term 'principal' throughout this chapter to signify both.
2. The team working with me in New Zealand and Australia on this project included Janne Pender, Eileen Henderson, Colleen Roche and Chris Faisandier.
3. Note that we are talking throughout this discussion of secondary school principals. We also assessed a number of roles held by primary school principals in schools of 300 to 500 students, which did not emerge at Level 4 and hence are not included in this chapter.
4. Note that the roles of assistant and deputy principal need to be assessed very critically in development terms, as these are often merely status titles and sometimes have no accountabilities beyond Level 2. The titles are endemic in the profession and are potentially the more misleading because of that.
5. *North & South* magazine, New Zealand (January 2007)
6. This approach is variously called 'assessment' or 'development'. Some organizations feel that a 'development' process is less threatening than one featuring an 'assessment'. It really depends on the culture of the organization as to which aspect is emphasized. Arguably one cannot devise an effective development programme until assessment and identification of needs for an individual has taken place.
7. See chapter 8 of *The Healthy Organization*.
8. A name has been chosen deliberately that could be either male or female, but the contents of this report are based on an actual assessment.

11 Tracking a successful leader

'Restricting themselves to actions in their comfort zone means CEOs will remain effective only as long as the best opportunities fall there.'

Lucier, C, Wheeler, S and Habel, R (2007)

The era of the inclusive leader

The first few chapters of this book underlined the importance of the link between accountability and leadership, and how this connection applies at different operational levels of an organization. The way to use the concept of accountability to construct a meaningful leadership development programme has also been described.

How then can we use the principles outlined in this book to map out the development of an individual leader's career over a lifetime?

The following example illustrates a classical track to the top of a major global organization; from Level 1 to Level 8 over a period of about 35 years. This journey encompasses boundary moves, dwell-time and other essential aspects of the principles of leadership accountability.

A Level 8 career track

A gifted student, John went to university in the 1950s, straight after leaving school and a brief period of compulsory military training.[1] A degree in languages followed at a world-class university.

Following graduation, John decided to join a major multinational, feeling that this would allow him to use his degree in languages. Over the next 35 years he climbed up through the hierarchies to become the CEO of the company, a huge organization whose products were sold in more than 150 countries around the world, and which employed about 300,000 people.

Level 1: entry level

John was already learning leadership lessons, albeit passively, prior to joining his chosen organization, where he would be expected to exercise positive leadership throughout his career. At school he had noted that the weaker the leader, the more the resort to sanctions – either in the form of officially condoned punishments, or bullying.

On leaving school, John undertook compulsory military training in his late teens. 'The two years I spent as an "other rank" were among the most useful and instructive years of my life. The quality of leadership I experienced was decidedly not high', he says. 'Men were led by a combination of strict discipline and tough sanctions. Their greatest interest in life, I soon discovered, was doing as little as possible and staying out of trouble. The commissioned officers I came across took little interest in anyone else, conscious of their superiority and determined to stay aloof. In those two years I learnt a great deal about how not to lead and I have sought to apply those lessons ever since.'

John then went on to university. 'At university I tried to forget the frustrations, indignities and disappointments of military service. But it had changed me forever. I now saw much of my past, at school, and so much of the lifestyle and attitudes that my fellow students still embraced, as narrow, privileged and non-inclusive. These formative years shaped my attitude to other people, and they laid the foundation for what in later business life became an obsession with concepts of customer orientation and human resource management.'

John is describing key boundary moves here; moves outside his initial comfort zone but not beyond his learning zone.

John joined his chosen company as a management trainee at Level 1.

A key job at Level 1, especially for young graduates, is a spell as supervisor. Supervisory jobs expose young recruits to people problems: issues such as induction, training, time-keeping and discipline. This is when they start to learn that most of the problems in an organization stem from people, not technology. This is a fundamental lesson for future leaders capable of moving up through the organization.

Level 2: promotion to managerial leadership

After about two years, and now in his mid-twenties, John became a manager at Level 2.[2] It is interesting to note that in some countries the new graduate recruits in this company went straight into management at Level 2. This was because in a number of countries the education process, combined with more extensive compulsory military training, took longer to complete. So these individuals were often into their mid- to late twenties by the time they started their corporate career. Age should not be the determining factor in deciding whether a young person joins as a management trainee or as a manager.

Although excited by the major promotion at the time, looking back John says: 'My first management job was a flop. I was helping to try and extend the brand equity of an international product. We were too inward focused. We did not succeed. It was my first lesson in the virtues of being true to consumer beliefs in the management of brand equity.'

It is worth noting here that already, from his experiences at school, the military and university, John was learning negative as well as positive lessons about the realities of leadership. As this case demonstrates, John was a person of exceptional innate ability, able to learn from what was happening to him and around him. The leader with potential sees beyond the present role, even though they may not yet be given the accountability to resolve the issues they can see. This is why it is very important to carefully assess the opinions, breadth of view and recommendations of potential leaders.

Research indicates that individuals with high potential as leaders do not need to spend too long in Levels 1 and 2.[3] This is partly because management jobs in Level 2 invariably only have a piece of the operational cake. In terms of operational accountabilities, the full cake usually comes at Level 3. So after two years, John was promoted to Level 3 and to another country at the same time. Two boundary moves. Not long after that he enjoyed another key boundary move.

My research indicates that two boundary moves at the same time is a lot of change to absorb. Only the most talented can cope with two boundary moves at the same time. Three such moves at the same time is probably taking an undue risk with your best talent and courting disaster.

Given the different types of boundary moves, described in Chapter 9, it is not possible to give an overall guideline for their timing. Clearly some are more critical than others; crossing a leadership level is at the top end of complexity and challenge. It does not seem to be possible to skip or slip a level. Moves across levels of accountability should not be rushed. This is particularly important at Levels 3 and 5, where dwell-times of five or more years seem most beneficial, provided that there are lateral moves within those respective levels during an individual's tenure.

Level 3: Managing managers

Moving to another country, John decided to learn the local language. 'That was when I learnt the value of what I call "cultural access", the vital importance of being right inside the culture in which one works. I have seen far too many examples of expatriate managers who never did succeed in penetrating the real culture of an unfamiliar market, with the result that nimble local competitors could dance rings round them.'

A move to corporate office

While at Level 3, John also had a stint at the corporate head office. A well-thought-out move to the corporate head office is an excellent form of development, especially for those who are not of the home country nationality. It increases their exposure to key decision-makers.

But more importantly, the ideal time for a short spell in the centre is when a manager at Level 3 has been identified as having Level 4+ potential. The essence of a good manager at Level 3 with potential to go further is the ability to see the wider issues and therefore make important contributions to policy and strategy. This ability can be keenly tested at head office.

A well-designed headquarters should not have too many jobs at Levels 1 and 2, as these do not add value to the field. The same can be said in large measure for Level 3 roles, except where these are clearly part of a team led by a Level 4+ manager working on strategic problems calling for new solutions. The Level 3 manager will not be accountable for the solutions but can be assessed on the quality of their strategic input.

The timing of John's first move to the centre, in a marketing support role, seems to have been carefully thought through to ensure maximum learning and meaningful exposure to top management. It is interesting to note that a marketing stint at headquarters in this particular organization was one of two types of head office career exposure that correlated very highly with success at Levels 5+.

Dwell-time at Level 3

Dwell-time at Level 3 is of critical importance for those aspiring to be promoted to strategic levels of accountability. The common tendency is to short-circuit this experience with accelerated development, but experience suggests this does not work.

By this stage John had been informed that he was considered a future top manager in the company with excellent prospects, but nevertheless he was at Level 3 for about eight years. This period did, however, include at least three boundary moves.

Level 4: heading up a function

After eight years at Level 3, John was promoted to an important Level 4 role as a national marketing director in Asia. He was held to account for the market share and margin of the group's international brands in his designated region. This was a major promotion as he now crossed the dividing line from operational to strategic accountability. He also acquired a working knowledge of another language.

Interestingly, the lessons from the earlier boundary moves quickly bore fruit. John noticed that the expatriate managers around him were making major assumptions and decisions about what would work in the Asian market. They had decided that products and services from the developed world would be appropriate in Asia. They did not really understand their consumers and John, still sensitive from his first management experience, proved that they were spectacularly wrong.

After about three years at Level 4, John was promoted to country manager at Level 5.

Strategic Level 4 roles have much in common with Level 2 roles, in that they are only part of a bigger picture. An operational leader at Level 3 often runs a complete unit, such as a call centre, distribution centre, factory or hypermarket, with direct subordinates at Level 2. Typically a Level 5 leader also has the whole picture, such as a country, whereas the Level 4 manager shares in a part of that national accountability.

Hence it seems to be well established that high-calibre leaders with potential can move relatively quickly through Levels 2 and 4 (in two to four years, for example) but not through Levels 3 and 5. In fact, as this example will show, the quality and extensiveness of his experience at Level 5 proved to be really critical for John's strategic and global leadership roles at Levels 7 and above.

If the leadership levels are not clearly identified, this development process is essentially hit or miss for an individual.

Level 5: national CEO

John was now in the role of national profit-accountable manager for the country in which he was working.

There are two schools of thought on promoting someone from within the team to become the new leader, in this case the national CEO. Most international companies favour taking the new potential leader out of the team for training prior to appointment.

But sometimes direct promotion can be justified. In this case the main reason was that the company was growing successfully but was getting to a key stage in the consolidation of that trend, and momentum might have been lost by bringing in a new expatriate on a steep learning curve. At the time, a local manager was not yet available in the business and part of John's assignment was to identify, propose and help develop his successor from among local management.

His assessment of this posting was as follows. 'Local management and I built a successful business that thrives to this day in that country. The huge lesson to draw from this episode was the key importance of good local managers. We recruited the best young people we could find, trained them and gave them early progressive accountabilities. My number two (a local) went on to become the CEO.

'Conclusion: the recruitment and retention of outstanding local managers is a crucial success factor for international business. (Ideally, with more than one per level.) There is no better route to complete cultural access.

'The next conclusion follows with inexorable logic. You will only retain outstanding people if they are fully motivated. Such motivation includes the proven and demonstrated knowledge that every post is open and accessible. Commitment and loyalty have to be earned. Earning the respect of local people is the toughest test of leadership for an expatriate manager.'

In my experience this is the one test where most multinationals short-change their people, by adopting a colonial approach and only selecting home country candidates for the top jobs. Nothing undermines a company's reputation more quickly in these days of stateless managers seeking truly international careers. Today a young Thai will attend a university such as UCLA and expect to start her career in say Brazil, with an international company that might be headquartered in New York, Tokyo or Mumbai.

First boundary move at Level 5

After a successful four years in this job, John was moved again, to become CEO in a Latin American country noted then for its terrorism and hyperinflation. In his words it was: 'A sideways move, and a long way sideways at that!'

But note the quality of the assignment. By now John was being viewed as a potential contender for the top global executive. The company had operations in every continent in the world. Hyperinflation, mainly in Latin America, was a new and major challenge facing the business at the time; but a gap in John's portfolio of experience. 'Inflation was running at 800 per cent and rising on the day of my arrival', he says. 'I was driven from the airport in a bullet-proof car, accompanied by armed bodyguards who followed me everywhere I went for the next couple of years.'

He was therefore confronted with a whole new series of business challenges or opportunities for learning. He was still at Level 5 but in a very different situation.

'The business issues were very different from what I had grappled with in Asia', he says. 'The company's market position was relatively strong but inflation was destroying value rapidly. In a way I was the wrong guy for the job. I was a business builder. What was needed was strong cash management and even stronger financial discipline.'

Given top management's emerging leadership development plan for John, it is clear that his inexperience in the area of financial discipline was exactly why he had been sent to Latin America. Building another business was not going to be a major lesson for him given his earlier success in Asia.

'We quickly decided that we had to completely redefine corporate objectives, goals and targets. In a nutshell, the single most important objective had to be to preserve the substance of the business. No more striving for bigger market shares by volume of goods sold, but instead by value of goods sold. Before the crisis, sales were measured by volume, tonnes or units sold. After my arrival we measured sales by inflation-adjusted cash value only, and we set pricing and measured profits in constant money only.

'We developed the ability to assess the full replacement costing of every one of the hundreds of items we sold every week. Prices were reset at the national exec meeting every Thursday and every package unit in every shop in the land was re-priced every Monday.'

This was before the days of the internet and online pricing. 'Head office did not believe it was possible but we did it. The situation was brought under control and the national company still prospers to this day. The key lesson to be drawn from this is management by selected information. If the boss asks for a particular topic or statistic, that is the one we all focus on. That is the one measurement we all watch.'

Tight focus on prioritized goals is a key tool of leadership. What you measure is what you get.

Oh, and John learnt another language on this assignment as he grappled with the business problems. He still has friends in the country to this day and regularly visits them in his retirement.

This is an excellent example of a boundary move at Level 5. The mother company had a problem at the time with a new, emerging and very threatening problem: hyperinflation. It had global implications for the financial health of the business. The company did not have an answer. This was a new phenomenon in those days.

So, it sent one of its best Level 5 leaders to solve the problem, even though technically it was a financial problem and John was not an accountant. As this was a new problem, noone at CHQ could guide him. It needed a person with the intellect to be able to address the essence of a new, potentially global problem and think from first principles to produce an answer that others could then apply elsewhere in the world.

It was also a crisis situation, not only in business terms, but also in personal terms, as the danger of kidnap was very real. It was a daunting challenge for a close family man and his wife. It also gave John credibility when later he would ask some of his managers to take on assignments in the less salubrious parts of the world, together with an insight into what was required.

Second boundary move at Level 5

As John then put it: 'The obvious antidote for the indiscipline of Latin America provided my next challenge: Japan. Probably the most self-disciplined nation on Earth, certainly the most successful economy on the planet when I was sent there.'

This was another change of qualitative experience, but still at Level 5. The Japanese business of this Western company, like most at the time, was small and struggling to maintain a foothold in markets dominated by huge, fiercely competitive Japanese incumbents.

'To witness it [the Japanese economic miracle] at first hand was to have all one's convictions about quality, customer focus, employee commitment and motivation, efficiency and cost-effectiveness massively reinforced. Everything that was sadly wrong about Latin America was brilliantly right in Japan.

'This covered the work ethic, commitment to national and corporate goals, social and financial discipline, and, above all, dedication to customer satisfaction. I can't say I learnt much that was new in Japan, but I was reminded of the key importance of a great many business truths that the rest of the world had let slip.'

As the Berlin Wall was about to come down and global competition was about to be unleashed on an unprecedented scale, this was a good time to have key management lessons reinforced. But John did learn one big new lesson in Japan.

'I learnt a lot about leadership, Japanese style. The painstaking process of building consensus for important decisions ensured full commitment to the decision once taken, throughout the business. It was a huge source of corporate strength and rapid action.

'Japan also produced the businessman I admired most – Akio Morita [CEO of Sony, the consumer electronics giant], the engineer of Sony Walkman fame, who was arguably the greatest marketing man of his generation.'[4]

But John, once again, could also see negative lessons worth heeding. 'The one dark shadow which hung over Japan in those years was the wall of protection behind which the country blockaded itself (*à la* the EEC of today). As a direct result, alongside the industrial brilliance there were massive inefficiencies in banking, distribution and retailing. A national xenophobia fed by a growing sense of industrial invincibility was already showing signs of creating the complacency which later produced economic collapse.'

John's final conclusion is very significant given that this was his third job at Level 5. People fixated on a grading system often worry about the loss of administrative promotions if they do away with their myriad of grades and introduce leadership levels. However, John says: 'I spent far too short a time in Japan. Just two years. I went there to deal with an emergency (my predecessor had died suddenly).'

Needless to say, although John gained immensely from the Japanese experience (as will be further demonstrated in his Level 7 role described later in the chapter), and of course gained a good working knowledge of Japanese while there, he felt he needed more time to gain the full value of his posting. It is difficult to have much lasting impact at Level 5+ if the tenure is too short. In light of this it is disconcerting to note that the average time in the CEO's role is getting shorter. This is a serious erosion of the quality of strategic leadership and general management.

Level 6: leading a regional headquarters

After a good 10 years' experience at Level 5 (and we now know that dwell-time at Level 5 is a vital ingredient of success at Levels 7 and 8), John was promoted to run a regional headquarters (RHQ). This covered an area of the globe in which he had no direct experience and in a business that was totally new to him. At least from here on in his career, he did not have to master any new languages. He was now fluent in five, with a good working knowledge of two others. You could say he was well equipped on that front to run a global organization.

As for his new challenge, now at Level 6, he had this to say. 'In leadership terms this was my most difficult experience. My brief was to salvage a business needing severe surgery. I had progressed from business builder to corporate mortician.

'The business consisted of traders who saw me as an outsider with little knowledge or experience of their business. They were right. They knew I was there, to misquote the bard, not to praise them but to bury them. Nonetheless we managed it together.'

This was the first time John was directly accountable for more than one country and one line of international business. The job therefore introduced him to new variables of complexity that had to be managed simultaneously. The nature of the people problems and the inevitable industrial relations dimensions introduced him to another important part of leadership of which he had previously had little direct experience. In short he was still learning plenty.

He summarizes another lesson during this period as: 'understanding that the essentials of all businesses are the same whether trading trinkets or tractors'.

After four years in this Level 6 role, he was appointed to his first truly global assignment.

Level 7: leading at Level 7

John now had accountability for a global business line that the company planned to build into a more substantial part of its activities. This was in large measure to offset some of the businesses he had divested in his previous role.

So now both the quality and the complexity of the new role represented a step up in accountability. He had to seek out a large acquisition or two, in line with the corporate strategic review. What, who and how was left to him to fathom.

He also had to fight head-to-head with two of the best companies in the world who were his direct competitors. One was on a par in size and complexity, the other slightly less so. Both had equally aggressive targets for growth and global market domination, so all three companies would naturally have the same potential takeover targets.

However, as you might by now expect, John successfully secured more than one successful takeover, sometimes on a hostile basis, to fight off the global competitors. He increased the company's global footprint to the extent that this line of business is now part of the company's successful heartland.

He also discovered that he had entered an arena where marketing was the critical factor in the success equation. He was now dealing with a business where emotional factors outweighed the purely functional ones. His experience of generating success in Japan in the face of fierce competition was invaluable. He had learnt the importance of good market research in understanding the consumer. It also gave him the courage of his convictions to stress unrelentingly issues such as quality. He initiated a major quality initiative in his business, which later migrated across the group.

Notwithstanding the above, John summarized the first key lesson of this Level 7 role as: 'The key to success lay in constant and remorseless innovation. The life cycle of products (not brands) was shortening. They were also very culture, lifestyle and youth related. To succeed you had to be at the forefront of the youth culture. That means you had to empower your own young people to be your own change agents.'

Given that this was John's first global job, his next comment is another revealing lesson. 'This reality has important consequences for globalization. You can run your successful new products round the world, repeating the success in market after market. But the successful idea has to originate somewhere, not just the dominant home market. For a truly global company, success must originate from anywhere in the world.

'The art of global leadership is how to ensure the right resources of research, development and advertising skills are on hand to support that reality. That sort of innovation is the lifeblood of international business success.'

Level 8: the Level 8 leader

By now it should be clear why there are very few Level 8 leadership jobs in the world. It is also apparent that only a tiny percentage of people have the capability to be successful at this level.

It must be apparent that John is an exceptional person. Gifted at school, mastering many languages, he also had an extraordinary ability to rise above his current experience and learn from both the good and bad practices he witnessed. And he was already doing this in his teens.

His experience also demonstrates the value and importance of appropriate boundary moves at key stages in leadership development. John kept getting jobs with real, challenging accountability throughout his career.

Imagine for a moment if the Latin American posting had been as a COO, compressed in the same leadership level as the local president. Most companies faced with such a problem would typically send out a heavyweight manager with a brief to solve the problem, and do just that. If that had been the case John could not have taken the rapid, unilateral and innovative action already outlined. He would have been dogged by political considerations and the massaging of egos, with much of his work overlapping that of others, such as the CFO and the president, and subject to duplication and second guessing. In short he could not have been effective in the timescale available. The lost opportunity would have affected both the country's need to survive and that of the group to be able to apply the lessons learnt in other parts of the world, as subsequently happened.

Advising leaders at Levels 6 and above

Not surprisingly, given his immense experience and ability, John has subsequently worked as a non-executive director on the board of a number of international companies. Interestingly, he again highlights the one case where leadership failed and what can be learnt from that.

He was a non-executive director of a company where both the CEO and CFO had to resign as a result of a US$1 billion hole in the accounts. The company in question had grown at an average of 15 per cent per annum for some time. Annual growth of that magnitude was a driver both of the share price and of the market's willingness to finance more acquisitions. Thus 15 per cent top line growth became not merely a means to an end, but an end in itself.

The missing money was mostly in a newly acquired subsidiary. Due diligence had not revealed the problem. The fraud, once found, was several layers of management down from the top.

The main problems were:

- too many layers of management;
- corporate over-stretch;
- too much power in the hands of a single individual.

John felt that an important lesson was about the tone at the top. The CEO was popular. His leadership was unquestioned and he had the short-term track record to prove it. He took little advice, and rejected most outside comment, however well informed. Given his record, challenges to his views were readily deflected. Whenever he took greater risks his judgement was trusted. He built a house of cards based on reckless acquisitions, which would have collapsed irrespective of the fraud.

Having observed this series of sorry events, John concluded that it is important to 'keep your feet on the ground, not to believe your own publicity and to surround yourself with capable people who can dare to tell you when you are wrong'.

The Accountable Leader Chapter 11: Key points

The example of the successful leader in this chapter, where moving through positions of leadership in the company helped to groom him to become the leader of the organization, demonstrates why a well-constructed leadership development programme needs to be built upon a platform of well-defined accountabilities.

It is currently fashionable to believe that, since the job for life is supposedly no longer an option, then leaders learn best by jumping from company to company. However, what they really need is a series of well-constructed boundary moves, which enable them to learn and grow. The best international companies have carefully nurtured and guarded this secret. They realized some time ago that their competitors can copy everything they do except the way their leaders behave. That, in the final analysis, is their only true competitive advantage.

Every successful organization needs a distributed network of capable leaders in real jobs with clear accountabilities, at every level from the front line to the C-Suite. In other words, in order to be successful in the long haul you need to know how to hold leaders to account throughout your organization. You need both an effective leader of the organization and competent leaders throughout the organization. And as a starting point you need to know how many leadership levels are required in your organization.

Notes

1. Although this is a real example, the true identity of the individual has been kept anonymous.
2. The grading system in the organization did not consist of leadership levels but by studying the roles and the organization it was possible to identify retrospectively the levels underpinning John's career.
3. For example, see chapter 8 of *The Healthy Organization*.
4. Morita, A, Reingold, A and Shimomana, M (1987) *Made in Japan*, Fontana, Reading

12 The accountable leader: 20 key ideas

'Mine ear is open and my heart prepar'd.'

Shakespeare, King Richard the Second

20 key ideas in this book

1. Everyone has a right to real work and a real job; a real job is one in which the person in that job is held to account. The need to be held to account stems from the right to be free.
2. An individual can only be held to account if the organization has clearly demarcated levels of accountability, or leadership levels.
3. The Decision Making Accountability (DMA) Solution Set maps how leaders are held to account throughout an organization.
4. The principles of DMA form the basis for effective organization design.
5. A programme to assess potential leaders needs to rest on a sound foundation of clear accountabilities.
6. The DMA Solution Set provides that platform.
7. An administrative promotion occurs when an individual is moved to another grade at the same level of accountability.
8. Boundary moves occur when individuals are taken out of their comfort zone, but not beyond their learning zone.

9. A bureaucracy is an unhealthy organization that has lost contact with both its purpose and its customers. It is disconnected from performance and its

members are not held to account as their actions have limited or even no personal consequences.

10. An accountability level is justified when the leader in it makes decisions that members of the team cannot make, and that are different in substance and quality from those of the manager to whom that leader reports.

11. Only one layer of management is needed for each level of accountability above the front line.

12. Compression occurs when there are two or more layers of management at the same level of accountability, or two or more tiers of supervision at Level 1. Compression is the opposite of empowerment.

13. A good engineer might not be a good manager because leadership behaviours are required in addition. These qualities can be identified by means of the DMA Leadership Competencies.

14. Values are badges of belonging – important for the life of an organization and contentment of the individual, but not indicators of potential leadership.

15. Outstanding performance at one level of accountability does not guarantee good performance at the next level.

16. Beware of accelerated development programmes. Evidence shows that exposure to genuine Level 3 accountability is critical preparation for strategic and governance roles. Insufficient experience at Level 3 correlates with failure on promotion.

17. Potential leadership is best assessed by differentiating behaviours (differentiating competencies) linked to the Seven Elements of the levels of accountability.

18. A differentiating competency identifies those behaviours that help ensure a person can perform effectively at the next level of accountability.

19. One must know where the operational-strategic divide occurs in the organization in order to devise an effective leadership development programme.

20. Apply these two tests to your organization:
    1. Is the average span of control less than six?
    2. Do any of the following apply?
       - Revenues or costs up to US$5 billion, with six or more layers of management.

- Revenues or costs up to US$15 billion with seven or more layers.
- Revenues or costs up to US$45 billion with eight or more layers.
- Revenues or costs up to US$150 billion with nine or more layers.
- An organization in a country with a GDP of up to US$100 billion with more than five layers of management.

If the answer is 'yes', then there are too many managers and they cannot be held to account clearly as leaders. In other words:

Your organization is over-managed and under-led.

References

Adair, J (2005) *How To Grow Leaders*, Kogan Page, London

Bains, G *et al* (2007) *Meaning Inc.: The blueprint for business success in the 21st century*, Profile Books, London

Bennis, W (1989) *Why Leaders Can't Lead*, Jossey-Bass, San Francisco, California

Berlin, I (2001), ed H Hardy, *Liberty*, Oxford University Press, Oxford

Bett, M *et al* (1995) *Independent Review of the Armed Forces' Manpower, Career and Remuneration Structures*, HMSO, London

Bevan, J (2002) *The Rise and Fall of Marks and Spencer*, Profile Books, London

Bloch, S and Whiteley, P (2003) *Complete Leadership*, Pearson Education, London

Boal, K B and Hooijberg, R (2000) Strategic leadership research moving on, *Leadership Quarterly* **11** (4).

Boam, R and Sparrow, P (1992) *Designing and Achieving Competency: A competency-based approach to developing people and organizations*, McGraw-Hill, London

Bridges, W (1996) *Job Shift: How to prosper in a world without jobs*, Nicholas Brearley, London

Brousseau, K R *et al* (2006) The Seasoned Executive's Decision Making Style, *Harvard Business Review*, February

Brown, W (1971) *Organization*, Heinemann, London

Bungay, S and McKinney, D (2003) Mission Leadership, *Ashridge Journal*, Spring

Burns, J M (1978) *Leadership*, Harper & Row, New York

Campbell, A, Goold, M and Alexander, M (1995) The Value of the Parent Company, *California Management Review*, **38** (1), Fall

Chan Kim, W, Mauborgne, R and van der Heyden, L (2003) *General Failings in Mastering Leadership*, PWC/FT, London

Chandler, A (1962) *Strategy and Structure: Chapters in the History of the Industrial Enterprise*, MIT Press, Cambridge

Charan, R, Drotter, S and Noel, J (2001) *Leadership Pipeline: How to build the leadership powered company*, Jossey-Bass, San Francisco, California

Collingwood, H (2001) Personal Histories: Leaders remember the moments and people that shaped them, in *Harvard Business Review on Breakthrough Leadership, Harvard Business Review*

Collins, J (2001) *From Good to Great: Why some companies make the leap and others do not*, HarperCollins, London

Cooper, C L (2005) (ed) *Leadership and Management in the 21st Century*, Oxford University Press, Oxford

Czikszcentmihalyi, M C (1991) *Flow: The psychology of optimal experience*, Harper and Row, New York

Darling, J R (1999) Organizational Excellence and Leadership Strategies: Principles followed by top multinational executives, *Leadership and Organization Development Journal*, **20** (6)

Davis, S M and Lawrence, P R (1977) *Matrix*, Addison-Wesley, Reading, Massachusetts

Dawes, S (2006) Case Study: Organisational redesign separate from new pay structure at Orange, *e-reward.co.uk Research Report no 47*.

Day, D V (2000) Leadership Development: A review in context, *Leadership Quarterly*, **11**

de Pree, M (1989) *Leadership is an Art*, Doubleday/Currency, New York

Dive, B J (1989) *Competitive Structures for the 90s*, Unilever Personnel Division, London

Dive, B J (2003a) How to Design a Healthy Regional Headquarters, in *Regional Headquarters Roles and Organization*, The Conference Board, New York

Dive, B J (2003b) When is an organization too flat? *Across The Board*, July–August

Dive, B J (2004a) *The Healthy Organization: A revolutionary approach to people and management*, Kogan Page, London

Dive, B J (2004b) Winning principals and how to pick them, *New Zealand Management*, September.

Dive, B J (2005a) Problems with job evaluation and organization design, *Croner Pay and Benefits Briefing*, (307) 3 November

Dive, B J (2005b) Job evaluation and organization design – the solution, *Croner Pay and Benefits Briefing*, (308) 22 November

Dive, B J (2005c) Grade, rank and status: issues and challenges, *Croner Pay and Benefits Briefing*, (309) 14 December

Dive, B J (2007) Is there a principal crisis in Australian secondary schools? *Independence – The Journal of the Association of Heads of Independent Schools of Australia*, **31** (2)

Donaldson, L (1995) *American Anti-management Theories of Organization*, Cambridge University Press, Cambridge

Drucker, P (1967) *The Effective Executive*, Harper & Row, New York

Earley, P C and Erez, M (1997) *The Transplanted Executive*, Oxford University Press, Oxford

Fisch, G G (1963) Stretching the span of management, *Harvard Business Review*, September–October

Franks, O (2003) *Introduction to Mastering Leadership*, FT/PWC, London

French, W L and Bell, C H Jnr (1973) *Organization Development: Behavioural science interventions for organization improvement*, Prentice Hall, Englewood Cliffs, New Jersey

Galbraith, J R (2000) *Designing the Global Corporation*, Jossey-Bass, San Francisco, California

Gladwell, M (2000) *The Tipping Point: How little things can make a big difference*, Little Brown & Co, New York

Gobillot, E (2007) *The Connected Leader*, Kogan Page, London

Goffee, R and Jones, G (2003) *The Character of a Corporation*, Profile Books, London

Goleman, D (1999) *Working and Emotional Intelligence*, Bloomsbury, London

Goold, M, Campbell, A and Alexander, M (1994) *Corporate-level Strategy*, John Wiley & Sons, New York

Goold, M and Campbell, A (2002) *Designing Effective Organizations*, Jossey-Bass, San Francisco, California

Graicunas, V A (1937) Relationships in organization, in *Papers on the Science of Administration*, eds L Gulick and L Urwick, Colombia University, New York

Gratton, L (2004) *The Democratic Enterprise: Liberating your business with individual freedom and shared purpose*, FT Prentice Hall, London

Grint, K (2005) Twenty-first-century leadership – The God of Small Things: Or putting the 'ship' back into 'leadership', in *Leadership and Management in the 21st Century*, ed C L Cooper, Oxford University Press, Oxford

Handy, C (1997) *The Hungry Spirit*, Hutchinson, London

Hilmer, F G and Donaldson, L (1996) *Management Redeemed: Debunking the fads that undermine corporate performance*, The Free Press, New York

Hoebeke, L (1994) *Making Work Systems Better*, John Wiley & Sons, UK

Homer (1984) *The Odyssey*, translated by R Fitzgerald, Oxford University Press, New York

Huff, A S and Moeslein, K (2005) *An Agenda for Understanding Individual Leadership in Corporate Leadership Systems,* in *Leadership and Management in the 21st Century,* ed C L Cooper, Oxford University Press, Oxford

Janger, A R (1989) *Measuring Structure: Comparative benchmarks for management structure,* The Conference Board, New York

Jaques, E (1989) *Requisite Organization,* Cason Hall & Co, Arlington, Virginia

Jaques, E and Cason, K (1994) *Human Capability,* Cason Hall & Co, Arlington, Virginia

Jaques, E and Clement, S D (1991) *Executive Leadership,* Cason Hall & Co, Arlington, Virginia

Jaques, E *et al* (1978) *Health Services: Their role and organization and the role of patients, doctors, and the health professions,* Heinemann, London

Kakabadse, A and Kakabadse, N (1999) *Essence of Leadership,* International Thomson, London

Kaplan, R S and Norton, D P (1996) *The Balanced Scorecard: Translating strategy into action,* Harvard Business School Press, Boston, Massachusetts

Katzenbach, J R (1997) The myth of the top management team, *Harvard Business Review,* November–December

Kennedy, C (2002) *Guide to the Management Gurus: The best guide to business thinkers,* Random House Business Books, London

Klatt, B, Murphy, S and Irvine, D (1999) *Accountability: Practical tools for focusing on clarity, commitment and results,* Kogan Page, London

Kleiner, A (2003) *Who Really Matters,* Doubleday, New York

Kraines, G A (2001) *Accountability Leadership,* Career Press, Franklin Lakes, New Jersey

Kramer, R J (2003) *Regional Headquarters Roles and Organization,* The Conference Board, New York

Kramer, R J (2006) *The Role of COOs,* The Conference Board, New York

Kressler, H W (2003) *Motivate and Reward,* Palgrave Macmillan, Hampshire

Lala, R M (2004) *The Creation of Wealth – The Tatas from the 19th to the 21st century,* Penguin Books India, New Delhi

Landes, D (1998) *The Wealth and Poverty of Nations,* Abacus, London

Larson, V (2007) Our best schools: how to find them, *North and South,* February

Lawrence, P R and Lorsch, J W (1986) *Organization and Environment: Managing differentiation and integration,* Harvard Business School Press, Cambridge, Massachusetts

Lucier, C, Wheeler, S and Habel, R (2007) The Era of the Inclusive Leader, *Strategy and Business,* (47), Summer

McCall, M W Jnr (1998) *High Fliers: Developing the next generation of leaders,* Harvard Business School Press, Boston, Massachusetts

McCall, M W Jnr and Holenbeck, G P (2002) *Developing Global Executives*, Harvard Business School Press, Boston, Massachusetts

McCall, M W Jnr, Lombardo, M M and Morrison, A M (1988) *The Lessons of Experience*, Lexington Books, New York

McClelland, D C (1998) *Human Motivation*, Cambridge University Press, New York

McMorland, J (2005) Are you big enough for your job? Is your job big enough for you? *University of Auckland Business Review*, **7** (2)

Maslow, A, Stephens, D C and Heil, G (1998) *Maslow on Management*, John Wiley & Sons, New York

Michaels, E, Handfield-Jones, H and Axelrod, B (2001) *The War for Talent*, Harvard Business School Press, Cambridge, Massachusetts

Mintzberg, H (1988) Crafting Strategy, *Harvard Business Review*, June–July.

Mintzberg, H (2003) *Managers not MBAs: A hard look at the soft practice of managing and management development*, Berrett-Koehler, San Francisco

Morita, A, Reingold, A and Shimomana, M (1987) *Made in Japan*, Fontana, Reading

Mourkogiannis, N (2006) *Purpose: The starting point of great companies*, Palgrave Macmillan, New York

Neilson, G L and Pasternack, B A (2006) *Results: Keep what's good, fix what's wrong and unlock great performance*, Capstone, Chichester

Neuschel, R P (2005) *The Servant Leader: Unleashing the power of your people*, Kogan Page, London

Nibly, H (1984) Leadership versus Management, *BYU Today*, February

Olivier, M (2003) *The Working Journey*, M. J. Litho, Cape Town

O'Neill, O (2002) *A Question of Trust: The BBC Reith Lectures 2002*, Cambridge University Press, Cambridge

Pascale, R T and Athos, A (1981) *The Art of Japanese Management*, Victor Gollancz, London

Paterson, T T (1972) *Job Evaluation*, Business Books, London

Perkins, S J and Shortland, S M (2006) *Strategic International Human Resource Management, Choices and Consequences in Multinational People Management*, Kogan Page, London

Pettigrew, A and Fenton, E (2000) *The Innovating Organisation*, Sage, London

Popper, K (2002) *The Open Society and its Enemies, Volume 1*, Routledge Classics, London

Reese, T J (1996) *Inside the Vatican*, Harvard University Press, Cambridge, Massachusetts

Rhind, D (2005) Herding Cats or Luxuriating in Talent? Leadership and Management of Universities, in *Leadership and Management in the 21st Century*, ed C L Cooper, Oxford University Press, Oxford

Roes, R R (1979) *The Effectiveness of Company Organization Structures,* Unilever Personnel Division, London

Rowbottom, R (1977) *Social Analysis: A collaborative method of gaining useable scientific knowledge of social institutions,* Heinemann, London

Schein, E H (1969) *Process Consultation: Its role in organization development,* Addison-Wesley, Reading, Massachusetts

Schell, M S and Solomon, C M (1997) *Capitalizing on the Global Workforce,* McGraw-Hill, New York

Senge, P M (1990) *The Fifth Discipline: The art and practice of the learning organization,* Doubleday Currency, New York

Sirota, D, Misckind, L A and Meltzer, M I (2005) *The Enthusiastic Employee: How companies profit by giving workers what they want,* Wharton Ideas Publishing, New Jersey

Tannen *et al* (2007) *HR Coping with Change,* CIPD, UK

Taylor, C (2005) *Walking the Talk: Building a culture for success,* Random House, London

Tichy, N M and Devanna, M A (1986) The Transformational Leader *Sloan Review,* July

Tichy, N M and Cardwell, N (2002) *The Cycle of Leadership: How great leaders teach their companies to win,* Harper Business, New York

Wind, J R and Main, J (1998) *Driving Change: How the best companies are preparing for the 21st century,* Kogan Page, London

Yeats, W B (1950) *The Collected Poems,* Oxford University Press, Oxford

Zenger, J H and Folkman, J (2007) *The Handbook for Leaders: 24 lessons of extra-ordinary leadership,* McGraw-Hill, Maidenhead

Index